Second Edition

Children's Mathematics

Cognitively Guided Instruction

Thomas P. Carpenter
Elizabeth Fennema
Megan Loef Franke
Linda Levi
Susan B. Empson

HEINEMANN
Portsmouth, NH

D1293050

Heinemann
145 Maplewood Ave., Suite 300
Portsmouth, NH 03801
www.heinemann.com

Offices and agents throughout the world

Library of Congress Cataloging-in-Publication Data
Children's mathematics : cognitively guided instruction.—Second edition / Thomas P. Carpenter [and four others].
    pages   cm
  ISBN 978-0-325-05287-8
    1. Mathematics—Study and teaching (Primary)   I. Carpenter, Thomas P.
QA135.5.C4947 2014
372.7'044—dc23   2014035840

Editor: Katherine Bryant
Production: Sonja S. Chapman
Typesetter: Kim Arney
Cover and interior designs: Suzanne Heiser
Manufacturing: Steve Bernier

Printed in the United States of America on acid-free paper
12 13 14   PAH   24 23 22
May 2022 Printing / PO 34358

DEDICATION

Cognitively Guided Instruction (CGI) teachers frequently talk about how they learn from their students. We have been fortunate to be able to learn from both teachers and their students. The teachers we have worked with have truly been partners in our research. They have helped to extend our understandings of children's mathematical thinking, shown us what is possible as they support student learning in classrooms, and inspired us to continue our research and professional development.

We dedicate this book to all the teachers, children, and teacher leaders who have helped to make CGI what it is today. This really is their story, and we are grateful to them for helping us tell it.

The continuing popularity of this book is testimony to the importance of its central message: Young children *can* think mathematically and instruction that builds on their thinking takes them further and deeper into the core concepts of arithmetic than teachers might imagine.

—James Hiebert,
Robert J. Barkley Professor of Education,
University of Delaware

The training we have had in Cognitively Guided Instruction and through *Children's Mathematics* has shown us that understanding "how" children think mathematically is so much more valuable to their ongoing development than trying to "give" them the way to think. Our students have flourished!

—Kathy Goecke, principal

Cognitively Guided Instruction not only changed the way I teach and restored my passion for teaching, it has had a positive impact on thousands of children.

—Debbie Gates, elementary mathematics specialist

This exemplary resource is essential for teachers, professional developers, and researchers who are interested in understanding, supporting, and extending children's ways of reasoning.

—Vicki Jacobs,
Yopp Distinguished Professor of Mathematics Education,
UNC Greensboro

Children's Mathematics is by far the most powerful and practical book that I have used in my work with teachers. The potential it has to not only deepen students' conceptual understanding of mathematics but their teachers' as well is unparalleled . . . it is essential reading for every teacher who teaches mathematics.

—Andrew Jenkins, principal

I am far more engaged and excited about teaching math myself because *Children's Mathematics* helped me understand what questions to ask and what student comments to listen for that will lead to student discovery.

—Lesley Wagner, teacher

CONTENTS

Foreword *by Mary M. Lindquist*   xiv

Introduction to the Second Edition   xviii

1. *Children's Mathematical Thinking*   1

2. *Addition and Subtraction: Problem Types*   7

3. *Addition and Subtraction: Children's Solution Strategies*   17

4. *Multiplication and Division: Problem Types and Children's Solution Strategies*   49

5. *Beginning to Use Cognitively Guided Instruction*   76

6. *Base-Ten Number Concepts*   84

7. *Children's Strategies for Solving Multidigit Problems*   96

8. *Problem Solving as Modeling*   129

9. *Developing Classroom Practice: Posing Problems and Eliciting Thinking*   134

10. *Developing Classroom Practice: Engaging Students with Each Other's Ideas*   153

11. *Mathematical Principles Underlying Children's Mathematics*   173

12. *The Conceptual Basis for Cognitively Guided Instruction*   184

13. *Conclusion: Keep on Learning*   198

Appendix A: The Research Base of Cognitively Guided Instruction   200

Appendix B: Answers to Selected Questions for Reflection   210

References   214

HOW TO ACCESS ONLINE VIDEO CLIPS

You can access individual clips by scanning the QR codes in the margins of the book or entering the corresponding URLs in your browser. If you'd like to access all the clips at once, follow these instructions.

- Step 1. Go to www.heinemann.com
- Step 2. Click on "Login," to open or create your account. Enter your email address and password or click "Register" to set up an account.
- Step 3. Enter keycode CHMATH2E and click "Register."

You're in!

When a child's strategy or classroom example in the text is also viewable on the accompanying video, a QR code and URL link in the margin will send you directly to the clip.

All video is not to be shared, duplicated, reproduced, or further distributed.

VIDEO CONTENTS

Chapter 3

CLIP 3.1: Direct Modeling strategy for a Join (Change Unknown) problem   19
  * http://smarturl.it/CM3.1

CLIP 3.2: Direct Modeling strategy for a Separate (Result Unknown) problem   19
  * http://smarturl.it/CM3.2

CLIP 3.3: Direct Modeling strategy for a Separate (Result Unknown) problem,   19
in which a teacher responds to a miscount
  * http://smarturl.it/CM3.3

CLIP 3.4: Direct Modeling strategy for a Separate (Change Unknown) problem   20
  * http://smarturl.it/CM3.4

CLIP 3.5: Direct Modeling strategy for a Compare (Difference Unknown) problem   20
  * http://smarturl.it/CM3.5

CLIP 3.6: Direct Modeling strategy for a Join (Start Unknown) problem   21
  * http://smarturl.it/CM3.6

CLIP 3.7: A child who has directly modeled for other problems is given   21
a Join (Start Unknown) problem
  * http://smarturl.it/CM3.7

CLIP 3.8: Count On from Larger strategy for addition   25
  * http://smarturl.it/CM3.8

CLIP 3.9: Count On from Larger strategy for a Join (Result Unknown) problem   25
  * http://smarturl.it/CM3.9

CLIP 3.10: Counting strategy for a Join (Change Unknown) problem   26
  * http://smarturl.it/CM3.10

CLIP 3.11: Counting strategy for subtraction   26
  * http://smarturl.it/CM3.11

CLIP 3.12: Counting strategy for a Separate (Result Unknown), in Spanish   26
  * http://smarturl.it/CM3.12

CLIP 3.13: Counting strategy for a Join (Change Unknown) problem, with written notation   28
- http://smarturl.it/CM3.13

CLIP 3.14: Derived Fact strategy based on doubles   29
- http://smarturl.it/CM3.14

CLIP 3.15: Derived Fact strategy based on doubles   30
- http://smarturl.it/CM3.15

CLIP 3.16: Derived Fact strategy using ten as a benchmark   30
- http://smarturl.it/CM3.16

CLIP 3.17: Derived Fact strategy for subtraction using ten as a benchmark   30
- http://smarturl.it/CM3.17

CLIP 3.18: Gilberto uses strategies for adding and subtracting, using ten as a benchmark   31
- http://smarturl.it/CM3.18

CLIP 3.19: Karen uses a variety of Number Fact strategies for adding and subtracting   32
- http://smarturl.it/CM3.19

CLIP 3.20: Aaliyah solves a Join (Result Unknown) problem   47
- http://smarturl.it/CM3.20

CLIP 3.21: Aaliyah solves a Join (Change Unknown) problem   47
- http://smarturl.it/CM3.21

CLIP 3.22: Aaliyah solves a Separate (Change Unknown) problem   47
- http://smarturl.it/CM3.22

CLIP 3.23: Jordyn solves a Join (Result Unknown) problem   47
- http://smarturl.it/CM3.23

CLIP 3.24: Melissa solves a Separate (Result Unknown) problem   48
- http://smarturl.it/CM3.24

CLIP 3.25: Melissa solves a Join (Change Unknown) problem   48
- http://smarturl.it/CM3.25

Chapter 4

CLIP 4.1: Direct Modeling strategy for a Multiplication problem   51
- http://smarturl.it/CM4.1

CLIP 4.2: Direct Modeling strategy for Measurement Division, total counted first   52
- http://smarturl.it/CM4.2

CLIP 4.3: Direct Modeling strategy for Measurement Division, total counted later   52
- http://smarturl.it/CM4.3

CLIP 4.4: Direct Modeling strategy for a Partitive Division problem 53
* http://smarturl.it/CM4.4

CLIP 4.5: Counting strategy for a Multiplication problem 57
* http://smarturl.it/CM4.5

CLIP 4.6: Derived Fact strategy for multiplication 61
* http://smarturl.it/CM4.6

CLIP 4.7: Derived Fact strategy for multiplication 61
* http://smarturl.it/CM4.7

CLIP 4.8: Derived Fact strategy for Multiplication problem, in which amount in a group 61
is partitioned
* http://smarturl.it/CM4.8

CLIP 4.9: Direct Modeling strategy for Measurement Division with a remainder 64
* http://smarturl.it/CM4.9

CLIP 4.10: Direct Modeling strategy for Measurement Division with a remainder, 64
adjusted for child
* http://smarturl.it/CM4.10

CLIP 4.11: Watch Austin solve a Multiplication and Measurement Division problem 75
* http://smarturl.it/CM4.11

CLIP 4.12: Now watch Austin solve a Partitive Division problem 75
* http://smarturl.it/CM4.12

Chapter 5

CLIP 5.1: Watch the first-graders in Ms. Hassay's classroom share their strategies for 83
a Multiplication problem
* http://smarturl.it/CM5.1

Chapter 6

CLIP 6.1: Counting by Ones strategy to solve a base-ten Multiplication problem 87
* http://smarturl.it/CM6.1

CLIP 6.2: Counting by Tens strategy for a base-ten Multiplication problem 87
* http://smarturl.it/CM6.2

CLIP 6.3: Counting by Tens strategy for a base-ten Multiplication problem 87
* http://smarturl.it/CM6.3

CLIP 6.4: Counting by Tens strategy for base-ten Measurement Division 87
* http://smarturl.it/CM6.4

CLIP 6.5: Direct Place Value strategy for base-ten Measurement Division 87
- http://smarturl.it/CM6.5

CLIP 6.6: Direct Place Value strategy for a base-ten Multiplication problem 88
with follow-up questions
- http://smarturl.it/CM6.6

CLIP 6.7: Counting by Tens strategy for base-ten Measurement Division 89
of more than 100 objects
- http://smarturl.it/CM6.7

CLIP 6.8: Direct Place Value strategy for base-ten Measurement Division 89
of more than 100 objects, in Spanish
- http://smarturl.it/CM6.8

CLIP 6.9: Using a Direct Place Value strategy to solve base-ten Measurement 90
Division of more than 100 objects
- http://smarturl.it/CM6.9

CLIP 6.10: Watch Emma solve a base-ten Measurement Division problem 95
- http://smarturl.it/CM6.10

CLIP 6.11: Now watch Emma solve a Partitive Division problem with similar numbers 95
- http://smarturl.it/CM6.11

CLIP 6.12: Evan solves a base-ten Multiplication with extras problem for the first time 95
- http://smarturl.it/CM6.12

Chapter 7

CLIP 7.1: Direct Modeling with Tens strategy for a Join (Result Unknown) problem 98
- http://smarturl.it/CM7.1

CLIP 7.2: Direct Modeling with Tens strategy for a Separate (Result Unknown) 99
problem, with no trading
- http://smarturl.it/CM7.2

CLIP 7.3: Direct Modeling with Tens strategy for a Separate (Result Unknown) 99
problem, with no trading
- http://smarturl.it/CM7.3

CLIP 7.4: Solving a Separate (Result Unknown) problem with an emergent 101
understanding of ten as a unit
- http://smarturl.it/CM7.4

CLIP 7.5: An Incrementing Invented Algorithm for addition 104
- http://smarturl.it/CM7.5

CLIP 7.6: Combining the Same Units Invented Algorithm for addition   104
- http://smarturl.it/CM7.6

CLIP 7.7: Combining the Same Units Invented Algorithm for addition,   104
with an error that is addressed
- http://smarturl.it/CM7.7

CLIP 7.8: Combining the Same Units Invented Algorithm for addition,   104
supported by student written notation
- http://smarturl.it/CM7.8

CLIP 7.9: Incrementing Invented Algorithm for subtraction with student notation   105
- http://smarturl.it/CM7.9

CLIP 7.10: Incrementing Invented Algorithm for subtraction with teacher   105
notation of child's thinking
- http://smarturl.it/CM7.10

CLIP 7.11: Combining the Same Units Invented Algorithm for subtraction   106
- http://smarturl.it/CM7.11

CLIP 7.12: Incrementing Invented Algorithm for Join (Change Unknown)   107
- http://smarturl.it/CM7.12

CLIP 7.13: Incrementing Invented Algorithm for Join (Change Unknown),   107
with a follow-up question
- http://smarturl.it/CM7.13

CLIP 7.14: Compensating Invented Algorithm for addition   107
- http://smarturl.it/CM7.14

CLIP 7.15: Direct Modeling with Tens strategy for a Multiplication problem   111
- http://smarturl.it/CM7.15

CLIP 7.16: Adding strategy for Multiplication, in Spanish   114
- http://smarturl.it/CM7.16

CLIP 7.17: Adding strategy for Multiplication   114
- http://smarturl.it/CM7.17

CLIP 7.18: Invented Algorithm for a Multiplication problem   114
- http://smarturl.it/CM7.18

CLIP 7.19: Invented Algorithm for a Multiplication problem, with follow-up questions   114
- http://smarturl.it/CM7.19

CLIP 7.20: Elijah uses a Direct Modeling by Tens strategy for a harder problem   120
- http://smarturl.it/CM7.20

CLIP 7.21: Elijah uses an Invented Algorithm for an easier problem,   120
with follow-up questions
- http://smarturl.it/CM7.21

CLIP 7.22: Zakyla solves a multidigit Multiplication problem, and her thinking is extended   128
- http://smarturl.it/CM7.22

CLIP 7.23: Emma solves a multidigit Multiplication problem, and her thinking is extended   128
- http://smarturl.it/CM7.23

Chapter 8

CLIP 8.1: A kindergartner uses Direct Modeling to solve a variety of problems   131
- http://smarturl.it/CM8.1

Chapter 9

CLIP 9.1: Unpacking the problem context in Ms. Scott's class   136
- http://smarturl.it/CM9.1

CLIP 9.2: Unpacking the problem context to personalize the problem for a student   137
- http://smarturl.it/CM9.2

CLIP 9.3: Unpacking the problem context to help a student get started   137
- http://smarturl.it/CM9.3

CLIP 9.4: Ms. Byron, Ms. Hassay, and Ms. Grace begin by posing the problem   139
- http://smarturl.it/CM9.4

CLIP 9.5: Ms. Byron works with a student who has a partially correct strategy   143
- http://smarturl.it/CM9.5

CLIP 9.6: Ms. Dominguez works with a student who has an error   147
- http://smarturl.it/CM9.6

CLIP 9.7: Ms. Byron elicits a student's thinking about an invented algorithm   147
- http://smarturl.it/CM9.7

CLIP 9.8: Ms. Grace works with a student to extend a mathematical idea   148
- http://smarturl.it/CM9.8

CLIP 9.9: Ms. Barron works with students to extend a mathematical idea   148
- http://smarturl.it/CM9.9

CLIP 9.10: Ms. Scott explains how she decided to pose the marbles problem   151
- http://smarturl.it/CM9.10

Chapter 10

CLIP 10.1: Students in Ms. Grace's class share and compare strategies　　　156
- http://smarturl.it/CM10.1

CLIP 10.2: Ms. Byron supports students to engage with each other's ideas　　　166
- http://smarturl.it/CM10.2

CLIP 10.3: Ms. Barron's class discusses a student's Invented Algorithm　　　166
- http://smarturl.it/CM10.3

CLIP 10.4: Ms. Dominguez's class engages with each other's ideas　　　171
- http://smarturl.it/CM10.4

CLIP 10.5: Ms. Scott engages her class in a student's shared strategy　　　171
- http://smarturl.it/CM10.5

Chapter 11

CLIP 11.1: Juliet uses a fundamental property of addition in her strategy　　　183
- http://smarturl.it/CM11.1

CLIP 11.2: The teacher extends Roger's thinking about multiplication and elicits the use of a fundamental property　　　183
- http://smarturl.it/CM11.2

FOREWORD

Cognitively Guided Instruction (CGI) has moved the discussion of learning and teaching elementary school mathematics from the ABCs to the SRQs. This monumental change has been made through the thoughtful and persistent leadership of the CGI research and development group and their many colleagues. CGI is a tribute to all the children, teachers, and administrators who have experienced and contributed to this approach. This is my interpretation of CGI as viewed from one who has followed and learned from those who have been intimately involved in its development. My hope is that you, too, will learn from this publication.

I would like to thank Linda Jaslow, Mathematics Specialist, Northwest Arkansas Education Service Cooperative; John Johnson, Principal of Downtown School in Des Moines, Iowa; and Nick Johnson, Orange County Department of Education, California. They willingly responded to my request for their views about what CGI has meant to those with whom they have worked in quite diverse settings.

S IS FOR *SENSE MAKING*

Sense making is at the heart of all aspects of CGI. First, CGI expects and allows children to make sense of mathematics. As children solve problems that are appropriate for their development, which is often beyond what a traditional curriculum expects, they are grappling with what makes sense for them. You will see many examples of this aspect of learning in this book, so I will not belabor this point although it is, in my mind, the most important *S*.

Students are not the only ones making sense of mathematics. Teachers also make sense of the mathematics in the process of making sense of children's mathematical thinking. Teachers make sense of how to use knowledge of children's mathematical thinking to help children learn mathematics and to reach diverse students.

Sense making builds a firm foundation, allowing students to learn new mathematics using what they already know. These connections are essential to seeing mathematics as a coherent whole, not as a collection of isolated rules.

In summary, the sense-making underpinning of CGI affects students, teachers, and the mathematics they are learning and teaching.

S IS FOR *STANDARDS*

Recently, as I listened to interviews of teachers using CGI, I was struck with the consistent reaction to the Common Core State Standards for School Mathematics (CCSSM). As Linda Jaslow said, "When the CCSSM were released, many of our teachers and administrators felt like it was nothing new to them; they have been doing it for years." Although I was well acquainted with these standards, these reactions made me reread the Standards for Mathematical Practice. It is evident that CGI embodies the practice standards such as "make sense of problems and persevere in solving them." I know of no approach other than CGI that embeds this standard and the other practice standards in all instruction.

R IS FOR *RESEARCH*

Appendix A includes a summary of the research associated with CGI; it is research that I believe is exemplary in the mathematics education field. First, research on children's mathematical thinking is central to CGI. Second, it has been a long journey, over thirty years, that began with specific research-based knowledge of the development of children's basic number concepts and skills. The research included inquiry about how to help teachers use this research-based knowledge to build on the children's thinking. The research was conducted to learn and to adjust the next route according to what the children learned. Third, the research was also unique because teachers are partners, both formally and, importantly, informally as they become researchers of their own students' thinking and sense making.

R IS FOR *RESPECT*

First, there is respect for the students. It is a different way to think about who can do mathematics and what type of mathematics they can do. Linda Jaslow said, "CGI has changed the mathematical culture and expectations for student learning in many of our schools across Arkansas." This respect for students who can learn mathematics is reflected by Nick Johnson: "I see supporting teachers (and administrators) who inquire into their students' thinking, as an entry point into rethinking what mathematics is, who can do meaningful mathematics, and how opportunities to participate in mathematics are structured in our classrooms and schools."

Second, the students learn to respect the thinking of other students as they discuss and critique strategies. They not only learn from each other, they learn how to react to different ways of thinking and different explanations. This book describes this critical role, another example of the continual learning of all involved with CGI.

Third, there is respect for teachers, their views, and their expertise. Look at the number of teachers who are quoted in the book because they have important insights and because they are the ones who can make change in how students learn and view mathematics.

Fourth, there is respect for the professional development of teachers. As Nick Johnson said, "CGI completely changed not only how I think about the teaching and learning of mathematics, but also how I think about the goals and processes of professional development. Professional development in CGI is unique in that it supports teachers to inquire into and build upon children's thinking in ways that value the expertise and sense making that teachers bring with them." And John Johnson said, "I can honestly say that CGI provides the best professional development I have ever seen. It has a profound impact on the way teachers teach."

Last, there is respect for mathematics and why we learn mathematics—to solve problems.

Q IS FOR *QUESTIONING*

Central to instruction in CGI is the art of questioning. CGI teachers use questioning in many ways. They question to help them understand a child's mathematical thinking. They question to help a child articulate his or her strategies so classmates can understand and, in turn, the child develops better understanding. They encourage students to ask questions of other students.

When I wrote the foreword to the first book, *Children's Mathematics,* I posed many questions. The reflection questions included in this book are much deeper and more specific. They will guide your journey as you become more adept in helping children learn mathematics. Listen to the view of a principal: "Once teachers become better skilled at asking thoughtful questions to help children move to the next level in mathematical thinking, they also get better at their questioning skills in other curriculum areas" (John Johnson).

Q IS FOR *QUEST*

As this journey continues to provide mathematics instruction that benefits all children and to provide professional development that empowers teachers to build on children's mathematical thinking, I hope you will join or continue that journey with many others across the United States. When a child presented with a new problem or a challenge to his or her thinking says, "I can do this," all of us will benefit.

—Mary Montgomery Lindquist
Fuller E. Callaway Professor of Mathematics Education, Emeritus
Columbus State University, Columbus, Georgia
Past President, The National Council of Teachers of Mathematics

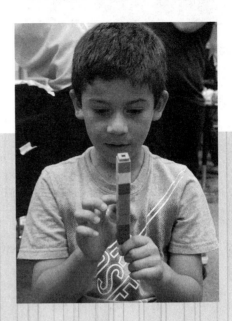

Introduction

The better I get at listening to children, the clearer I hear them tell me how to teach them.

—Elementary school teacher

Over the past thirty years, we have observed how much children are capable of learning when their teachers truly understand children's thinking and provide them an opportunity to build on their own thinking. We also have learned from teachers how important it is for them to have explicit knowledge of children's mathematical thinking. One of the first teachers we worked with commented, "I have always known that it was important to listen to kids, but I never knew what questions to ask or what to listen for."

This book provides a detailed account of the development of children's mathematical thinking and how teachers can promote this development in ways that honor children's thinking. It provides a framework for understanding children's thinking in whole number arithmetic and describes how this thinking evolves over time. It also illustrates how teachers have created powerful learning communities in which students engage with one another's ideas to build their understanding of mathematics.

We have revised *Children's Mathematics* to reflect what we have learned through research and experience talking with children, participating in classrooms, and leading professional development over the past fifteen years. But the central story remains the same. The second edition continues to focus on understanding children's mathematical thinking. As was the case in the first edition, we do not provide specific directions for how to organize a classroom or how to implement instruction. Teaching is a complex problem-solving endeavor. Because of the intimate knowledge that you have of your own students, you are most qualified to make immediate decisions about supporting your students' mathematical learning.

That said, in the fifteen years since the publication of the first edition, we have learned a great deal about what classrooms look like when teachers' mathematics instruction is guided by children's thinking. We now have much more explicit knowledge of features of successful Cognitively Guided Instruction (CGI) classrooms than we did when we wrote the first edition, and this is reflected in two new chapters on classroom instruction. It is not easy to describe a typical CGI classroom because each one is unique. Our goal is not to provide models of classroom instruction to serve as a template for you to apply to your own classroom. Rather, we present specific cases that embody first principles of successful CGI classrooms. Our goal is for teachers individually and in collaboration with other teachers to make sense of the principles in relation to their own classes and teaching styles.

In addition to the revisions and new chapters on teaching, this edition also includes a new chapter that examines the mathematical principles underlying children's strategies and a new chapter addressing the conceptual basis for CGI. It also includes reflection questions with many of the chapters. Together these additions provide opportunities for digging into the content, relating children's thinking to practice, and making sense of the rationale for the ideas presented.

A major contribution of the second edition is an entirely new, greatly expanded collection of video interviews of children and cases of classrooms supporting the development of children's mathematics. Whereas the first volume included video examples of children solving selected problems, the second edition provides a much more extensive collection of examples that cover most of the major problem types and strategies for solving them. Our growing understanding of critical features of classroom interactions is reflected in video cases that embody first principles of successful CGI classrooms. Over ninety episodes include interviews of children solving problems, interviews illustrating extended interactions between a child and the individual interviewing the child, and classroom cases.

THE CGI TRILOGY

Children's Mathematics focuses on the development of whole-number arithmetic in the primary grades, but there is more to learning basic arithmetic than we can cover in this one book. Learning about whole numbers should provide a foundation for learning about fractions and decimals, and it should involve a seamless transition to learning algebra.

It has been proposed that the learning of fractions is a critical juncture in students' learning of mathematics and that many students' difficulties with mathematics in later grades can be traced to their basic misconceptions about fractions. We suggest, however, that most students' difficulties with fractions and decimals is grounded in their limited understanding of whole number arithmetic and the fact that traditional arithmetic instruction on fractions does not build on children's intuitive notions of sharing. We introduce the concept of sharing (Partitive Division) in Chapter 4. The initial focus is on sharing that results in whole number answers, but the activity of sharing lays the foundation for solving similar problems that establish basic fraction concepts.

The treatment of addition and subtraction of multidigit whole numbers emphasizes combining the same units (ones, tens, hundreds, etc.). Unlike a procedural knowledge of adding and subtracting whole numbers that starts with lining up the numbers on the right, understanding that it is necessary to combine the same units can be directly extended to adding and subtracting decimal numbers. It also supports understanding why it is necessary to add and subtract fractions with common denominators. The extension of whole number concepts to fractions and decimals is discussed in greater detail in *Extending Children's Mathematics: Fractions and Decimals* (Empson and Levi 2011).

CGI also provides a foundation for the transition to learning algebra by engaging children in developing practices based on the powerful ideas that underlie both arithmetic and algebra. The artificial separation of arithmetic and algebra is avoided by an emphasis on building and expressing relations rather than practicing inflexible step-by-step procedures. These ideas are discussed in more detail in Chapter 11 and in *Thinking Mathematically: Integrating Arithmetic and Algebra in Elementary School* (Carpenter, Franke, and Levi 2003).

NATIONAL REPORTS ON SCHOOL MATHEMATICS

Since the publication of the first edition of *Children's Mathematics*, a number of reports have been issued that present a broad consensus about research findings, curriculum standards, and/or instructional practices for mathematics instruction. These reports include *Adding It Up* (National Research Council 2001), *Principles and Standards for School Mathematics* (National Council of teachers of Mathematics 2000), *Curriculum Focal Points for Kindergarten Through Grade 8 Mathematics* (National Council of Teachers of Mathematics 2006), and *The Common Core State Standards for Mathematics* (National Governors Association Center for Best Practices, and Council of Chief State School Officers 2010). A common theme running through all of these reports is the critical importance of learning with understanding. Although CGI predates these reports, it draws on and has contributed to the same research base that grounds their recommendations. Teachers who understand how children think about mathematics are well equipped to teach for understanding regardless of the specific reform initiatives. For example, consider reflections from two CGI teachers on the relationship between CGI and the Common Core State Standards for Mathematics in their teaching.

I teach CGI Professional Development Classes for a State-Funded Education Co-op that serves seventeen school districts. Over the past eight years, we have provided CGI PD to over 700 teachers. Our teachers love the results they are seeing with their students. Before seeing the Common Core math standards, some teachers were a little anxious about what this would mean for their CGI math instruction. When the Common Core math standards were released, our teachers just smiled. They felt like this is what they have been doing for the past 8 years both in content (CGI) and in the pedagogical practices (the Standards of Mathematical Practice). This was not new for them. The CCSSM were just another confirmation of the importance of using CGI in their classrooms.

—Linda Jaslow, Math Specialist

I don't think you can do the Common Core justice without knowledge of children's thinking. Good teaching isn't just about giving children problems or knowing the standards; good teaching starts with knowing what the children understand and then purposefully crafting problems to deepen and extend that knowledge. I think it is much easier to craft problems to meet the needs of students because of my work with CGI. For me, the Problem Type and Solution Strategy frameworks along with understanding children's base-ten acquisition are key in terms of understanding what children know and any misconceptions they might have, and the frameworks provide purposeful next steps in instruction. I can't just look at the CCSS, I also need to know what the children know and understand. CGI gives me the framework to do just that. The CGI problem types are a vehicle for both assessment and further learning.

—Annie Keith, teacher

1

Children's Mathematical Thinking

It is only when you build from within that you really understand something. If children don't build from within and you just try to explain it to a child, then it's not really learned. It is only rote, and that's not really understanding.

—Ann Badeau, teacher

Initially, young children's conceptions of addition, subtraction, multiplication, and division are quite different from adults'. This does not mean that their conceptions are wrong or misguided. In fact, their conceptions make a great deal of sense, and they provide a basis for learning basic mathematical concepts and skills with understanding.

This chapter provides a picture of the overarching principles underlying children's thinking. This perspective provides a unifying structure for understanding the more detailed analyses of children's thinking in addition, subtraction, multiplication, and division with single- and multidigit numbers in the following chapters.

MODELING THE ACTION AND RELATIONS IN PROBLEMS

Consider the following problems:

> *Eliz had 12 cookies. She ate 5 of them. How many cookies does Eliz have left?*

> *Eliz has 5 dollars to buy cookies. How many more dollars does she need to earn to have 12 dollars?*

> *Eliz has 5 dollars. Tom has 12 dollars. How many more dollars does Tom have than Eliz?*

Most adults would solve all three of these problems by subtracting 5 from 12. For young children, however, these are three different problems, which they solve using different strategies. For example, Tanya, a beginning first-grader, solved the first problem with physical objects by putting out 12 cubes and removing 5 of them. She found the answer by counting the cubes that remained. For the second problem, she started with a set of 5 cubes and added more until there was a total of 12 cubes. She counted the 7 cubes that she had added to the initial set to find the answer. For the third problem, she made two sets, one containing 5 cubes and one containing 12. She lined them up so that the set of 5 matched the first 5 cubes in the set of 12, and she counted the unmatched cubes in the set of 12. Tanya's strategies for solving these problems are typical of the way that most children her age solve them.

The different solutions to these three problems illustrate that, in the eyes of children, not all addition or subtraction problems are alike. There are important distinctions between different types of addition problems and between different types of subtraction problems, which are reflected in the way that children think about and solve them. However, although Tanya used a different strategy for each problem, there is a common thread that ties the strategies together. In each case, she *directly modeled* the action or relationship described in the problem. The first problem involved the action of removing 5 from 12, and that is how Tanya modeled the problem. In the second problem, the action was additive, and Tanya started with a set representing the initial quantity and added cubes to it. The third problem involved a comparison of two quantities, so Tanya used a strategy for comparing two sets.

Now look at how Tanya solved the following division problems:

> *Ramon had 12 gumdrops. He put 3 gumdrops on each cupcake. How many cupcakes was he able to put gumdrops on?*

There are 20 children in the first-grade class. The teacher wants to divide the class into 4 teams with the same number of children on each team. How many children will be on each team?

For the first problem, Tanya put out 12 cubes. Then she put 3 of them in one group, 3 more in another, 3 more in a third group, and the final 3 made the fourth group. To find the answer, she counted the *groups*. For the second problem, she first put out 20 cubes. Then she dealt the cubes one by one into 4 piles. To find the answer, she counted the *cubes* in one of the piles.

Again, Tanya directly modeled the action described in the problems. In the first case, she made groups of a specified size and counted the groups to find the answer. In the second, she made a given number of groups with the same number in each group and counted the cubes in one of the groups to find the answer. The differences in the strategies used to solve the two problems reflect the different actions described in the problems. Although adults may recognize both as division problems, young children initially think of them in terms of the actions or relationships portrayed in the problems.

USING COUNTING STRATEGIES AND DERIVED NUMBER FACTS

The action and relationships in a problem tend to influence the strategies that children use for an extended period of time, but older children do not always represent all the quantities in a problem with physical objects. Over time, Direct Modeling strategies give way to more efficient Counting strategies, which are generally more abstract ways of modeling a problem. For example, José, another first-grader, solved the same problem that Tanya physically modeled by counting on from 5 to 12:

Eliz has 5 dollars to buy cookies. How many more dollars does she need to earn to have 12 dollars?

José started at 5 and counted, "5 [pause] 6, 7, 8, 9, 10, 11, 12." As he counted from 6 to 12, he extended a finger with each count. When he reached 12, he counted the extended fingers to get 7 dollars. What distinguishes this solution from Tanya's is that José realized that he did not have to make the initial set of 5 objects. He could represent the extra dollars needed by the numbers in the counting sequence from 6 to 12. The trick was to figure out how many numbers there were in that sequence, which he did by keeping track on his fingers. This is a more abstract solution than Tanya used, but the counting sequence still parallels the action in the problem. He solved the problem in which Eliz ate 5 cookies by counting back from 12, "12 [pause], 11, 10, 9, 8, 7. She has 7 left."

No one taught these Counting strategies to José. He invented them himself. The invention of increasingly efficient procedures for representing addition, subtraction, multiplication, and division problems is another kind of problem solving for which young children demonstrate remarkable facility and creativity. Children also demonstrate this skill in the ways they use their developing knowledge of number facts. For example, Zena, another first-grade student, could not recall the number fact 8 + 5 in solving a problem, but she knew that 8 + 2 is 10, so she said, "I know 8 plus 2 is 10 and then I just have 3 more from the 5 to add. 10 plus 3 is 13, so 8 plus 5 is 13."

DOING WHAT COMES NATURALLY

All of the strategies we have described come naturally to young children. Children do not have to be taught that a particular strategy goes with a particular type of problem. With opportunity and encouragement, children construct for themselves strategies that model the action or relationships in a problem. Similarly, they do not have to be shown how to count on or be explicitly taught specific Derived Facts. In an environment that encourages children to use procedures that are meaningful to them, they will construct these strategies. This is not to say that all children individually construct these solutions by themselves. Children adapt strategies as they engage with other children using different strategies and discuss mathematical ideas with their teacher or other children. But the strategies we have described emerge in classrooms without direct instruction by the teacher. Numerous research studies have shown that virtually all children use the strategies described here at various times in the development of their understanding of basic number concepts (see Appendix A).

Children enter school with a great deal of informal or intuitive knowledge of mathematics that can serve as the basis for developing understanding of the mathematics of the primary school curriculum. Without direct instruction on specific number facts, algorithms, or procedures, children can construct viable solutions to a variety of problems. Basic operations of addition, subtraction, multiplication, and division can be defined in terms of these intuitive problem-solving processes, and symbolic procedures can be developed as extensions of them.

LOOKING AHEAD

The previous examples illustrate how the structure of a problem influences the strategies that children use to solve it. In order to understand how children think about addition, subtraction, multiplication, and division, it is necessary to consider differences among problems. In the chapters that follow, we set forth classification schemes for describing important differences among addition and subtraction problems and multiplication and division problems. These analyses provide a framework for understanding the strategies that children use to solve problems.

Our purpose is not simply to identify a collection of problems for children to solve using the strategies we describe. Our overarching goal is to provide a basis for developing understanding of basic number concepts and operations by connecting them to children's surprisingly rich intuitive conceptions and giving them an opportunity to extend those concepts in ways that make sense to them.

Chapter 2 leads off with an analysis of addition and subtraction problems. Using this analysis, we detail the evolution of children's strategies for solving these problems (Chapter 3). Initially, children model the action and relations in problems that reflect the distinctions portrayed in the analysis of problem types for the four operations. Over time, this physical modeling gives way to more efficient Counting strategies, which are generally more abstract ways of modeling a problem. Eventually children come to rely on number facts, but number facts are not learned by rote. Using number facts to solve problems is built upon an understanding of properties of operation and number sense, which develop as children abstract their Direct Modeling and Counting strategies. Chapter 4 portrays a similar picture of the development of multiplication and division concepts and procedures.

Base-ten number concepts and multidigit algorithms emerge as extensions of the concepts and strategies that children have learned for smaller numbers. The grouping and partitioning in which children engage for multiplication and division provide direct support for conceptualizing a group of ten as a unit, which is the basis for the base-ten system. As children develop familiarity with base-ten concepts, they extend their Direct Modeling strategies to use materials that include groups of ten. Over time, these Direct Modeling strategies are abstracted as children construct Invented Algorithms for carrying out calculations. The development of base-ten number concepts and strategies for solving multidigit problems are described in Chapters 6 and 7. In Chapter 8, we return to the notion of problem solving as modeling and examine it in a broader context.

In Chapters 5, 9, and 10, we discuss how Cognitively Guided Instruction (CGI) can be applied in the classroom. We first look at some broad principles to consider as you begin to implement CGI (Chapter 5). We placed this chapter in the midst of the children's thinking chapters to provide you the opportunity to think about the development of children's thinking in relation to classroom practice while you are extending your knowledge of children's mathematical thinking. In Chapter 9, we discuss how teachers pose problems to make sure their students can engage with the mathematics

We encourage you to ask children to solve some of the problems presented in this book as you read. Interacting with children is essential to learning about children's mathematical thinking. Connecting the information in this book with experiences with children will result in a far richer understanding of children's thinking than reading the book alone. Discussing these ideas with a colleague or group of colleagues will further enhance your understanding.

in the problem. We also discuss eliciting students' strategies and the questions teachers ask to encourage students to explain details of their strategies. In Chapter 10, we look at examples of students engaging with one another's strategies and how teachers support this engagement.

In Chapter 11, we examine the mathematical principles underlying children's strategies and consider how children's strategies contribute to their understanding of fundamental properties of number and operations. In Chapter 12, we discuss the conceptual framework for learning with understanding that has emerged from our research and represents the underlying principles of CGI. In Chapter 13, we conclude with the theme that learning to use CGI is a journey that continues throughout a teacher's career. Appendix A summarizes the research basis for CGI.

2

Addition and Subtraction: Problem Types

This chapter describes a classification scheme for addition and subtraction problems that provides a structure for interpreting how children solve different problems and for selecting problems for instruction. There are important distinctions among different types of addition and subtraction problems that are reflected in the ways that children think about and solve them.

One of the most useful ways of classifying word problems focuses on the types of action or relationships described in the problems. Research has shown this classification corresponds to the way that children think about problems. As a result, this scheme distinguishes among problems that children solve differently and provides a way to identify the relative difficulty of various problems.

For addition and subtraction problems, four basic classes of problems can be identified: *Join, Separate, Part-Part-Whole,* and *Compare*. The number size can vary, as can the theme or context of the problems; however, the basic structure involving actions and relationships remains the same. Join and Separate problems involve action. In Join problems, elements are added to a given set. In Separate problems, elements are removed from a given set. Part-Part-Whole and Compare problems do not involve actions. Part-Part-Whole problems involve the relationship between a set and its two subsets. Compare problems involve comparisons between two disjoint sets. Problems within a class all involve the same type of action upon quantities or relationships between quantities. Within each class, several distinct types of problems can be identified depending upon which quantity is the unknown.

JOIN PROBLEMS

Join problems involve a direct or implied action in which a set is increased by a particular amount. The following is an example of the type of Join problem that teachers commonly use to introduce addition:

> *4 birds were sitting in a tree. 8 more birds flew onto the tree. How many birds were in the tree then?*

The action in the problem takes place over time: There is a starting quantity at Time 1 (the 4 birds sitting in the tree); a second (or change) quantity is joined to the initial quantity at Time 2 (the 8 birds that flew onto the tree); the result is a final quantity at Time 3 (the 12 birds then in the tree).

Although the resulting set of birds is composed of the birds initially in the tree and the birds that joined them, the two sets of birds take on quite different roles in the problem because of the temporal nature of the action. These distinctions are important because children may not initially realize that 8 birds joining 4 birds gives the same result as 4 birds joining 8 birds. Furthermore, three distinct types of Join problems can be generated by varying which quantity is the unknown (Figure 2.1). Each of these problems represents a different problem to young children. Children use different strategies to solve them, and they vary in difficulty.

Join Problem Types

Unknown	Example
Result Unknown	*Robin had 6 toy cars. Her parents gave her 8 more toy cars for her birthday. How many toy cars did she have then?*
Change Unknown	*Robin had 6 toy cars. Her parents gave her some more toy cars for her birthday. Then she had 14 toy cars. How many toy cars did Robin's parents give her for her birthday?*
Start Unknown	*Robin had some toy cars. Her parents gave her 8 more toy cars for her birthday. Then she had 14 toy cars. How many toy cars did Robin have before her birthday?*

FIGURE 2.1

SEPARATE PROBLEMS

Separate problems are similar to Join problems in many respects. There is an action that takes place over time, but in this case the action in the problem is one in which the initial quantity is decreased rather than increased. As with Join problems, there are three distinct quantities in Separate problems, any one of which can be the unknown. There is a starting quantity, a change quantity (the amount removed), and the result. Figure 2.2 gives examples of the three distinct types of Separate problems that can be generated by varying the unknown.

Separate Problem Types

Unknown	Example
Result Unknown	*Colleen had 13 pencils. She gave 4 pencils to Roger. How many pencils does Colleen have left?*
Change Unknown	*Colleen had 13 pencils. She gave some pencils to Roger. Then she had 9 pencils left. How many pencils did Colleen give Roger?*
Start Unknown	*Colleen had some pencils. She gave 4 pencils to Roger. Then she had 9 pencils left. How many pencils did Colleen have to start with?*

FIGURE 2.2

PART-PART-WHOLE PROBLEMS

Part-Part-Whole problems involve static relationships among a particular set and its two disjoint subsets. Unlike the Join and Separate problems, there is no direct or implied action, and there is no change over time. Because one set is not being joined to the other, both subsets assume equivalent roles in the problem. Therefore, only two Part-Part-Whole problem types exist. The problem either gives the two parts and asks one to find the size of the whole, or gives one of the parts and the whole and asks the solver to find the size of the other part (see Figure 2.3).

Part-Part-Whole Problem Types

Unknown	Example
Whole Unknown	*8 boys and 7 girls were playing soccer. How many children were playing soccer?*
Part Unknown	*15 children were playing soccer. 8 were boys and the rest were girls. How many girls were playing soccer?*

FIGURE 2.3

COMPARE PROBLEMS

Compare problems, like Part-Part-Whole problems, involve relationships between quantities rather than a joining or separating action, but Compare problems involve the comparison of two distinct, disjoint sets rather than the relationship between a set and its subsets. Because one set is compared to the other, one set is labeled the *referent set* and the other, the *compared set*. The third entity in these problems is the difference, or the amount by which one set exceeds the other. The following comparison situation illustrates these different elements:

Mark has 8 mice.	*Referent set*
Joy has 12 mice.	*Compared set*
Joy has 4 more mice than Mark.	*Difference*

In a Compare problem, any one of the three entities can be the unknown—the difference, the referent set, or the compared set. Figure 2.4 gives an example of each type of problem.

Compare Problem Types

Unknown	Example
Difference Unknown	*Mark has 8 mice. Joy has 12 mice. Joy has how many more mice than Mark?*
Compared Set Unknown	*Mark has 8 mice. Joy has 4 more mice than Mark. How many mice does Joy have?*
Referent Unknown	*Joy has 12 mice. She has 4 more mice than Mark. How many mice does Mark have?*

FIGURE 2.4

NUMBER SENTENCES: ANOTHER PERSPECTIVE ON PROBLEM TYPES

Another way to think about the distinctions among certain problem types is to consider number sentences that can be used to represent them. This is particularly useful with Join and Separate problems. The three terms in addition and subtraction number sentences, such as $6 + 8 = 14$ and $13 - 4 = 9$, correspond to the three quantities in Join and Separate problems. As with the word problems, any of the terms can be the unknown, yielding a number sentence that corresponds to a particular Join or Separate problem. In Figure 2.5, we present number sentences representing the word problems in Figures 2.1 and 2.2. These problems clearly illustrate the distinction between problems with different unknowns. It is not possible to make such a clear correspondence between each of the Part-Part-Whole or Compare problems and number sentences because there is no action in the problems and thus no clear starting quantity, change quantity, or resulting quantity.

Join/Separate Problems Number Sentence Correspondence

Unknown	Join	Separate
Result Unknown	$6 + 8 = \square$	$13 - 4 = \square$
Change Unknown	$6 + \square = 14$	$13 - \square = 9$
Start Unknown	$\square + 8 = 14$	$\square - 4 = 9$

FIGURE 2.5

OTHER CONSIDERATIONS

Children's ability to solve word problems depends to a great degree on their ability to understand and model the action or situation in the problem. Variations in the wording of the problems and in the situations they depict can make a problem more or less difficult for children to solve.

We can make problems easier for children by making the action or relationships in the problems as clear as possible and using contexts that are familiar to the children in the class such as games some children play at home, things that a child in the class collects, or a trip that a child may be taking. Sometimes teachers use a common classroom experience such as a read-aloud book, a science or social studies project, or a field trip to set the context of a collection of problems. Teachers also write problems around out-of-school experiences of a child or groups of children to help children see how math is related to their home and community life.

Problems also are easier if their wording corresponds to the action sequence. Compare the following problems:

Janice had 9 cookies. She ate 3 of them. How many cookies does Janice have left?

Janice just ate 3 cookies. She started with 9 cookies. How many cookies does Janice have now?

In the first problem, the starting quantity is given first. In the second problem, the change quantity is given before the starting quantity. This requires a more careful analysis of the problem. Consequently, the first problem tends to be easier, but the second problem provides a more rigorous test of whether children are carefully analyzing the problem or just mechanically operating on the numbers given in the problem.

Other changes in wording also help make the action sequence more apparent to children, although it is sometimes difficult to point to the factor that makes one problem easier than another. Join (Change Unknown) problems that ask, "How many more are needed?" are generally easier than related problems in which the action has taken place in the past. For example, the first Join (Change Unknown) problem given below is easier for children than the second:

> *Tom has 7 stickers. How many more stickers does Tom have to get to have 11 stickers?*

> *Tom had 7 stickers. His sister gave him some more stickers. Now he has 11 stickers. How many stickers did Tom's sister give him?*

Another way that each of the problems described in the preceding sections can vary is whether or not the quantities described in the problems represent identifiable, discrete sets of objects. All of the problems presented in the preceding sections included quantities that could be directly represented using counters. Each counter could be used to represent a pencil, a mouse, or a sticker described in the problem. Such is not the case with problems involving continuous measures. For instance, consider this Join (Change Unknown) problem:

> *Cheryl's puppy weighed 3 pounds when she bought him. The puppy now weighs 12 pounds. How many pounds has the puppy gained?*

The pounds of puppy are not clearly identifiable objects. Using counters to represent the 12 pounds of puppy involves a more abstract representation than the representation of mice or pencils.

SUMMARY

We have identified four basic classes of addition and subtraction word problems. Each of the problems within each class involves the same general context, but has a different unknown. By varying the unknown within each class, a total of eleven distinct types of problems can be constructed. This classification of problem types is based on years of research on how children think about addition and subtraction.

We name the problem types in order to facilitate teachers' reflections about students' thinking and professional discussions among educators. We do not recommend that problem type names be used with students or that students be expected to learn them. A major thesis of CGI is that children solve these problems naturally by attending to the context. Having students learn problem type names or identify the problem type would be counterproductive, because it would distract students from attending to and reasoning about the context. Similarly we do not recommend that children be taught key-word strategies to help them solve problems. Such strategies are ineffective in dealing with anything but a narrow set of problem situations and discourage children from making sense of the problems they solve.

In Figure 2.6, we present examples of each basic problem type. The differences among the eleven problem types is important because they are related to how children solve the problems, which in turn affects the difficulty level of different problems. We discuss the relationship between problem structure and children's solution strategies in the next chapter.

Addition and Subtraction Problem Types

Join (Result Unknown)	Join (Change Unknown)	Join (Start Unknown)
Connie had 5 marbles. Juan gave her 8 more marbles. How many marbles does Connie have altogether?	Connie has 5 marbles. How many more marbles does she need to have 13 marbles altogether?	Connie had some marbles. Juan gave her 5 more marbles. Now she has 13 marbles. How many marbles did Connie have to start with?
Separate (Result Unknown)	**Separate (Change Unknown)**	**Separate (Start Unknown)**
Connie had 13 marbles. She gave 5 to Juan. How many marbles does Connie have left?	Connie had 13 marbles. She gave some to Juan. Now she has 5 marbles left. How many marbles did Connie give to Juan?	Connie had some marbles. She gave 5 to Juan. Now she has 8 marbles left. How many marbles did Connie have to start with?
Part-Part-Whole (Whole Unknown)	**Part-Part-Whole (Part Unknown)**	
Connie has 5 red marbles and 8 blue marbles. How many marbles does she have?	Connie has 13 marbles. 5 are red and the rest are blue. How many blue marbles does Connie have?	
Compare (Difference Unknown)	**Compare (Compare Quantity Unknown)**	**Compare (Referent Unknown)**
Connie has 13 marbles. Juan has 5 marbles. How many more marbles does Connie have than Juan?	Juan has 5 marbles. Connie has 8 more than Juan. How many marbles does Connie have?	Connie has 13 marbles. She has 5 more marbles than Juan. How many marbles does Juan have?

FIGURE 2.6

QUESTIONS FOR FURTHER REFLECTION

1. CGI teachers find it important to write problems using contexts that are familiar and interesting to their students. Choose a book that you are reading with your students or a topic that you are studying. Write one problem for each of the problem types that relate to the story or topic. Here are some examples of problems that Annie Keith, a second- and third-grade teacher, wrote when her students were studying rocks and fossils.

   a. *Join (Change Unknown):* Russ has 143 rocks in his collection. His sister Christie gave him a box of rocks for his birthday. Now Russ has 182 rocks in his collection. How many rocks did his sister give to him?

   b. *Part-Part-Whole (Whole Unknown):* On our walk, we found 145 pieces of sandstone and 76 pieces of granite. We didn't find any other types of rocks. How many rocks did we find on our walk?

   c. *Part-Part-Whole (Part Unknown):* Takara brought his rock collection in for us to look at. He has 35 rocks. 17 of those rocks are granite and the rest are agates. How many agates does Takara have?

   d. *Compare (Difference Unknown):* Ms. Wiesner's class has 139 fossils. We have 206 fossils. How many fewer fossils does Ms. Wiesner's class have than we do?

2. Identify the problem type for each of the following problems. You might want to start by identifying the action (joining or separating) or situation (part-part-whole or compare) and then decide what is unknown.

   a. *Aubrey had 22 books. Her grandma gave her 8 books for her birthday. How many books does Aubrey have now?*

   b. *Peter has 8 paperback books and 4 hard cover books in his book bag. How many books does Peter have in his book bag?*

   c. *Zach is 11 and Finn is 8. How many years older is Zach than Finn?*

   d. *Karen had 7 dollars. Her mother gave her some money for mowing the lawn and now she has 13 dollars. How much money did Karen's mother give her for mowing the lawn?*

   e. *Bob had a full box of crayons. He lost 4 crayons and now he has 8 crayons. How many crayons were in the full box that Bob had to start with?*

3. For an additional challenge, identify the problem type for each of these problems:

   a. *Saul had 21 candies. He ate some of them. Then he had 6 candies left. How many candies did Saul eat?*

   b. *When I left the mall I had 12 dollars. I know I spent 3 dollars at the mall. How much money did I have before I went into the mall?*

   c. *Juan had 15 boxes of candy. There were 4 candies in each box. He ate all of the candies in 3 of the boxes. How many full boxes of candy did Juan have left?*

   d. *After her birthday party, Melissa counted her books and told her dad that she now has 50 books. Melissa's dad knows that Melissa had 39 books before her birthday party. How many books did Melissa get for her birthday?*

   e. *Madison has 3 sticker books. There are 6 stickers in one book. There are 9 stickers in another book. There are 7 stickers in the third book. How many stickers does Madison have?*

   f. *Liam had 8 chocolate chip cookies and 9 sugar cookies. He ate 3 chocolate chip cookies. How many cookies did Liam have left?*

4. Below are some pairs of problems. For each pair of problems:

   a. Decide how the problems are alike and different from each other.

   b. Pose both problems to some children.

   c. After you have watched the children solve the problem, think about whether you have anything to add about how the problems are alike and different.

   A1: Andy has 9 rocks. How many more rocks would he need to get to have 13 rocks?

   A2: Andy had 13 rocks. He gave 9 of them to Todd. How many rocks does Andy have now?

   B1: David had 14 cookies. He ate 6 cookies. How many cookies does David have left?

   B2: David has 14 cookies. Liz has 6 cookies. How many more cookies does David have than Liz?

   C1: Makayla had some erasers in a box. She gave 9 erasers to her friend. Now she has 7 erasers in the box. How many erasers did Makayla give to her friend?

   C2: Makayla has a box of erasers. The erasers in her box are either pink or purple. She has 9 pink erasers and 7 purple erasers. How many erasers does Makayla have before she gave some to her class?

3

Addition and Subtraction: Children's Solution Strategies

In this chapter, we discuss the strategies that children use to solve the addition and subtraction problems described in Chapter 2. Research has identified a remarkably coherent picture of the strategies that children invent to solve addition and subtraction problems and how they evolve over time. The distinctions among problem types are reflected in children's solution processes. For the most basic strategies, children use physical objects (counters), pictures, tally marks, or fingers to directly model the action or relationships described in each problem. Over time, children's strategies become more abstract and efficient. Direct Modeling strategies are replaced by more abstract Counting strategies, which in turn are replaced with Number Fact strategies.

DIRECT MODELING STRATEGIES

Children invent Direct Modeling strategies to solve many of the problem types discussed in Chapter 2. The Direct Modeling strategies vary based on the action or relationships described in the problems and the location of the unknown.

Joining All

The Direct Modeling strategies for the Join (Result Unknown) and Part-Part-Whole (Whole Unknown) problems are similar. To solve Join (Result Unknown) or Part-Part-Whole (Whole Unknown) problems, children use objects or fingers to represent each of the addends, and then they count the union of the two sets. We illustrate this strategy, called *Joining All*, in the following example:

> *Robin had 4 toy cars. Her friends gave her 7 more toy cars for her birthday. How many toy cars did she have then?*
>
> Karla makes a set of 4 cubes and a set of 7 cubes. She pushes them together and then counts them, "1, 2, 3, 4, 5, 6, 7, 8, 9, 10, 11," pointing to a cube with each count. Karla then responds, "She had 11 cars."

Joining To

A similar strategy is used to solve Join (Change Unknown) problems. The primary difference is that the goal is to find the number of objects added to the initial set rather than the total. The child makes a set equivalent to the initial quantity and adds objects to it until the new collection is equal to the total given in the problem. The number of objects added is the answer. This strategy, called *Joining To*, is illustrated in the following example and in Figure 3.1.

FIGURE 3.1 Carl uses a Direct Modeling strategy to solve a Join (Change Unknown) problem

> *Robin has 9 toy cars. How many more toy cars does she need to get for her birthday to have 12 toy cars altogether?*
>
> Carl makes a set of 9 cubes. He adds additional cubes, counting, "10, 11, 12" until there is a total of 12 cubes. He keeps the cubes that he adds separate from the initial set of 9 cubes so that he can count them separately. He then counts the 3 cubes he added. Carl responds, "She needs 3 more."

One important difference between this strategy and the Joining All strategy is that children must plan ahead and anticipate that they will need to distinguish the counters that they join to the initial set from the counters in the initial set so that they can count them separately. They may do this by keeping the counters physically separate or by using different-colored counters. This requires some advanced planning that the Joining All strategy does not.

CLIP 3.1 Direct Modeling strategy for a Join (Change Unknown) problem http://smarturl.it/CM3.1

Separating From

The strategy that best models the Separate (Result Unknown) problem involves a subtracting or separating action. In this case, the larger quantity in the problem is initially represented, and the smaller quantity is subsequently removed from it. We give an example of this strategy, called *Separating From*, below:

> *Colleen had 12 pencils. She gave 5 pencils to Roger. How many pencils does Colleen have left?*
>
> Karla makes a set of 12 cubes and removes 5 of them. She counts the remaining cubes. Karla then responds, "She has 7 left."

CLIP 3.2 Direct Modeling strategy for a Separate (Result Unknown) problem http://smarturl.it/CM3.2

Separating To

The Separate (Change Unknown) problem also involves a separating action. The strategy generally used to solve this problem is similar to the Separating From strategy except that objects are removed from the larger set until the number of objects remaining is equal to the smaller number given in the problem. The following example illustrates this strategy, called *Separating To*:

CLIP 3.3 Direct Modeling strategy for a Separate (Result Unknown) problem in which a teacher responds to a miscount http://smarturl.it/CM3.3

> *Roger had 11 stickers. He gave some to Colleen. He has 3 stickers left. How many stickers did he give to Colleen?*
>
> Karla makes a set of 11 cubes. She slowly removes cubes one by one until she sees that there are only 3 cubes left. She then counts the 8 cubes that were removed. Karla then responds, "He gave her 8."

Separating To involves a certain amount of trial and error because the child can't simply count objects as they are physically removed but must check the initial set to determine whether the appropriate number of objects remains. Children can most easily apply this strategy when there are a small number of items remaining so that the child

CLIP 3.4 Direct Modeling strategy for a Separate (Change Unknown) problem http://smarturl.it/CM3.4

can perceive whether there are 2 or 3 objects left without needing to count them. This strategy is not as commonly used by children as the Direct Modeling strategies described above for Join and Separate (Result Unknown) and Join (Change Unknown) problems.

Matching

Compare (Difference Unknown) problems describe a matching process. The strategy used to solve these problems involves the construction of a one-to-one correspondence between two sets until one set is exhausted. Counting the unmatched elements gives the answer. We illustrate the Matching strategy in the following example and in Figure 3.2.

> *Mark has 6 mice. Joy has 9 mice. Joy has how many more mice than Mark?*
>
> Karla counts out a set of 6 cubes and another set of 9 cubes. She puts the set of 6 cubes in a row. She then makes a row of the 9 cubes next to the row of 6 cubes so that 6 of the cubes are aligned with the 6 cubes in the initial row. She then counts the 3 cubes that are not matched with a cube in the initial row. Karla responds, "She has 3 more."

CLIP 3.5 Direct Modeling strategy for a Compare (Difference Unknown) problem http://smarturl.it/CM3.5

FIGURE 3.2 Karla uses a Direct Modeling strategy to solve a Compare (Difference Unknown) problem

Trial and Error

It is difficult to model the Start Unknown problems because the initial quantity is unknown and therefore cannot be represented. A few children attempt to solve these problems using a Trial and Error strategy.

The following example shows one such attempt:

Robin had some toy cars. Her friends gave her 5 more toy cars for her birthday. Then she had 11 toy cars. How many toy cars did Robin have before her birthday?

Karla counts out 3 cubes. She then adds 5 cubes to the original set and counts the total. Finding that the total is 8 rather than 11, she puts the cubes back with the unused cubes and starts over. Next she makes a set of 5 cubes and adds 5 more to it. Again she counts and realizes her original estimate is too low. This time she appears to recognize that she is only off by 1, so she adds 1 to her original set of 5 and then joins the other set of 5 to it. Counting the total, she finds that it is now 11. She recounts the first set of 6 cubes. She responds, "She had 6 before her birthday."

CLIP 3.6 Direct Modeling strategy for a Join (Start Unknown) problem http://smarturl.it/CM3.6

CLIP 3.7 A child who has directly modeled for other problems is given a Join (Start Unknown) problem http://smarturl.it/CM3.7

This example of Trial and Error illustrates a reasonably systematic attempt to solve the problem. When the first two estimates were too low, Karla increased them. Most children do not attempt to use Trial and Error for Start Unknown problems. They simply are unable to solve them. Many children who do attempt Trial and Error are less systematic than Karla.

Figure 3.3 summarizes the six Direct Modeling strategies described above. It is important to note that it takes more than the use of manipulative materials for a strategy to be considered Direct Modeling. For a strategy to be labeled as "Direct Modeling" the strategy has to explicitly model the action or relationships in the problem. For example, using a Separating From strategy to solve a Compare (Difference Unknown) is not considered Direct Modeling, although it should be accepted as a valid strategy.

Direct Modeling Strategies

Problem	Strategy Description
Join (Result Unknown) *Ellen had 3 tomatoes. She picked 9 more tomatoes. How many tomatoes does Ellen have now?*	**Joining All** The child constructs a set of 3 objects and a set of 9 objects. He finds the answer by counting all the objects in the two sets.
Join (Change Unknown) *Chuck has 3 dollars. How many more dollars does he need to buy a stuffed animal that costs 12 dollars?*	**Joining To** The child constructs a set of 3 objects. She adds objects to this set until there is a total of 12 objects. She finds the answer by counting the number of objects added.
Separate (Result Unknown) *There were 12 seals playing. 9 seals swam away. How many seals were still playing?*	**Separating From** The child constructs a set of 12 objects and then removes 9 objects. She finds the answer by counting the remaining objects.
Separate (Change Unknown) *There were 12 people on the bus. Some people got off. Now there are 3 people on the bus. How many people got off the bus?*	**Separating To** The child counts out a set of 12 objects. He removes objects from the set until the number of objects remaining is equal to 3. He finds the answer by counting the objects he removed.
Compare (Difference Unknown) *Megan has 3 stickers. Randy has 12 stickers. How many more stickers does Randy have than Megan?*	**Matching** The child makes a set of 3 objects and a set of 12 objects. The two sets are matched one-to-one until one set is used up. She finds the answer by counting the unmatched objects remaining in the larger set.
Join (Start Unknown) *Deborah had some books. She went to the library and got 9 more books. Now she has 12 books altogether. How many books did she have to start with?*	**Trial and Error** The child constructs a set of objects. He adds a set of 9 objects to the set, and counts the objects in the resulting set. If the final count is 12, then the number of objects in the initial set is the answer. If it is not 12, he tries a different initial set.

FIGURE 3.3

Paper-and-Pencil Representations of Direct Modeling Strategies

Children can model problems using tally marks or pictures as well as concrete objects. In this case, paper-and-pencil representations are a tool that children can use in solving the problem in the same way that they use concrete objects. There are some differences between the use of manipulative materials and paper-and-pencil representations. Manipulative materials can be moved around whereas paper-and-pencil representations provide a more static picture of a problem. This may require children to think ahead about what they want their paper-and-pencil representations to look like. One of the most important differences between the two is that paper-and-pencil representations provide a more permanent record of children's strategies.

Many teachers find it productive to ask children to make a written record of the strategies they have used when the problem was actually solved with concrete objects. In this case, the strategies recorded on paper serve a very different purpose than the use of paper and pencil to solve a problem. Whether written solutions are generated in actually solving a problem or are a record of a solution with manipulative materials, paper-and-pencil representations can help a teacher understand how a child solved a problem if the teacher was not able to observe that child during problem solving. Written solutions can be useful when children share their strategies and compare them with the strategies of other children. They also provide a record of the strategies that children have used at various times. Finally, being asked to generate a written representation of a strategy may encourage a child to reflect on the strategy that she has produced. Figure 3.4 is an example of how a kindergartener recorded a Direct Modeling strategy for the problem:

Carson brought 17 crackers for snack. He ate 9 crackers. How many does he have now?

FIGURE 3.4 A paper-and-pencil representation of a Direct Modeling strategy for a Separate (Result Unknown) problem

COUNTING STRATEGIES

Counting strategies are more efficient and abstract than modeling with physical objects. In applying these strategies, a child recognizes that it is not necessary to physically construct and count the two sets described in a problem.

Counting On from First

Children often use two related Counting strategies to solve Join (Result Unknown) and Part-Part-Whole (Whole Unknown) problems. With the Counting On from First strategy, a child begins counting forward from the first addend in the problem. The sequence ends when the number of counting steps that represents the second addend has been completed. The following example illustrates this strategy:

> *Robin had 4 toy cars. Her friends gave her 8 more toy cars for her birthday. How many toy cars did she have then?*
>
> Jasmine counts, "4 [pause], 5, 6, 7, 8, 9, 10, 11, 12. She has 12 cars." As Jasmine counts, she extends a finger with each count. When she has extended 8 fingers, she stops counting and gives the answer. (See Figure 3.5.)

FIGURE 3.5 Using a Counting On from First strategy to solve a Join (Result Unknown) problem

Counting On from Larger

The Counting On from Larger strategy is identical to the Counting On from First strategy except that the child begins counting with the larger of the two addends. George uses this strategy in response to the problem:

> *Robin had 4 toy cars. Her friends gave her 7 more toy cars for her birthday. How many toy cars did she have then?*
>
> George counts, "7 [pause], 8, 9, 10, 11—11 toy cars." George also moves his fingers as he counts, but the movement is very slight, and it is easy to miss his use of them to keep track.

George's strategy indicates that he understands that adding 4 toy cars to 7 toy cars is the same as adding 7 toy cars to 4 toy cars. This understanding is obvious to adults but isn't always obvious to young children.

Note that in order to know when to stop counting, these two Counting strategies require some method of keeping track of the number of counting steps that represent the second addend. Children often use their fingers to keep track of the number of counts. A few may use counters or tallies, but a substantial number of children give no evidence of any physical action accompanying their counting. When a Counting strategy is carried out mentally, it is difficult to determine how a child knows when to stop counting. Some children appear to use some sort of rhythmic or cadence counting such that counting words are clustered into groups of 2 or 3. Others explicitly describe a double count (e.g., 6 is 1, 7 is 2, 8 is 3), but children often have difficulty verbalizing this process.

CLIP 3.8 Count On from Larger strategy for addition
http://smarturl.it/CM3.8

CLIP 3.9 Count On from Larger strategy for a Join (Result Unknown) problem
http://smarturl.it/CM3.9

When fingers or other objects are used in Counting strategies, they play a very different role than they do in Direct Modeling strategies. In this case, the fingers do not represent the second addend per se but are used to keep track of the number of steps incremented in the counting sequence. Sometimes children may not appear to count their fingers; they recognize familiar finger patterns and can immediately tell when they have used a given number of fingers.

Counting On To

A similar strategy is used to solve Join (Change Unknown) problems. Rather than the number reached being the answer, the answer is the number of steps in the counting sequence. The child initiates a forward counting strategy beginning with the smaller given number. The sequence ends with the larger given number. By keeping track of the number of counting words uttered in the sequence, the child determines the answer. This strategy, which is called *Counting On To*, is the counting analogue of the Direct Modeling strategy Joining To. The following example illustrates the Counting On To strategy:

> *Robin had 8 toy cars. How more toy cars would she have to collect to have 13 toy cars?*
>
> Ann counts, "8 [pause], 9, 10, 11, 12, 13." She extends a finger with each count as she says the sequence from 9 to 13. She looks at the extended fingers and responds, "She would need 5."

CLIP 3.10 Counting strategy for a Join (Change Unknown) problem http://smarturl.it/CM3.10

Without counting, Ann recognized that she had extended 5 fingers. Other children may have to actually count the extended fingers.

Counting Down

To reflect the action in the Separate (Result Unknown) problems, a backward counting sequence is used. The child starts counting at the larger number given in the problem and counts backward. This strategy, called *Counting Down*, is analogous to Separating From. Counting Down may take either of two forms:

Colleen had 11 pencils. She gave 3 pencils to Roger. How many pencils did she have left?

Ann counts, "11, 10, 9 [pause], 8. She had 8 left." Ann uses her fingers to keep track of the number of steps in the counting sequence.

Bill counts, "11 [pause], 10 [raises 1 finger], 9 [raises a second finger], 8 [raises a third finger]. She had 8 left."

CLIP 3.11 Counting strategy for subtraction http://smarturl.it/CM3.11

CLIP 3.12 Counting strategy for a Separate (Result Unknown), in Spanish http://smarturl.it/CM3.12

Ann said "11" as she mentally took away the eleventh pencil, "10" as she took away the tenth pencil, and "9" as she took away the ninth pencil. The answer was the next (fourth) number in the backward sequence, 8. Bill's counting was different. As he took 1 away, he said, "10," referring to the 10 that remained and then "9" for the 9 that remained. Finally, he said, "8" for the 8 that remained as he removed the third pencil.

Counting Down To

A backward counting sequence is also used to represent the action in a Separate (Change Unknown) problem. But the backward counting sequence in the *Counting Down To* strategy continues until the smaller number is reached; the number of words in the counting sequence is the solution to the problem. The following example illustrates this strategy, which is the counting counterpart of Separating To.

Colleen had 12 pencils. She gave some pencils to Roger. Then she had 8 pencils left. How many pencils did Colleen give to Roger?

Ann counts, "12 [extends one finger], 11 [extends a second finger], 10 [extends a third finger], 9 [extends a fourth finger and pauses], 8." She does not extend a finger for the 8. She looks at the 4 extended fingers and answers, "She gave 4 to Roger."

Bill counts, "12 [pause], 11 [extends one finger], 10 [extends a second finger], 9 [extends a third finger], 8 [extends a fourth finger]." He looks at the 4 extended fingers and answers, "She gave 4 to Roger."

In Figure 3.6, we summarize the above Counting strategies.

Counting Strategies for Addition and Subtraction Problems

Problem	Strategy Description
Join (Result Unknown) *Ellen had 3 tomatoes. She picked 9 more tomatoes. How many tomatoes does she have now?*	**Counting On from First** The child begins counting with 3 and continues on 9 more counts. The answer is the last number in the counting sequence.
Join (Result Unknown) *Ellen had 3 tomatoes. She picked 9 more tomatoes. How many tomatoes does she have now?*	**Counting On from Larger** The child begins counting with 9 and continues on 3 more counts. The answer is the last number in the counting sequence.
Join (Change Unknown) *Chuck has 9 dollars. How many more dollars does he need to save to buy a stuffed animal that costs 12 dollars?*	**Counting On To** The child counts forward starting from 9 and continues until reaching 12. The answer is the number of counting words in the sequence.
Separate (Result Unknown) *There were 12 seals playing. 3 seals swam away. How many seals were still playing?*	**Counting Down** The child counts backward starting from 12. The sequence continues for 3 more counts. The last number in the counting sequence is the answer.
Separate (Change Unknown) *There were 12 people on the bus. Some people got off. Now there are 3 people on the bus. How many people got off the bus?*	**Counting Down To** The child counts backward from 12 and continues until reaching 3. The answer is the number of counting words in the sequence.

FIGURE 3.6

Written Representations of Counting Strategies

Children generally use their fingers to keep track of the numbers in a Counting strategy, but if children are asked to record their strategies, they need to have some way to represent them. There is some danger that children may record a Direct Modeling strategy

CLIP 3.13 Counting strategy for a Join (Change Unknown) problem, with written notation
http://smarturl.it/CM3.13

even though they used a Counting strategy simply because records of Direct Modeling strategies are easier to generate and explain. However, children can be encouraged to represent their Counting strategies by describing the strategy and/or listing the numbers in their counting sequence.

Figure 3.7 depicts an example of how Sally recorded her solution to the problem:

Tom has 8 rocks. How many more rocks would he need to collect to have 12 rocks altogether?

When Sally's teacher asked her how she solved this problem, she said, "I started with 8 [points to the numeral 8], and then went 9, 10, 11, 12, I looked and saw that it was 4 more, so I wrote 4."

Figure 3.8 shows Ammar's solution to the following Separate (Result Unknown) problem,

Carson brought 17 crackers for snack. He ate 9 crackers. How many does he have now?

When asked how he solved this problem, Ammar said, "Carson had 17, take away 1, that's 16, take away 2, that's 15, take away 3, that's 14, take away 4 that's 13, take away 5, that's

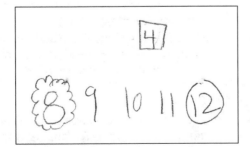

FIGURE 3.7 Sally's written representation of a Counting strategy for a Join (Change Unknown) problem

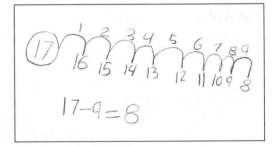

FIGURE 3.8 A written representation of a Counting strategy for a Separate (Result Unknown) problem

12, take away 6, that's 11, take away 7 that's 10, take away 8 that's 9 and take away 9, that's 8. Carson had 8 crackers left."

These examples show that even when children record their thinking, it can be useful to also ask the child to explain their solution.

DISTINCTION BETWEEN COUNTING AND MODELING STRATEGIES

It is important to note the distinction between Direct Modeling and Counting strategies. Direct Modeling is distinguished by the child's explicit physical representation of each quantity in a problem and the action or relationship involving those quantities before counting the resulting set. In using a Counting strategy, a child essentially recognizes that it is not necessary to actually construct and count sets. The answer can be figured out by focusing on the counting sequence itself. Counting strategies generally involve some sort of simultaneous double counting, and the physical objects a child may use (fingers, counters, tally marks) are used to keep track of counts rather than to represent objects in the problem.

Although children frequently use fingers with Counting strategies, the use of fingers does not distinguish Counting strategies from Direct Modeling strategies. As illustrated in the following examples, fingers may be used to directly model a problem or to keep track of the steps in a counting sequence:

> *Peter had 5 daisies. His sister gave him 3 more daisies. How many daisies did he have then?*
>
> Angela uses a Direct Modeling strategy: She puts up 3 fingers on one hand and 5 fingers on the other hand. She then counts her fingers, bending each one slightly with each count, "1, 2, 3, 4, 5, 6, 7, 8. He has 8 daisies."
>
> Jerry uses his fingers in a Counting On strategy: He says, "5 [pause], 6, 7, 8," extending one finger for each count. "He has 8 daisies."

NUMBER FACT STRATEGIES

Children's solutions to word problems are not limited to Modeling and Counting strategies, as children do learn number facts both in and out of school and apply this knowledge to solve problems. Children learn certain number combinations before others, and they often use a small set

CLIP 3.14 Derived Fact strategy based on doubles http://smarturl.it/CM3.14

CLIP 3.15 Derived Fact strategy based on doubles http://smarturl.it/CM3.15

of memorized facts to derive solutions for problems involving other number combinations. Children often learn doubles (e.g., 4 + 4, 7 + 7) and sums to 10 (e.g., 7 + 3, 4 + 6) before other combinations. They generally use doubles for problems that involve addends that differ from a double by 1 or 2 as illustrated in the following examples:

> *6 frogs were sitting on lily pads. 8 more frogs joined them. How many frogs were there then?*

Lisa, Jackson, Jamal, and Madison each answer, "14," almost immediately.

> **Ms. J:** *How do you know there were 14?*
> **Lisa:** Because 6 and 6 is 12, and 2 more is 14.
> **Jackson:** Well, I took 1 from the 8 and gave it to the 6. That made 7 and 7, and that's 14.

CLIP 3.16 Derived Fact strategy using ten as a benchmark http://smarturl.it/CM3.16

CLIP 3.17 Derived Fact strategy for subtraction using ten as a benchmark http://smarturl.it/CM3.17

Children use sums to 10 by partitioning one of the addends so that they first calculate a sum to 10 and then add on the remainder. This strategy depends on children being able to decompose numbers less than 10 into two addends, and on recognizing pairs of numbers that add to 10. This strategy can be applied to any number combination with a sum greater than 10 as is shown in the following strategies for the above problem about frogs on lily pads.

> **Jamal:** 6 and 4 is 10 and then 4 more is 14.
> **Madison:** 8 and 2 more is 10, and 4 more is 14.

Children use Derived Facts to solve all problem types. Here are some examples of children's use of Derived Facts for a Separate (Result Unknown) problem:

> *Todd had 16 crayons. He gave 9 crayons to his sister. How many crayons does Todd have left?*

> **Tessa:** He has 7 crayons left, 16 minus 6 is 10 and then minus 3 more is 7.
> **Ms. F:** *Why did you take away 6 and then 3 more?*

Tessa: 6 and 3 more make 9, I took away 6 and then I needed to take away 3 more to take away 9 altogether.

Ms. F: *Joshua, can you tell me why Tessa started by taking away 6?*

Joshua: I didn't do it that way.

Ms. F: *Can you think about why Tessa might have started by taking away 6 from 16?*

Joshua: Probably because it is easy, 16 minus 6 is 10, 16 is 10 plus 6, that was a good idea to take away 6.

Ms. F: *How did you solve this problem, Joshua?*

Joshua: I added, I did 9 plus what is 16? 9 plus 1 is 10, and then 10 plus 6 is 16.

Ms. F: *Tessa, will Joshua get the same answer as you?*

Tessa: Did he get 16?

Ms. F: *I don't think he told us his answer yet, did you Joshua?*

Joshua: No, I just said how I did it, I thought 9 plus what is 16, 9 plus 1 is 10 and then plus 6 is 16.

Tessa: I think it is going to work, because now he will add 1 plus 6, that is 7.

Joshua: Yes, so 9 plus 7 is 16, he had 7 crayons left.

Ms. F: *Does anyone have another way that they solved this?*

Juan: I know that 8 and 8 is 16, so 7 and 9 is also 16. So the answer is 7.

CLIP 3.18 Gilberto uses strategies for adding and subtracting using ten as a benchmark
http://smarturl.it/CM3.18

Notice that both Joshua and Tessa used 10 as a benchmark in their solution to this problem. Using 10 as a benchmark is a more flexible strategy than using Doubles for both addition and subtraction Derived Facts. It can be applied to all number combinations with sums greater than 10 whereas Doubles strategies generally are only used for number combinations that are near doubles such as 6 + 7 and 6 + 8. The use of 10 as a benchmark is especially helpful for subtraction Derived Facts. When children use Doubles strategies for subtraction problems, they generally do so by relating the subtraction fact to the related addition fact as illustrated by Juan's solution.

It might be expected that Derived Facts are used by only a handful of very bright students. This is not the case. Even without specific instruction, most children use Derived Facts before they have mastered all their number facts at a recall level. In a three-year longitudinal study of non-CGI classes, over 80 percent of the children used Derived Facts at some time in grades 1 through 3, and Derived Facts represented the primary strategy of 40 percent of the children at some time during this period

(Carpenter and Moser 1984). When children have the opportunity to solve problems using their own strategies, discuss their strategies with their teacher and classmates, and discuss their classmates' strategies, the use of Derived Facts becomes even more prevalent.

WRITTEN REPRESENTATIONS OF NUMBER FACT STRATEGIES

Number Fact strategies can be represented with equations or other notation using written numerals. Figures 3.9 and 3.10 show examples of Colette's written representations of Number Fact strategies.

Colette used an arrow ($\rightarrow$) rather than an equal sign (=) to represent Number Facts strategies. This is a notation that the teacher introduced to students by using it to record a Derived Fact solution that a child shared with the class. She introduced this notation to record the incremental nature of children's strategies while avoiding using the equal sign incorrectly. Consider Colette's strategy for $6 + 7 = \square$ in Figure 3.9. It would be mathematically incorrect to represent this strategy as $6 + 4 = 10 + 3 = 13$ because the equal sign expresses a relation between two equal quantities, and $6 + 4$ is not equal to $10 + 3$. This

FIGURE 3.9 Colette's written representations of her Derived Fact strategy for the problem $6 + 7 = \square$

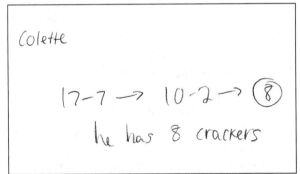

FIGURE 3.10 Colette's written representation of her Derived Fact strategy for the problem: *Carson brought 17 crackers for snack. He ate 9 crackers. How many does he have now?*

use of the equal sign should be avoided, and students should be discouraged from using the equal sign in this way.[1]

When Colette was asked to describe how she solved this problem, she said, "I know that 7 is 4 and 3. Six and 4 is 10 and then 3 more is 13." Colette could have written her strategy as follows.

$$7 = 4 + 3$$
$$6 + 4 = 10$$
$$10 + 3 = 13$$

Although adults tend to be more comfortable with using equations to represent these strategies, children often see the notation with the arrow symbol as a better representation of strategies like Colette's in which they start with one quantity and add on in parts until they arrive at the desired quantity. She also could have represented her solution by writing the equation $6 + 4 + 3 = 13$, but it may be easier for other children to understand the solution if the 10 is included in the written representation. As is shown in Figure 3.10, Colette uses a similar representation of her derived fact for the SRU story problem.

Figure 3.11 shows Rachael's written representation of her Doubles Derived Fact strategy.

Rachael explained how she solved $6 + 7 = \square$ as follows, "I knew that 6 plus 6 is 12, so 6 plus 7 would be 13." She used equations to represent her thinking. In this example, Rachael related one number fact to another number fact so equations provide an easy way to represent her strategy.

Recording Number Fact strategies is important for the development of children's understanding for several reasons. First, recording Number Fact strategies helps children learn to use notation that they will eventually need as a tool for problem solving. Although children can solve problems such as $8 + 5$ without writing anything down, later when they solve problems with bigger numbers they often will need to write something down. Second, as is the case for all written representations of strategies, the notation becomes a tool for reflection.

FIGURE 3.11 Rachael's written representation of her Doubles Derived Fact strategy

1. For more information on developing an understanding of the equal sign, see Carpenter, Franke, and Levi (2003).

Children can examine their notation to determine if (a) the strategy is correct, (b) they could apply the strategy to different problems, or (c) they could make the strategy more efficient. Finally, notation is a means for communicating with others. Children learn best when they discuss each other's strategies. Some children are able to understand another student's Number Fact strategy if they have the support of a written representation.

RELATION OF STRATEGIES TO PROBLEM TYPES

We summarize the relation between strategies and problem types in Figure 3.12

Younger children generally select strategies that directly represent the action or relationships described in problems. For some problem types, the action dominates the problem more than others. Almost all children use Join To or Count On To strategies to solve Join (Change Unknown) problems. Children consistently solve Separate (Result Unknown) problems with the Separating From strategy. Because it is relatively difficult, children use the Counting Down strategy less frequently. As a consequence, some children who use Counting strategies that involve forward counting for other problems may continue to use Separate From to solve Separate (Result Unknown) problems. Matching is used for Compare problems, but there is no counting extension of Matching. Separating

Relations Between Strategies and Problem Types

Problem Type	Direct Modeling	Counting
Join (Result Unknown) *Part-Part-Whole (Whole Unknown)*	Joining All	Counting On
Join (Change Unknown)	Joining To	Counting On To
Separate (Result Unknown)	Separating From	Counting Down
Separate (Change Unknown)	Separating To	Counting Down To
Compare (Difference Unknown)	Matching	*
Join (Start Unknown) *Separate (Start Unknown)*	Trial and Error	Trial and Error
Part-Part-Whole (Part Unknown)	*	*

*There is no commonly used strategy corresponding to the action or relationship described in the problem.

FIGURE 3.12

To is not used universally although some younger children use it. Children use Trial and Error strategies even less frequently.

With experience in solving problems, children become more flexible in their selection of strategies so that they can select strategies that do not always correspond to the action in a given problem. However, even older children tend to select strategies that model the action or relationships for certain problems. Children generally model the very dominant action in a Separate (Result Unknown) or Join (Change Unknown) problem for an extended period of time. On the other hand, most older children replace the Matching strategy for Compare problems with one of the other common strategies that do not directly model the comparison relation described in Compare problems. As there is no counting analogue of Matching, children must select a strategy that does not model the Compare problem if they want to use a Counting strategy.

LEVELS OF DEVELOPMENT OF STRATEGIES

There is a great deal of variability in the ages at which children use different strategies. When they enter kindergarten, most children can solve some word problems using Direct Modeling strategies even when they have had little or no formal instruction in addition or subtraction. A number of entering first-graders are able to use Counting strategies, and a few use Number Fact strategies consistently.

Most children pass through three levels in acquiring addition and subtraction problem-solving skills. Initially they solve problems exclusively by Direct Modeling. Over time, Direct Modeling strategies are replaced by Counting strategies, and finally most children come to rely on Number Fact strategies. The transition from Direct Modeling to using Counting strategies does not take place all at once, and for a time children may use both Direct Modeling and Counting strategies. Similarly, children learn a few number facts quite early, when they are still relying primarily on Direct Modeling or Counting strategies, and the use of Number Facts strategies evolves over an extended period of time.

Direct Modeling Strategies

At first, young children are limited in their modeling capabilities. They do not plan ahead and can only think about one step at a time. This causes no problems with the Joining All and Separating From strategies, but it can cause difficulties in Joining To. Consider the following example:

> *Robin had 5 toy cars. How many more toy cars does she have to get for her birthday to make 9 toy cars?*

> Nick makes a set of 5 cubes and then adds 4 more cubes to the set counting,
> "6, 7, 8, 9," as he adds the cubes. He is not careful to keep the new cubes
> separate, so when he finishes adding them, he cannot distinguish them from
> the original set of 5 cubes. He looks confused for a moment and then counts
> the entire set of 9 cubes and responds, "9?"

Nick modeled the action in the problem, but he did not recognize that he needed to keep the 4 cubes that he added on separate from the 5 cubes in the initial set. As a consequence, he had no way to figure out how many cubes he added. In other words, he simply modeled the action described in the problem without planning ahead how he was going to use his model to answer the question.

The only strategies available to children who only think about one step at a time are Joining All and Separating From. Therefore, they can only solve problems that can be modeled with these strategies: Join (Result Unknown), Part-Part-Whole (Whole Unknown), and Separate (Result Unknown) problems. With experience solving simple problems, children learn to reflect on their Modeling strategies. This gives them the ability to plan their solutions to avoid the errors illustrated in Nick's example above. Thus the ability to think about the entire problem—the question to be answered as well as the action in the problem—allows children to solve Join (Change Unknown) problems by using a Joining To strategy.

Compare (Difference Unknown) problems are slightly more difficult to model than Join (Change Unknown) problems. However, if the context or wording of the Compare problems provides cues for matching, direct modelers can solve them. Graphing problems in which two quantities, like the number of boys and the number of girls in the class, are represented on a bar graph provides situations in which quantities can be compared. Children at this level quite readily solve such problems. The bar graph is a way of matching so that quantities can be compared in much the same way that the Matching strategy is applied to any Compare problem.

Most direct modelers have difficulty solving Start Unknown problems with understanding. Because the initial set is unknown, they cannot start out representing a given set. The only alternative for modeling the problem is Trial and Error, and Trial and Error is a difficult strategy for most direct modelers to apply. Direct modelers find the Part-Part-Whole (Part Unknown) problem difficult for a slightly different reason. Because there is no explicit action to represent, many of them have difficulty using concrete objects to represent the part-whole relationship described in the problem.

Counting Strategies

Gradually over a period of time, children replace concrete Direct Modeling strategies with more efficient Counting strategies, and the use of Counting strategies is an important marker in the development of number concepts. Counting strategies represent more than efficient procedures for calculating answers to addition and subtraction problems. They indicate a level of understanding of number concepts and an ability to reflect on numbers as abstract entities.

Initially, children may use both Direct Modeling and Counting strategies concurrently. At first, they use Counting strategies in situations in which they are particularly easy to apply, such as when the second addend is a small number or the first addend is relatively large:

Sam had 24 flowers. He picked 3 more. How many flowers did he have then?

Even after children become quite comfortable with Counting strategies, they may occasionally fall back to Direct Modeling strategies with concrete objects. Most children come to rely on the Counting On strategies, but not all children use Counting Down consistently because of the difficulty in counting backward.

Flexible Choice of Strategies

There were 13 birds in the tree. 9 birds flew away. How many birds were in the tree?

Ms. L: *Jay, do you want to share first?*

Jay: I took 13 blocks [shows the other children his blocks as he counts them], 1, 2, 3, . . . 12, 13, and then I took away 9 of them [pushes 9 of the 13 blocks to the side as he counts] 1, 2, 3, . . . 9, and then these are the ones still in the tree, 1, 2, 3, 4. There are 4 in the tree.

Ms. L: *Your explanation helped me understand exactly what you did, Jay. Margie, do you want to share your way now?*

Margie: I did 13 [holds up a finger for each of the next counts], 12, 11, 10, 9, 8, 7, 6 ,5, 4, I got 4.

Ms. L: *Why did you stop when you said 4?*

Margie: Because 9 flew away, I knew this many [holds up 9 fingers] is 9.

Ms. L: *Jay, how is Margie's strategy like yours?*

Jay: We both took away 9.

Ms. L: Yes, you both did. Carrie, will you share what you did?

Carrie: I did 9 [holds up a finger for each of the next counts], 10, 11, 12, 13, that is 4, so I knew that 4 birds were left.

Ms. L: Your way seems different to me, could you say it again? [Carrie repeats her strategy]

Ms. L: [ensures that the other children can see Carrie's fingers as she counts] Margie, is Carrie's way like yours?

Margie: No, we both got 4 but she counted more. I don't get it. The birds flew away.

Carrie: I started with 9, those are how many birds flew away, and I knew if I added more until I got all the 13 birds, I could see how many birds were left. I counted from 9 to 13 to see how many more I would need to get all the birds, 9, 10, 11, 12, 13, that is 4 birds. Those are the birds that are left.

Ms. L: Carrie, was that my story?

Carrie: No, it wasn't the story but counting backward messes me up. The birds that flew away plus the birds that were left would make all of the birds.

Initially, children use Counting strategies that are consistent with the action or relationships described in problems. In other words, the Counting strategies are abstractions of the corresponding Direct Modeling strategies they used previously. In the previous example, Margie's Counting strategy is an abstraction of Jay's Direct Modeling strategy. Both strategies follow the take away action in the problem. Jay used blocks to represent the birds in the story and Margie was able to abstract quantities as counts, but both children started with 13, took away 9, and ended up with 4. Margie's and Jay's solutions follow the structure of the problem. Over time, however, many children learn to solve problems with strategies that do not follow the structure of the problem. Carrie's strategy is an example of such a strategy. She has developed an understanding of part-whole relationships, which allows her to think about the problem holistically in terms of the part of the birds that flew away and the part that stayed in the tree. Margie, who said she didn't get Carrie's strategy, has not yet developed this understanding.

Understanding part-whole relationships not only helps children be more flexible in their strategies, it also helps children solve problems that are challenging to model as illustrated by Kisha's solution to this Separate (Start Unknown) problem.

Some birds were sitting on a wire. 3 birds flew away. There were 8 birds still sitting on the wire. How many birds were sitting on the wire before the 3 birds flew away?

Kisha: [counts] 8 [pause], 9, 10, 11. There were 11.

Ms. K: *I understand how you found the answer, but how did you know to count on like that?*

Kisha: Well, there were the 3 birds that flew away, and the 8 birds that were still sitting there. And I want to know how many there were altogether. The 3 and the 8 together were how many birds there were on the wire. So I put them together. I counted on from 8 to get 11.

Another basic principle that allows children to be more flexible in dealing with Join and Separate problems is an understanding that actions can be reversed. In other words, the act of joining objects to a set can be undone by removing the objects from the resulting set. For example, the following Separate (Start Unknown) problem can be solved by reversing the action:

Colleen had some stickers. She gave 3 stickers to Roger. She had 5 stickers left. How many stickers did Colleen have to start with?

Eve: I thought about this for a long time. Then I thought, what if I take the 5 stickers she had at the end and put back the 3 that she gave away, I would get what she started with. 5 plus 3 is easy, I know that is 8. So Colleen had 8 stickers before she gave some away.

Analyzing the problem as Eve did allows children to think of this problem in terms of a joining action so they can solve it without using a Trial and Error strategy.

Children eventually come to understand that in most addition and subtraction problems, two parts are joined together to make a whole. Compare problems, on the other hand, involve the comparison of two distinct sets and therefore do not fit directly into a part-whole representation. However, in a Compare problem the subset of the larger set that matches the smaller set can be thought as one part and the unmatched objects the other part. Thus, with a little extra work, even compare problems can be related to a part-whole analysis.

Once a part-whole relation has been established, problems can be solved more flexibly. If the whole is missing, the problem can be thought of as an addition problem, which can be solved by starting with either of the parts and adding the other part to it to find the whole. If one part is missing, the problem can be thought of as a subtraction problem, which can be solved by either starting with the whole and taking away the known part or starting with the known part and adding to it to find the missing part. Derived Fact strategies draw implicitly on some level of understanding of problems in terms of part-whole relations.

As powerful as part-whole analysis can be, we recommend letting children come to this understanding over time. Trying to get them to use part-whole relations before they are ready runs the risk that translating problems into parts and the whole becomes a mechanical procedure. It is preferable that they use modeling and counting procedures that make sense to them rather than try to learn a procedure they do not understand.

When children do understand problems in terms of parts and the whole, they can be quite purposeful in their use of strategies for particular problems. Consider how Peter solved these problems:

> **Ms. J:** *Sally had 14 cookies. She ate 3 of them. How many cookies does Sally have left?*
> **Peter:** 14 [holds up a finger for each count], 13, 12, 11, she has 11 cookies left.
> **Ms. J:** *How would you solve this problem: Sally had 12 cookies. She gave away 9 cookies. How many cookies does Sally have left?*
> **Peter:** 9 [holds up a finger for each count], 10, 11, 12 [looks at his fingers], 3, she has 3 cookies left.

Peter used a Counting Down strategy when the set he was taking away was small. When the set was larger, he Counted On To. Thus, Peter chose the most efficient strategy based on the numbers in the problem.

Understanding part-whole relationships, understanding that actions can be reversed, and developing the capacity to analyze problems to choose an efficient strategy for that particular problem are essential for understanding addition and subtraction. Children with these understandings have a firm foundation for learning later mathematics.

Number Fact Strategies

Some children continue to use Counting or Derived Facts strategies for an extended period of time, and it should not be assumed that children know facts from memory simply because they obtain answers quickly. Children can become very efficient in using Counting strategies and can apply them very quickly. But Counting strategies do not lead directly to learning number facts. Derived Facts strategies, on the other hand, support children to look at relations among numbers and operations in ways that support learning to know number facts from memory. Children who use Derived Facts strategies gradually start knowing more and more facts from memory. It is important to recognize that number facts are learned at a recall level over a much longer period of time than previously has been assumed. Through experience solving problems and reflecting on their strategies and the strategies of their classmates, children begin to know many number facts from memory. Children will develop fluency with addition and subtraction with repeated experience with addition and subtraction problems with single-digit numbers and ample opportunities to discuss Derived Facts with their classmates. Students who know facts from memory after going through Direct Modeling strategies, then Counting Strategies, then Derived Facts strategies have a stronger understanding of addition and subtraction than children who learn facts through rote memorization.

INTEGRATION OF SOLUTION STRATEGIES AND PROBLEM TYPES

The relationships between strategies and problem types and the levels at which strategies may be used are represented in the Children's Solution Strategies chart (Figure 3.13). This figure presents a somewhat simplified version of what we have described. Derived Fact

Children's Solution Strategies

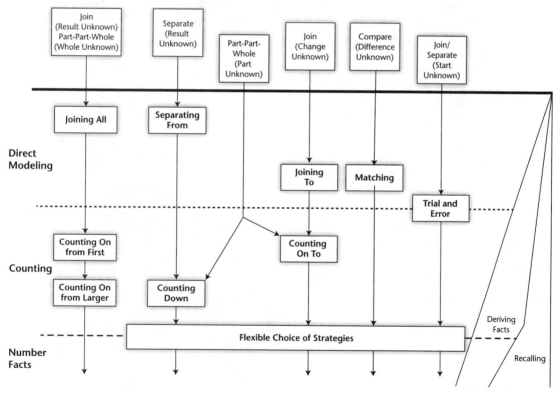

FIGURE 3.13

and Recall of Number Fact strategies are portrayed as cutting across all levels. Children use some number facts at all levels, and the use of number facts increases until Number Fact strategies become the dominant strategy.

QUESTIONS FOR FURTHER REFLECTION

1. Identify the problem type and produce a written representation of a Direct Modeling strategy, a Counting strategy, and a Derived Fact strategy for each of these problems. Do your strategies follow the action in the problem? It is often helpful to arrange your strategies in a grid like the one below so that you can see how the strategies progress.

Problem	Direct Modeling Strategy	Counting Strategy	Derived Fact Strategy
There are 5 ducks in the pond. If 7 more ducks landed in the pond, how many ducks would be in the pond? Problem type: _____			
I have 12 dollars. If I spend 4 dollars on lunch, how many much money would I have left? Problem type: _____			

Problem	Direct Modeling Strategy	Counting Strategy	Derived Fact Strategy
Bob has 9 apples. How many more apples would he need to buy to have 17 apples? Problem type: _____			

2. Choose one of the Join (Change Unknown) problems below that you think would be appropriate for your students. Describe the strategies students are most likely to use to solve this problem. Predict which of these strategies your students might use.

   a. *Sashi has 5 rocks. How many more rocks would she need to find to have 9 rocks?*
   b. *Rico has 8 books. How many more books would he need to buy to have 15 books?*
   c. *Margie has 23 erasers. How many more erasers would she need to buy to have 34 erasers?*

   Pose the problem you chose from the preceding list to your students. Choose three or four students who are likely to use different strategies and ask them how they solved the problem. Did the students do what you expected? Did any of your students use Direct Modeling, Counting, or Number Fact strategies?

3. Which of the following problems would be more challenging for your students? Pose both of these problems to see if your prediction is correct.

   a. *Martha had 14 jelly beans. She ate 8 of them. How many jelly beans does Martha have left?*
   b. *Martha has 13 jelly beans. 7 are red and the rest are yellow. How many yellow jelly beans does Martha have?*

4. Consider the following problem:

Shana has 12 baseball caps. Silvia has 8 baseball caps. How many more baseball caps does Shana have than Silvia?

Suppose you posed this problem and it was too hard for a student to solve. Think of two different ways you could change the problem to make it easier.

5. Figures 3.14 through 3.18 show some examples of what students wrote on their paper after solving the following problem:

Allison and her brother frosted all of the cookies that their mom made for the party. Allison decorated 20 cookies. Her brother decorated 3 cookies. How many cookies will there be at the party?

FIGURE 3.14 Margie's strategy

FIGURE 3.15 Reiner's strategy

FIGURE 3.16 Bob's strategy

FIGURE 3.17 Carrie's strategy

   a. Identify each strategy as Direct Modeling, Counting, or Number Fact strategy.

   b. For each example, write a question that would help the student explain the strategy. The question could either be thought of as one that could encourage the student to reflect on the strategy or help other students to understand the strategy.

6. If your students were to produce the work shown in question 5, which students would you choose to explain their strategies to the class? In what order would you have them share their strategies?

FIGURE 3.18 Jay's strategy

7. Consider how TJ and Dianne solve 8 + 7.

TJ: 8 plus 2 is 10 and then 5 more is 15.
Dianne: 8 plus 8 is 16, 1 less is 15.

TJ's Derived Fact strategy used 10 as a benchmark (8 + 2 → 10 + 5 → 15). Dianne's Derived Fact strategy used doubles (8 + 7 is 1 less than 8 + 8). For each of the following problems, generate a derived fact using doubles and a derived fact using 10 as a benchmark.

Number Fact	Derived Fact	
	Ten as a Benchmark	*Doubles*
6 + 7		
8 + 9		
4 + 8		
9 + 3		

When you are finished, circle the derived facts that are efficient for a given problem. Do you notice any patterns?

8. Consider how Charlie solved the problem 13 − 5. Charlie said, "13 minus 5. [pause] I know 13 minus 3 is 10, minus 2 more is 8." Figure 3.19 shows what he wrote.

See if you can use a strategy like Charlie's to solve these problems:

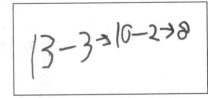

FIGURE 3.19 Charlie's strategy

a. *15 − 8*
b. *14 − 6*
c. *12 − 4*

9. Watch Aaliyah solve the following problems.

   Join (Result Unknown): Jayden had 3 flowers. She picked 8 more flowers. How many flowers does Jayden have now?

   Join (Change Unknown): Aaliyah has 6 dandelions. How many more dandelions does she need to pick so that she has 11 dandelions to make a big bunch?

   Separate (Change Unknown): Sam had 8 animal crackers. His sister ate some of them. Now Sam has 6 animal crackers. How many crackers did Sam's sister eat?

   a. Identify the strategy that Aaliyah used for each problem.
   b. What are some of the probing questions the teacher asked to reveal Aaliyah's understanding? What did these questions help the teacher learn about Aaliyah's thinking?

CLIP **3.20** Aaliyah solves a Join (Result Unknown) problem
http://smarturl.it/CM3.20

CLIP **3.21** Aaliyah solves a Join (Change Unknown) problem
http://smarturl.it/CM3.21

CIP **3.22** Aaliyah solves a Separate (Change Unknown) problem
http://smarturl.it/CM3.22

10. Watch Jordyn solve this Join (Result Unknown) problem:

    Angie had 2 pennies. She found 15 more pennies. How many pennies does Angie have now?

    a. Identify the strategy that Jordyn used.
    b. What are some of the probing questions the teacher asked to reveal Jordyn's thinking?
    c. As Jordyn was beginning to explain her thinking, she started to draw. Why do you think the teacher stopped her?

CLIP **3.23** Jordyn solves a Join (Result Unknown) problem
http://smarturl.it/CM3.23

CLIP 3.24 Melissa solves a Separate (Result Unknown) problem
http://smarturl.it/CM3.24

CLIP 3.25 Melissa solves a Join (Change Unknown) problem
http://smarturl.it/CM3.25

11. Watch Melissa solve these two problems:

Paco had 15 cookies. He ate 7 of them. How many cookies does Paco have left?

Camilla has 9 dollars. How many more dollars does she have to earn so that she'll have 17 dollars to buy a new book?

a. Identify the problem type for each problem.
b. Identify the strategy that Melissa used for each problem.
c. What kinds of probing questions did the teacher ask? What did these questions help the teacher learn about Melissa's thinking?

4

Multiplication and Division: Problem Types and Children's Solution Strategies

The analysis of addition and subtraction provides a framework that can be extended to multiplication and division. This chapter starts with a discussion of problem types that represent basic multiplication and division problems and the strategies that children generally use to solve them. These problems and strategies involve grouping or partitioning collections of countable objects. In the second part of the chapter, we examine some different problem types and the ways students may think about them.

GROUPING AND PARTITIONING PROBLEMS

Although not all real-life problems that can be solved by multiplication and division involve grouping or partitioning into equivalent sets without remainders, the initial discussion of multiplication and division considers only those problems in which collections can be grouped or partitioned into equivalent groups with no remainders. Grouping and Partitioning problems all involve three quantities, as illustrated by the following example:

> *Megan has 5 bags of cookies. There are 3 cookies in each bag. Altogether she has 15 cookies.*

The three quantities in the problem are the number of bags, the number of cookies in each bag, and the total number of cookies. In a problem, any one of the three quantities can be unknown. When the total number of cookies Megan has altogether is unknown, the problem is a *Multiplication* problem. When the number of groups or bags is unknown, the problem is called a *Measurement Division* problem. When the number of cookies in each bag or group is unknown, the problem is called a *Partitive Division* problem. The three problem types—Multiplication, Measurement Division, and Partitive Division—are illustrated in Figure 4.1.

Multiplication problems give the number of groups and the number of objects in each group, and the unknown is the total number of objects. Note that the two known numbers represent different things. One number represents the number of groups (number of bags), and one represents how many are in each group (the number of cookies in each bag). This distinction is important because it is reflected in the Direct Modeling and Counting strategies that children use to solve the problem.

Measurement Division problems give the total number of objects and the number of objects in each group. The number of groups (the number of bags of cookies) is the

Multiplication and Division Problem Types

Problem Type	Number of Groups	Amount per Group	Total
Multiplication Megan has 5 bags of cookies with 3 cookies in each bag. How many cookies does Megan have?	5	3	Unknown
Partitive Division Megan has 15 cookies. She puts the cookies into 5 bags with the same number of cookies in each bag. How many cookies does she put in each bag?	5	Unknown	15
Measurement Division Megan has 15 cookies. She puts 3 cookies in each bag. How many bags can she fill?	Unknown	3	15

FIGURE 4.1

unknown. Essentially, children use the number of objects in each group to measure the total number of objects, which is where the name *Measurement Division* comes from.

Partitive Division problems give the total number of objects and the number of groups, and the number of objects in each group (the number of cookies per bag) is unknown. Children partition the total number of objects into a given number of groups, hence the name *Partitive Division*. The distinctions between the Measurement and Partitive Division problems are critical because children initially solve them in very different ways, reflecting the different information given in the problem.

In summary, we have described three types of problems that represent multiplication and division. The three problem types are related but differ in what is known and what is unknown. In a Multiplication problem, the goal is to find the total number of objects. In a Measurement Division problem, the goal is to find the number of sets. In a Partitive Division problem, the goal is to find the number of objects in each set.

CHILDREN'S STRATEGIES FOR SOLVING MULTIPLICATION, MEASUREMENT DIVISION, AND PARTITIVE DIVISION PROBLEMS

As with addition and subtraction problems, children initially solve multiplication and division problems by directly modeling the action and relationships described in the problems. Over time, these Direct Modeling strategies are replaced by more efficient strategies based on counting, adding/subtracting, or the use of derived number facts.

Direct Modeling Strategies

Multiplication

Children first solve Multiplication problems by modeling each of the groups (using counters, tally marks, or other representations) and counting the total number of objects. This Grouping strategy is illustrated below:

Ms. Jenkins bought 7 boxes of cupcakes. There were 4 cupcakes in each box. How many cupcakes did Ms. Jenkins buy?

Carla counts out 1 set of 4 blocks, then another set of 4 blocks, then a third set and a fourth set, a fifth, a sixth, and a seventh. After she has finished making 7 groups with 4 blocks in each set, she counts all the blocks and says, "28. She bought 28 cupcakes."

CLIP 4.1 Direct Modeling strategy for a Multiplication problem
http://smarturl.it/CM4.1

Measurement Division

Children initially solve Measurement Division problems by directly modeling. Children construct a given number of sets, each containing the specified number of objects. They then count how many sets they made. This strategy is called a *Measurement* strategy. There are at least two variations of the Measurement strategy, depending on whether the total number is counted first or later. The following examples illustrate these variations:

> *There are 28 fish, with 7 fish in each fish bowl. How many fish bowls are there?*
>
> Geno counts out 28 linking cubes. He then connects them into groups of 7 and counts the groups. He says the answer is "4."
>
> Maricela connects a group of 7 linking cubes, another group of 7, and a third group of 7. She then counts all the cubes in the 3 groups and finds there are only 21. She then counts out another group of 7 and counts all the cubes again. She now finds the total is 28, so she counts the groups and says, "4."

CLIP 4.2 Direct Modeling strategy for Measurement Division, total counted first
http://smarturl.it/CM4.2

CLIP 4.3 Direct Modeling strategy for Measurement Division, total counted later
http://smarturl.it/CM4.3

Both children made 4 sets with 7 counters in each set. The difference between how Maricela and Geno solved this Measurement Division problem is that Geno first counted the 28 counters and then separated them into groups of 7 counters, whereas Maricela started by forming groups of 7 until she had counted 28 altogether. The strategies are just variants of the same basic Measurement strategy, and it is not necessary to worry about which variation a child might be using. Both children directly represented the action described in the problem.

Partitive Division

Children also directly model Partitive Division problems by constructing groups of objects. The solution requires finding the number of objects in the group rather than the number of groups. There are several ways that a child might do this. One way is to deal the objects into the correct number of groups one at a time, until the total number of objects is used up. The following example illustrates this strategy:

> *Mr. Franke baked 28 cookies. He gave all the cookies to 4 friends, being careful to give the same number of cookies to each friend. How many cookies did each friend get?*
>
> Ellen counts out 28 counters. She places the counters into 4 separate places 1 at a time. After she puts 1 counter in each spot, she starts over and adds another

counter to each set, continuing this process until she has used up all the counters. Then she counts the counters in 1 pile and says, "7 . . . each would get 7 cookies."

CLIP 4.4 Direct Modeling strategy for a Partitive Division problem http://smarturl.it/CM4.4

Many students do not systematically deal the counters out one by one. They start out putting more than 1 object in a group and then add or remove objects from each group as they find it necessary, as described below:

Kang counts out 28 counters. He places 4 counters in 1 group, 4 in another group, 4 in another, and 4 in another until he sees that there are 4 groups. At this point he sees that he has not used up all the counters, so he adds 2 counters to each group and then adds 1 until he has used up all the counters. Then he counts the counters in 1 of the groups and answers, "7."

Although Kang put 4 counters in each group, his strategy for solving this Partitive Division problem was very different from the strategy used to solve a Measurement Division problem. Kang's initial goal was not to put 4 counters in each group; it was to construct 4 groups with the same number in each group and to use all of the counters. When he saw that he had not used up the counters, he added more to each group. He may have started with 4 in each group because that number was mentioned in the problem, but he was able to adjust the number of objects in each group.

Children sometimes start to solve a Partitive Division problem by putting too many objects in a group. For example, Kang might have guessed that each friend got 8 cookies and put 8 counters in each group. In that case, there would not have been enough counters to make the required number of groups, and he would have removed counters from each group to complete the last group.

Sometimes children attempt to represent each group itself with an object that is not part of the group. This allows the child to model the given number of groups before they begin to deal with the objects in the group. This may seem confusing, but most children do not have difficulty distinguishing between the object representing the group and the objects in the group when they use this strategy. Jazmin's solution to the following Partitive Division problem illustrates this approach:

Mr. Gomez has 20 cupcakes. He wants to put them into 4 boxes so that each box has the same amount. How many cupcakes can he put in each box?

First Jazmin counts out 20 cubes. Then she selects 4 additional cubes that are not part of the 20 to represent the 4 boxes and puts them in a line in front of her. She deals the cubes one by one to each of the 4 separate "boxes" on the table. When she has used up all 20 cubes, she counts the number of cubes in 1 of the groups, not counting the first cube that she put out to identify the group and answers, "5."

Teacher: *Good. I see how you got the 5, but can you tell me why you didn't count this [indicates the cube that represented the group]?*
Jazmin: That's 1 of the boxes.

FIGURE 4.2 Jazmin uses Direct Modeling for a Partitive Division problem, using a cube to represent each group

As they do with Measurement Division problems, some children may not count out the total set first, but keep track of it as they are placing the counters into groups. Geri utilizes this approach to solve the following problem:

Linda had 12 cookies for the bake sale. She put them into 4 bags so that there were the same number of cookies in each bag. How many cookies were there in each bag?

Geri counts while she puts 4 counters in separate places on the table and says "1, 2, 3, 4." She then puts another counter by each of the first 4 counters and continues to count, "5, 6, 7, 8." She continues by adding another counter to each set and saying, "9, 10, 11, 12." She counts the counters in 1 set and says, "3."

These examples of strategies that children use for Partitive Division problems are just variations of the *Partitive* strategy. Basically, the Partitive strategy involves some form of directly modeling the action or relationships described in Partitive Division problems. A total number of objects are partitioned into a given number of sets, and the number of objects in one or more of the sets is counted to find the answer. Figure 4.3 contains a

Direct Modeling Strategies for Multiplication and Division Problems

Problem	Strategy Description
Multiplication Bart has 4 boxes of pencils. There are 6 pencils in each box. How many pencils does Bart have altogether?	**Grouping** Make 4 groups with 6 counters in each group. Count all the counters to find the answer.
Measurement Division Bart has 24 pencils. They are packed 6 pencils to a box. How many boxes of pencils does he have?	**Measurement** Put 24 counters into groups with 6 counters in each group. Count the groups to find the answer.
Partitive Division Bart has 6 boxes of pencils with the same number of pencils in each box. Altogether he has 24 pencils. How many pencils are in each box?	**Partitive** Divide 24 counters into 6 groups with the same number of counters in each group. Count the counters in one group to find the answer.

FIGURE 4.3

summary of the basic Direct Modeling strategies for Multiplication, Measurement Division, and Partitive Division problems.

To solve multiplication and division problems with Direct Modeling, children must recognize that they can count groups of objects as well as individual objects. They also must tacitly understand that an amount (such as 24) can be composed of equal groups of another amount (6 groups of 4). These principles may seem obvious to adults, but it takes children time and experience to develop this understanding. Understanding these principles has often been considered a major hurdle for young children, which has led to postponing the introduction of multiplication and division problem situations until middle grades. We have documented, however, that by kindergarten most children can successfully model and solve multiplication and division problems. Experiences solving multiplication and division problems in kindergarten and first grade can provide a foundation for understanding multiplication, division, and base-ten concepts in later grades.

Written Representation of Direct Modeling Strategies

As was the case with addition and subtraction problems, children can represent their Direct Modeling strategies for multiplication and division problems on paper (see

Figure 4.4). In fact, paper-and-pencil representations can clearly show the groupings as illustrated in the following example for the problem:

> Mrs. Leise has 5 aquariums. There are 6 fish in each aquarium. How many fish does Mrs. Leise have altogether?

Counting and Adding Strategies

As with addition and subtraction, children gradually replace Direct Modeling strategies with Counting strategies. However, it is more difficult to use Counting strategies for multiplication and division problems than it is for

FIGURE 4.4 Written representation of a Direct Modeling strategy

addition and subtraction problems. As a result, children generally do not use Counting strategies as early for multiplication and division problems as they do for addition and subtraction problems.

Counting strategies used for Multiplication and Measurement Division problems often involve some form of skip counting. The following is an example of a solution to a Grouping problem that involves skip counting:

> There are 3 tennis balls in a can. How many balls are there in 7 cans?

Linda: [mumbles to herself, putting up fingers 1 at a time until she has put up 7 fingers] 21—there are 21 balls.

Ms. K: OK. Can you tell me how you figured out that it was 21?

Linda: I counted up to 21.

Ms. K: Can you tell me the numbers you said?

Linda: 3, 6, 9, 12, 15, 18, 21. [With each count, she extends a finger to keep track of the number of threes she has counted.]

Ms. K: How did you know to stop at 21?

Linda: I kept track on my fingers.

Ms. K: How did you keep track?

Linda: I went 3 [clearly shows that she is putting up 1 finger], 6 [puts up a second finger]. [Linda continues skip counting and extending a finger until she has 7 fingers extended and has skip counted to 21.]

The use of Counting strategies for multiplication and division problems is similar to the use of Counting strategies for addition and subtraction problems. In both cases children are essentially counting the numbers in a counting sequence. The difference is that in the case of addition and subtraction, children are counting the numbers in the standard counting sequence whereas for multiplication and division strategies they are counting the numbers in a skip counting sequence. Solving problems with skip counting also requires additional conceptual knowledge that groups of objects be counted in the same way that single objects are counted. When Linda counted 3, 6, 9, 12, 15, 18, 21, she implicitly recognized that 3 balls would be 1 can, 6 balls would be 2 cans, 9 balls would be 3 cans, 12 balls would be 4 cans, and so on. She was essentially using her fingers to count groups of 3. This builds on the understanding shown in Direct Modeling strategies that an amount (such as 21) can be composed of equal groups of another amount (7 groups of 3).

Children generally are more proficient in skip counting by certain numbers, like three and five, than they are by other numbers, such as seven. Also, some children are only proficient at skip counting for the first three or four numbers in a sequence and need to complete their solutions by counting by ones. In this case they may use a combination of skip counting and Counting On by Ones. The following example illustrates this strategy:

The teacher has 5 sheets of stickers. There are 4 stickers on each sheet. How many stickers does the teacher have?

Jeannie counts, "Let's see, 4, 8, 12 [pause], 13, 14, 15, 16 [pause], 17, 18, 19, 20—20 stickers."

CLIP 4.5 Counting strategy for a Multiplication problem
http://smarturl.it/CM4.5

Jeannie could count by fours to 12. After that she had to count on by ones, which she did in two segments. Note that children skip count by the number of objects in each group, not by the number of groups. They keep track of the number of groups on their fingers or in some other way. This is a natural extension of the Direct Modeling strategy and corresponds to the way they put objects into groups when they directly model. Children do not easily recognize that they could skip count by either number given in a multiplication problem. For example, in the previous problem, it might have been easier to skip count by 5, but that is not what Jeannie did, because there were 4 objects in the groups.

Many children also use addition strategies to solve multiplication and division problems. For example, rather than skip counting, some children may repeatedly add the number representing the objects in each group. Skip counting is essentially repeated addition, but some children tend to think of their solution more in terms of counting, and others think of it more in terms of adding. Addition strategies, such as the doubling example that follows, offer other ways to solve problems.

A bottle of cola will fill 6 glasses. How many glasses can you fill with 7 bottles of cola?

Ji-hoon makes a drawing [Figure 4.5] and says, "42." [Keep in mind that the drawing is *Ji-hoon's* and represents his thinking. It is not an illustration used by a teacher.]

Mr. C: *How did you do that?*
Ji-hoon: I added 6 plus 6 three times, then I added the three 12s plus the extra 6 to get 42.

FIGURE 4.5 Ji-hoon's written representation of his Adding strategy

Counting Strategies for Measurement Division

Children use similar counting and addition and subtraction strategies to solve Measurement Division problems. The difference is that the children skip count or add or subtract until they reach the given number. The answer is the number of times they have counted, added, or subtracted, as shown in the following solution to a Measurement Division problem:

A restaurant puts 4 slices of cheese on each sandwich. How many sandwiches can they make with 24 pieces of cheese?

Susan counts, "Hmm, 4, 8, 12, 16, 20, 24." With each count, Susan extends 1 finger. When she is done counting, she looks at the 6 extended fingers and says, "6. They can make 6 sandwiches."

Note that, as with the counting example for the Multiplication problem above, Susan skip counted the number of objects in each group. This fits the context of the Measurement Division problem.

Counting Strategies for Partitive Division

It is much more difficult to use strategies involving counting or adding to solve Partitive Division problems than it is for Multiplication and Measurement Division problems. For both the Multiplication and Measurement Division problems, children skip count by the number of objects in each group. But for Partitive Division problems, the number of objects in each group is the unknown. Therefore, in order to use a Counting strategy that corresponds to the action or relationships in the problem, children tend to use a Trial and Error strategy to figure out which number to skip count by or to add. They know the number of groups and the total number of objects. The number of groups tells children how many numbers there should be in the skip counting sequence, and the total number of objects tells them where the skip counting sequence should stop. The problem is to figure out what to count by (the number in each group). That is where Trial and Error comes in, as the following example illustrates:

> There are 24 children in the class. We want to divide the class into 6 teams with the same number of children on each team. How many children will there be on each team?
>
> Susan counts, "Let's see, 3, 6, 9, 12, 15, 18." With each count, Susan extends 1 finger. When she has extended 6 fingers, she pauses. "No, that's not big enough. Let's try 4. 4, 8, 12, 16, 20, 24." Again, Susan extends a finger with each count. When she reaches 24, she sees that there are 6 fingers extended. "That's it. There would be 4 in each group."

Essentially, Susan's problem was to find a number to count by, such that when there were 6 numbers in the counting sequence, the total would be 24. She did not know what to count by, so she needed to guess. The first guess did not work. She had 6 fingers extended, indicating she had counted 6 times and she had not yet reached 24. Consequently, she had to start over again with another number. She could see that 3 was too small, so she tried 4. As this example illustrates, it is significantly more difficult to use a Counting strategy for a Partitive Division problem than for a Multiplication or Measurement Division problem.

Written Representation of Counting Strategies

As was the case with Counting strategies for addition and subtraction problems, Counting strategies used to solve multiplication and division problems can be represented by listing the numbers in the counting sequence. Figures 4.6 and 4.7 include a written representation of a counting strategy for a Multiplication problem and a Measurement Division

FIGURE 4.6 Written representation of a Counting strategy for the Multiplication problem: *Elliott has 5 packages of cards. Each package had 4 cards in it. How many cards does he have?*

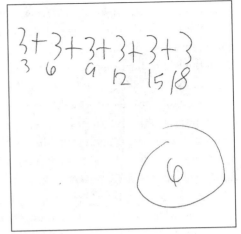

FIGURE 4.7 Written representation of a Counting strategy for the Measurement Division problem: *Ms. Bookout has 18 stickers in her sticker book. She puts 3 stickers on each page. How many pages will she use?*

problem. Although the notations look very similar, the answer for the Multiplication problem is the final count whereas the answer for the Measurement Division problem is the number of counts. Both students circle their answers in their written work.

Number Fact Strategies

As with addition and subtraction, children know some multiplication facts from memory before others. They can use facts they know from memory to derive other facts as shown in the following examples.

If there are 3 boxes of rocks with 8 rocks in each box, how many rocks would there be?

Luz: I know 2 eights is 16, so I added 1 more 8 to get 24.

If I had 8 boxes of peaches with 6 peaches in each box, how many peaches would I have?

Tanner: 4 sixes is 24, and another 4 sixes is 24, so 8 sixes is 48, 48 peaches. [See Figure 4.8.]

Maggie: I did it differently, and I also got 48. I know 6 sixes is 36 and then 2 sixes is 12, so 8 sixes is 36 plus 12, 48.

Jake: I have another way. I know 8 threes is 24, another 8 threes would be 24, add them together and that's the same as 8 sixes since 3 plus 3 is 6. 24 plus 24 is 48 peaches. [See Figure 4.9.]

CLIP 4.6 Derived Fact strategy for multiplication
http://smarturl.it/CM4.6

CLIP 4.7 Derived Fact strategy for multiplication
http://smarturl.it/CM4.7

Both Tanner and Maggie partitioned the number of groups. Jake, on the other hand, partitioned the amount in the group rather than the number of groups. In their initial Derived Fact strategies, children tend to partition one quantity or the other, but not both.

Some children use both multiplication and division in their derived facts.

9 people are going to the movies. If a movie ticket costs 5 dollars, how much would it cost for all 9 people to see the movie?

CLIP 4.8 Derived Fact strategy for Multiplication problem, in which amount in a group is partitioned
http://smarturl.it/CM4.8

Kevin: 9 tens is 90, but the tickets are 5 dollars, not 10 dollars so divide it in 2, that is 45.

$$4 \times 6 = 24$$
$$4 \times 6 = 24$$
$$40 + 8 = 48$$

answer

(48)

FIGURE 4.8 Tanner's representation of his strategy for 8 groups of 6

$$8 \times [3] = \$24$$
$$8 \times [3] = 24$$
$$3 + 3 = 6$$
$$24 + 24 = 48$$

FIGURE 4.9 Jake's representation of his strategy for 8 groups of 6

Because multiplication and division are related, the strategies children use to derive division facts are often related to their knowledge of multiplication facts.

Alana got 56 dollars for her birthday. She wants to use this money to buy books at the book fair. If each book costs 7 dollars, how many books could she buy?

Eve: 3 sevens is 21, another 3 sevens is 21, 21 plus 21 is 42, so I need, umm, 14 more to get to 56. 14 is 2 sevens. 3 sevens plus 3 sevens plus 2 sevens is 8 sevens. That means that 8 sevens is 56. She could buy 8 books.

Ms. L: *I don't understand what you did, Eve.*

Eve: I was trying to figure out how many sevens in 56. I didn't know that, but I know that 3 sevens is 21. So if she had 21 dollars, she could buy 3 books. Another 21 dollars would get her another 21 dollars would get her another 3 books and she would have 14 more dollars to spend. 2 sevens is 14, so she could buy 2 more books. 3 plus 3 plus 2 is 8. [See Figure 4.10.]

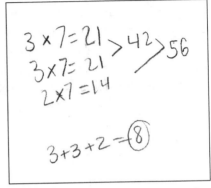

FIGURE 4.10 Eve's representation of her strategy for a Measurement Division problem

Note that Tanner, Eve and Kevin used the context of the story in the problem they were solving to describe their Derived Facts. As a consequence, they made a clear distinction between the number of groups and the size of the group in describing their strategies. Often a word problem supports a student better than an equation when communicating their use of Derived Facts because they can refer to the context of the story to explain their use of relationships.

Common Relationships Children Use to Derive Multiplication Facts

Children learn certain multiplication facts before others and can use these relationships to derive the facts they do not know. Some of the most common relationships children use to derive multiplication facts include the following.

Multiplying by 3. To multiply 3 times a number, children recognize that 3 groups of any number is the same as 2 groups of that number plus 1 more group. Luz's strategy for the word problem about 3 groups of 8 at the beginning of this section used this relationship.

Children who can use this strategy to multiply by 3 may not recognize that 3 times a number is the same as the number times 3. For example, they may count by threes to solve a problem about 7 groups of 3 ($7 \times 3 = 3 + 3 + 3 + 3 + 3 + 3 + 3$) but double 7 then add 1 more 7 to solve a problem about 3 groups of 7 ($3 \times 7 = 14 + 7 = 21$).

Multiplying by 4. Many children see that 4 times any number is the same as 2 times the number plus 2 times the number. For example, a child may see that 4 groups of 6 is the same as 2 groups of 6 plus another 2 groups of 6. If she knows that 2 groups of 6 is 12 then she can find 4 groups of 6 by adding 12 and 12 ($4 \times 6 = 12 + 12$).

Multiplying a number times 5. Many children learn the times 5 facts early because they can skip count easily by fives and these number facts follow a pattern. Multiplying times 5 tends to be easier for children when they can think of 5 as the number in a group, rather than the number of groups. For example, a child may figure 7 groups of 5 by relating it to facts learned by counting by fives ($7 \times 5 = 6 \times 5 + 5$) but have difficulty figuring the answer to 5 groups of 7 using a Derived Fact strategy. If he does not see how 5 groups of 7 relates to 7 groups of 5, he may think of 5×7 as repeated addition of 7 ($5 \times 7 = 7 + 7 + 7 + 7 + 7$).

Commutative property of multiplication. Children can be more flexible in applying the above Derived Fact strategies if they understand the commutative property of multiplication ($a \times b = b \times a$), but the commutative property of multiplication is harder for children to understand than the commutative property of addition. In the context of equal groups problems, it is not at all obvious why, for example, 6 groups of 9 items has the same number of items as 9 groups of 6 items. We return to the commutative property of multiplication later in this chapter as we discuss array and area problems.

As children's understanding of multiplication and division develops, they draw upon an increasingly larger set of memorized facts to derive facts they cannot recall. They become flexible in solving word problems as well as equations, such as $7 \times 8 = \square$, and they become fluent in the use of number facts to solve problems.

Allowing plenty of time for children to use, discuss, and reflect on derived fact strategies, without rushing the memorization of multiplication facts, has several long-term benefits. Children develop an understanding of the properties of multiplication (see Chapter 11) and the relationship between multiplication and division as they develop the ability to accurately and efficiently solve multiplication and division problems. The focus on making sense of number facts also contributes to helping children see that mathematics can be understood and reasoned about rather than learned as a collection of unrelated facts and procedures.

What to Do with What's Left Over

Because there are many situations in which the objects do not divide equally without any leftovers, children need to deal with remainders. Children can solve problems with remainders by using the strategies already described, and problems with remainders are not a great deal more difficult than problems without remainders.

In solving problems with remainders, it is necessary to take into account how the remainder relates to the problem. The context of the problem generally dictates how the remainder is treated in answering the question. There are four basic ways this may occur. In the following Measurement Division problem, an extra car must be included for the 2 people left over:

> *20 people are going to a movie. 6 people can ride in each car. How many cars are needed to get all 20 people to the movie?*

In each of the following Measurement and Partitive Division problems, the remainder is simply left over and is not taken into account:

> *It takes 3 eggs to make a cake. How many cakes can you make with 17 eggs?*

> *Ms. Franke has 21 marbles. She wants to share them equally among her 5 children so that no one gets more than anyone else. How many marbles should she give to each child?*

CLIP 4.9 Direct Modeling strategy for Measurement Division with a remainder
http://smarturl.it/CM4.9

CLIP 4.10 Direct Modeling strategy for Measurement Division with a remainder, adjusted for child
http://smarturl.it/CM4.10

From the context of these problems, it is clear that only 5 cakes can be made and 4 marbles can be given to each child. The child may either ignore the remainder or suggest that the 2 eggs can be put back into the refrigerator and that Ms. Franke can keep the last marble.

A third possibility is that the remainder is the answer to the problem, as in the following Measurement and Partitive Division problems:

> *A store has 26 basketballs, which they want to pack in boxes so that there are 3 balls in each box. If they fill as many boxes as possible, how many balls will be left over?*

> *Ms. Baker has 17 candies. She wants to share them equally among her 3 daughters so that no one gets more than anyone else. If she gives each daughter as many candies as possible, how many candies will be left over for Ms. Baker to eat?*

The fourth possibility is that the answer includes a fractional part. These problems can provide the basis for developing basic concepts of fraction and fraction equivalence. For a more complete discussion of how these problems can be used to develop fraction concepts see Empson and Levi (2011). The following is an example of a Partitive Division problem in which a fraction is included in the answer.

> Ms. Baker has 13 packages of clay that are all the same size. She wants 4 children to share the clay so that everyone gets the same amount. How much clay should each child get?

OTHER MULTIPLICATION AND DIVISION PROBLEMS

The multiplication and division problems discussed up to this point have dealt with grouping and partitioning collections of discrete objects that can be counted. There are related problems that involve multiplicative comparisons and/or quantities that are measures rather than collections of countable objects. These problems are similar in structure to the multiplication and division problems we have presented so far in that they also involve Multiplication, Partitive Division, and Measurement Division situations. For other problems, this is not the case. Problems involving areas, arrays, or combinations have completely different structures.

Problems Involving Measures

Some problems do not have countable groups. Instead they have measures of quantities that children can represent. Problems with quantities that can't be counted are a little more abstract than problems involving countable groups of objects, but when they follow the basic structure of grouping problems, they are not out of reach of young children. Consider the following problems:

> *Multiplication:* A baby elephant gains 4 pounds each day. How many pounds will the baby elephant gain in 8 days?

> *Measurement Division:* A baby elephant gains 4 pounds each day. How many days will it take the baby elephant to gain 32 pounds?

> *Partitive Division:* A baby elephant gained 32 pounds in 8 days. If she gained the same amount of weight each day, how much did she gain in 1 day?

These problems each involve a measure rather than a number of objects. In each case, the measure is pounds per day. Although the 8 days are not really 8 groups, and the 4 and

32 pounds are not countable objects, the problems do have some similarities to the basic Grouping and Partitioning problems discussed earlier in this chapter and can be thought of in much the same way. A child can think about how much the elephant gains in 1 day, in 2 days, and so forth. So the first problem might be solved by making 8 groups of counters with 4 counters in each group. Each group of 4 counters would represent how much the baby elephant gained each day, and the total number of counters would represent the total weight gained.

The second problem could be solved by counting out 32 counters, removing sets of 4, and counting the number of sets removed to determine how many days it would take to gain 32 pounds. The last problem could be solved by distributing the 32 counters into 8 piles, which represent the days, and counting the objects in each pile to determine how much the elephant gained daily. Thus, even though the problems do not describe actions involving discrete sets, children can solve them in much the same way that they solve the Grouping and Partitioning problems.

The following are some other common situations involving measures:

> *How many miles does a bicycle travel in 3 hours at an average speed of 12 miles per hour?*

> *A babysitter earns 3 dollars per hour for baby-sitting. How many hours will he have to baby-sit to earn 18 dollars?*

Multiplicative Comparison Problems

In problems described to this point, all of the numbers represent some sort of quantity: the number of groups; the number of objects in a group; the total number of objects; measures of time, speed, length; and so forth. For Multiplicative Comparison, this is not the case. Multiplicative Comparison problems involve a comparison of two quantities in which one is described as a multiple of the other. The relation between quantities is described in terms of how many times the larger quantity is compared to the smaller one. The number quantifying this relationship is not a measurable quantity. In the following problem, the animals' weights are measurable quantities, but the other quantity (three times as much) simply describes the relation between the measurable quantities. To solve this problem and other Multiplicative Comparison problems, children must understand the meaning of such terms as "3 times as much."

> *The first-grade class has a hamster and a gerbil. The hamster weighs 3 times as much as the gerbil. The gerbil weighs 9 ounces. How much does the hamster weigh?*

Multiplicative Comparison problems also can be constructed for any of the three basic problem types, as illustrated by the following examples.

Multiplication: *The giraffe in the zoo is 3 times as tall as the kangaroo. The kangaroo is 6 feet tall. How tall is the giraffe?*

Measurement Division: *The giraffe is 18 feet tall. The kangaroo is 6 feet tall. The giraffe is how many times as tall as the kangaroo?*

Partitive Division: *The giraffe is 18 feet tall. She is 3 times as tall as the kangaroo. How tall is the kangaroo?*

Common Features

The differences among all of these problems can be relatively minor, and it is not necessary to be concerned about whether a problem falls in one particular class or another. In general, the closer a problem follows a grouping situation with countable objects in each group, the easier it will be for young children. It is important for children to work with problems that reflect different conceptions of multiplication and division, but it is usually best to wait until children have a solid understanding of Grouping problems before moving to Multiplicative Comparison problems or problems with quantities that are measures.

Symmetric Problems: Area, Array, and Combination Problems

One important characteristic of all problem types discussed previously is that they are not symmetric; that is, the numbers in them are related to specific referents, and the referents are not interchangeable. When a problem talks about 5 bags of cookies with 7 cookies in each bag, young children initially think about the 5 in relation to the number of bags and the 7 in relation to the number of cookies in each bag. They solve the problem by making 5 groups with 7 objects in each group. It is not obvious to most young children that they also could solve the problem by making 7 groups with 5 objects in each group, or that they could count by fives.

At some point, children need to learn that $5 \times 7 = 7 \times 5$, but it is important to recognize that young children do not immediately understand that the two numbers in the Multiplication problems discussed above can be interchanged or that the methods used to solve a Measurement Division problem also can be applied to a Partitive Division problem. There are multiplication and division problems, however, in which the factors play equivalent roles. We call these problems *symmetric*. Area and Array problems and Combination problems are types of Symmetric problems.

Area and Array Problems

One important application of multiplication is calculating the area of a rectangular region by multiplying the length of the region by the width. This involves a very different conception of multiplication than has been discussed so far in this chapter. Unlike the Grouping/Partitioning, Rate, and Multiplicative Comparison problems, the two factors in an Area problem do not have distinctly different roles and are not attached to a specific referent. Although the longest side of a rectangle is frequently called the length and the shorter side the width, the length and width play essentially the same role in calculating the area of a rectangle.

Thus, Area problems represent a new type of multiplication and division problem. Because the two factors in an Area problem are interchangeable, there are not two distinct types of Area division problems. In other words, because the length and width play equivalent roles in area problems, it does not matter whether the length or the width is unknown. The following are examples of each basic type of Area problem:

> *A farmer plants a rectangular vegetable garden that measures 6 meters along 1 side and 8 meters along an adjacent side. How many square meters of garden did the farmer plant?*

> *A farmer plans to plant a rectangular vegetable garden. She has enough room to make the garden 6 meters along 1 side. How long does she have to make the adjacent side in order to have 48 square meters of garden?*

There is more to developing area concepts than multiplying the dimensions of a rectangle to calculate the area, but children can solve problems that introduce multiplication and division in area contexts before they have developed a complete understanding of area concepts. The following example is a problem that might be solved by modeling before children have developed a formal notion of area:

> *A baker has a pan of fudge that measures 6 inches on 1 side and 4 inches on another side. If the fudge is cut into square pieces 1 inch on a side, how many pieces of fudge does the pan hold?*

Children might model this problem by drawing a picture of the pan divided into 24 squares. They may count each of the squares, or they may find a more efficient way to figure out the number of pieces, like adding 6 four times or doubling (6, 12, 24). In these solutions, children need to construct some representation of the problem in order to solve it. In other problems, children might work directly with rectangular regions partitioned into square units. For example, they might find the number of floor tiles covering the floor of the classroom or work from a picture of a rectangular region partitioned into identical units.

Finding the number of items in a rectangular array involves the same basic conception of multiplication as finding the area of a rectangle. The primary difference is that arrays may be made up of discrete objects (cookies on a cookie sheet, rows of chairs, etc.). Array problems can be directly modeled in a systematic way by constructing a given number of rows of counters with the same number of counters in each row. Children may interpret some problems as either Array or Grouping problems. For example, the following problem could be thought of as an array of chairs or as groups of chairs in each row:

FIGURE 4.11 Using an Array to solve a Multiplication problem

> *For the second-grade play, the chairs have been put into 5 rows with 4 chairs in each row. How many chairs have been put out for the play?*

Some children might solve this problem by arranging counters into a 5-by-4 array (see Figure 4.11), whereas others may just make 5 groups of 4.

Although arrays provide natural representations for some types of multiplication and division problems, young children do not normally construct arrays unless a problem calls for them. Some textbooks use pictures of arrays to represent a wide variety of multiplication or division situations, including situations that children would not naturally represent as arrays. For example, in some textbooks a Grouping problem such as the following might be accompanied by a picture of an array with 4 rows of peanuts with 8 peanuts in each row:

> *How many peanuts would the monkey eat if she ate 4 bags of peanuts with 8 peanuts in each bag?*

In this case, a Grouping problem, which children usually think of as a certain number of groups with the same number in each group, has been represented as an array. This is not an incorrect representation of the problem, but it is not the form that young children generally use to model it. Textbook authors often use arrays because they provide a context for developing the principle that multiplication is commutative ($3\times5 = 5\times3$). But children do not naturally construct an array for a Multiplication problem unless an array is specifically described in the problem.

Thus, Array and Area problems provide a very different context for developing multiplication and division concepts than Grouping/Partitioning problems do. Furthermore, they illustrate important concepts that are not easily related to Grouping/Partitioning problems. Array problems can be used to help children understand that multiplication is commutative ($a\times b = b\times a$), and Area problems provide a basis for developing an understanding of multiplication and division of fractions.

Combination Problems

Another type of symmetric problem involves different combinations that can be constructed from given sets of objects, as this example does:

> The Friendly Old Ice-Cream Shop has 3 types of ice cream cones. They also have 4 flavors of ice cream. How many different combinations of an ice-cream flavor and cone type can you get at the Friendly Old Ice-Cream Shop?

This problem is symmetric because the cones and the ice-cream flavors can be interchanged in thinking about the problem. There is no real difference in thinking of the problem in terms of the number of flavors that go with each cone or in terms of the number of cones that go with each flavor. The problem might be solved by identifying 3 types of cones (sugar cones, waffle cones, and wafer cones) and 4 flavors (blue moon, bubble gum, double chocolate, caramel swirl) and actually making all the combinations (blue moon on a sugar cone, blue moon on a waffle cone, etc.). Many young children have difficulty constructing all the combinations in this way. They often are not systematic and only construct a few of the combinations. For example, they may concentrate on using each type of cone once, or they may not be systematic in constructing the combinations and then not recognize that they do not have them all. On the other hand, some children may recognize that it is not necessary to actually make all the combinations. They may see that for each cone, there will be 4 flavors, and be able to think of the problem as 3 groups of 4. Alternatively, they might see that for each flavor there will be 3 cones and relate the problem to 4 groups of 3.

Combination problems are not as central to developing concepts of multiplication and division in the primary grades as the other problems that we have discussed in this chapter. Because of their difficulty, they might be used sparingly in the primary grades.

They do, however, present a different type of challenging problem that can lead to a good discussion of strategies. Even though some children may have difficulty systematically organizing their combinations, the discussion may help children begin to see the need to organize results in systematic ways.

MULTIPLICATION AND DIVISION WORD PROBLEMS IN THE PRIMARY GRADES

There are good reasons for introducing multiplication and division word problems early in the mathematics curriculum. With experience, many kindergarten children can solve multiplication and division problems by using counters or drawings to model the groups described in the problems. By first and second grade, children often use a variety of strategies to solve multiplication and division word problems. Integrating the problems into the primary curriculum provides children a foundation for understanding multiplication and division as well as expanding their opportunities to solve problems in a variety of contexts. The variety that these problems provide encourages children to engage in problem solving rather than using superficial strategies to decide whether to add or subtract the numbers given in a problem. It is not necessary to introduce the symbols for multiplying and dividing ($\times$, $\div$) in the early grades, but that should not preclude engaging young children in solving the kinds of problems discussed in this chapter.

Multiplication and division problems also provide children the opportunity to develop a broad understanding of some of the fundamental grouping ideas underlying place value. In order to learn base-ten concepts with understanding, children must understand the concepts that underlie multiplication and division. In fact, base-ten problems are essentially multiplication or division problems involving groups of 10. For example, the problem "How many tens are there in 73?" is a Measurement Division problem. A common activity for introducing base-ten number concepts is to count collections of objects by organizing them into groups of 10. There is a direct parallel between this counting procedure and the strategy children use to solve a Measurement Division problem involving groups of 10.

When children have experiences with multiplication and division problems before they encounter place value concepts, they have the opportunity to develop an understanding of basic principles that are essential to understand base-ten numbers. As they learn principles of our base-ten number system, they only have to deal with the special characteristics of grouping by 10 and how such groupings are related to the names assigned to them. Thus, providing children the opportunity to solve a variety of multiplication and division problems can provide a context for them to develop a rich understanding of mathematics in a way that is meaningful to them. We will return to the learning of place value in Chapter 6, but first we discuss beginning to use CGI in your classroom.

QUESTIONS FOR FURTHER REFLECTION

1. Identify the problem type for each of these problems.

   a. *Alisha has 8 jars with 9 tadpoles in each jar. How many tadpoles does Alisha have?*
   b. *Mr. Rodriguez has 12 cookies that he is going to give to his 3 children. How many cookies should he give each child if he wants each child to have the same amount?*
   c. *3 people each have 5 cookies. How many cookies are there altogether?*
   d. *I have 30 stickers. If I use 5 stickers each day, how many days will my stickers last?*
   e. *23 children are going to the zoo. There is room for 3 children to ride in each car. How many cars will be needed to get all 23 children to the zoo?*
   f. *Freddie had 24 tangerines. She picked them after school at her aunt's house. She gave all 24 tangerines to 4 friends so that each friend got the same number of tangerines. How many tangerines did each of Freddie's friends get from Freddie?*
   g. *Gunter has 13 cookies. He is going to share his cookies with 3 friends so that everyone gets the same amount. How many cookies would each person get?*

2. Choose a book that you are reading with your students or a topic that you are studying. Write one problem for each of the problem types in Figure 4.1 that relate to the story or topic.

3. Identify the problem type and solve each problem with a Direct Modeling strategy, a Counting strategy, and a Derived Facts strategy.

Problem	Direct Modeling Strategy	Counting Strategy	Derived Fact Strategy
Jill has 4 boxes of books with 6 books in each box. How many books does Jill have? Problem type: _____			

Problem	Direct Modeling Strategy	Counting Strategy	Derived Fact Strategy
Fred has 30 dollars to spend on books. If each book costs 6 dollars, how many books could Fred buy? Problem type: _____			
Judy has 28 books. If she wants to put her books in 4 boxes with the same number of books in each box, how many books should she put in each box? Problem type: _____			

4. Predict how your students would solve these problems:

   a. *Josh has 4 bags with 3 rocks in each bag. How many rocks does Josh have?*
   b. *Sara has 24 pencils. She wants to put her pencils in 4 boxes with the same number of pencils in each box. How many pencils should she put in each box?*
   c. *If 6 people share 48 marbles so that each person gets the same number of marbles, how many marbles would each person get?*

5. Pose one or more of the problems from question 4 to your students. As long as your students do a reasonable job of counting objects, we encourage you to pose problems *a* and *b* even if this material isn't explicitly part of your grade-level standards.

Ask three or four students to explain how they solved the problems and take notes on what they say. Choose students who are likely to use different strategies and ask them how they solved the problem. Did the students do what you expected? Did any of your students use Direct Modeling, Counting, or Number Facts strategies? Describe the students' strategy in enough detail that someone reading your description could solve the problem the same way the students did.

6. Consider the following problem:

   If 8 tickets cost $56, how much would 1 ticket cost?

   Suppose you posed this problem and it was too hard for a student to solve. Think of two different ways you could change the problem to make it easier while still keeping the problem a division problem.

7. Figure 4.12 shows a strategy that a third-grader generated for the problem:

   I have 6 bags of books with 7 books in each bag. How many books do I have?

   a. How would you describe what this child did to another teacher?
   b. Write two questions that you would ask this child about her strategy. These questions can be either to help you understand her strategy, help her reflect on her strategy, or help her explain her strategy to other students.

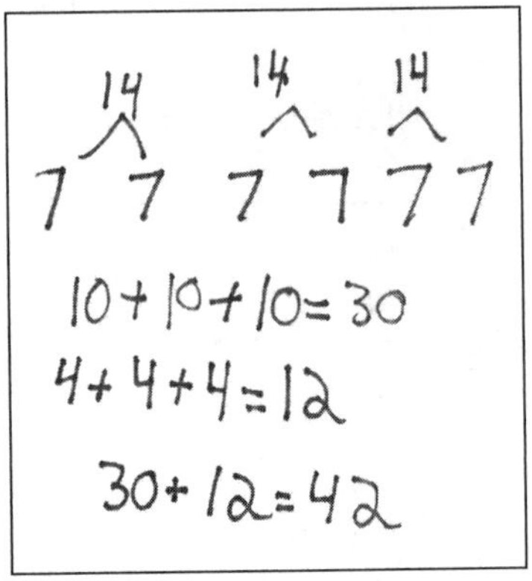

FIGURE 4.12

8. Figure 4.13 shows a strategy that the same third-grader generated for the problem:

   I have 7 bags of books with 8 books in each bag. How many books do I have?

   a. How would you describe what this child did to another teacher?
   b. How is her strategy for this problem different than her strategy for the problem about 6 groups of 7?
   c. Write two questions that you would ask this child about her strategy. These questions can be either to help you understand her strategy, help her reflect on her strategy, or help her explain her strategy to other students.

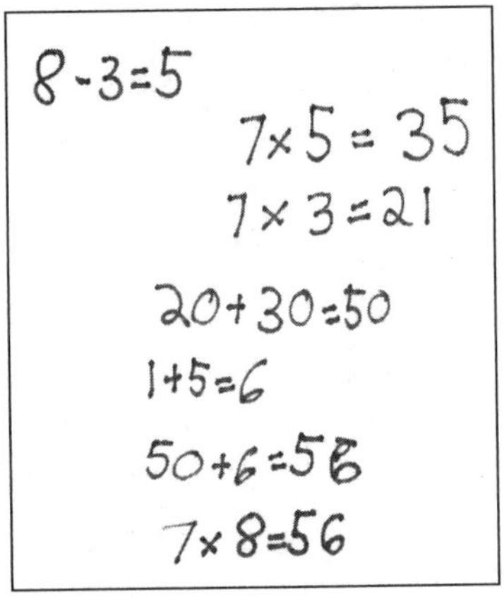

FIGURE 4.13

9. Write a Measurement Division problem and a Partitive Division problem that goes with the equation 35 ÷ 5 = □.

10. Write four word problems that are about 26 divided by 4, each of which has one the following different answers (a) 6, (b) 7, (c) 6½, (d) 2.

11. Watch Austin, a kindergartener, solve the following two problems:

   a. *Multiplication:* Robin has 3 package of gum. There are 6 pieces of gum in each package. How many pieces of gum does Robin have?
   b. *Measurement Division:* Tad had 15 ladybugs. He put 3 ladybugs in each jar. How many jars did Tad put ladybugs in?

   For each problem, describe the details of Austin's thinking and what he understands. Now, keeping in mind what you have learned about Austin's understanding of multiplication and division, predict how he might solve the following Partitive Division problem:

   c. *Partitive Division: There are 24 jelly beans in a bag. 4 children want to share them so they each get the same amount of jelly beans. How many jelly beans would each child get?*

   Now watch how Austin solved this problem. Was Austin's strategy similar to what you predicted he might do? Or something very different? Why do you think Austin solved the problem the way he did?

CLIP 4.11 Watch Austin solve a Multiplication and Measurement Division problem
http://smarturl.it/CM4.11

CLIP 4.12 Now watch Austin solve a Partitive Division problem
http://smarturl.it/CM4.12

5

Beginning to Use Cognitively Guided Instruction

My journey as a CGI teacher has been exciting, not only for me but for my students and colleagues. My students have taught me about math through their amazing thinking. I really enjoy learning, listening, and developing mathematical understanding with my students and colleagues.

—**Kathleen Bird, teacher**

Beginning to use CGI is all about making sense of children's thinking, listening to your students, and experimenting with your classroom practice. We offer in this chapter a brief overview of what to consider as you begin working with students. We purposefully placed this chapter in the midst of the children's thinking chapters to provide you the opportunity to think about the development of children's thinking in relation to classroom practice. Learning about children's thinking continues as you teach, and thinking about your teaching can help you see what more you want to learn about children's mathematical thinking.

Becoming a CGI teacher takes time. Changing your classroom practice so that you can draw on knowledge of the development of children's mathematical thinking can be challenging. Yet, teachers consistently report that although they felt uneasy as they started CGI, the rewards were worth the struggle for them and their students. We have found that one way to alleviate the uneasiness and to begin the journey that Ms. Bird describes is just to start. This chapter provides general information about starting your journey.

GETTING STARTED

I was really surprised by what kids can do without any help from me at all. . . . And even now when some of the kids tell you how they solve a problem, you have to admire that, because in your wildest dreams you wouldn't have thought about doing it that way.

—Jennifer Beard, teacher

Most teachers start to use CGI by asking students to solve problems like those discussed in Chapters 2–4 and 6 and 7. They choose word problems set in contexts with which their students are familiar. When teachers pose these problems, they do not demonstrate a strategy for solving a given problem type, although they may engage students in a discussion of the context in which the problem is set to be sure that students understand what the problem is about. Students are provided a variety of tools and encouraged to use a strategy that makes sense to them. As students solve the problem, teachers find it useful to move around and observe various students asking them about what they are doing, as a way to understand students' strategies and provide support when necessary.

There is no optimal way to organize a CGI class. Some teachers prefer to start by working with a small group of students. In other classes, the entire class is given a problem to solve and discuss. Sometimes teachers adapt the numbers in a problem or provide different problems for different students. Whatever organization enables you to support the students to solve problems using their own strategies and provides you opportunities to listen to the students' problem-solving strategies is an appropriate organization for you. Finding an organizational structure that works for you and your students may require you to experiment with how you pose problems and support students to share their ideas; and in turn, this experimentation and reflection will lead to ongoing learning for you and your students. (We will explore posing problems and eliciting students' ideas more in Chapters 9 and 10.)

Engaging Children in Problem Solving

Through problem-solving experiences, students have the opportunity to use and apply many mathematical skills and concepts. These skills and concepts are embedded in the different strategies that children use to solve problems. By listening to and observing students solving problems, I can better comprehend my students' ideas and make better instructional decisions that build on the student's understanding.

—Susan Gehn, teacher

In CGI classes, students learn most new content by engaging in problem solving. Solving and discussing a variety of problems supports students to develop both concepts and skills. Problems can be posed as word problems or symbolic problems or in other formats. The critical consideration is that students are engaged in deciding how to solve problems using what makes sense to them.

Unlike traditional instruction in which the content to be learned is clearly sequenced (addition before subtraction, etc.) and where students learn skills before they use them to solve problems, the curriculum in CGI classes is integrated. For example, students do not learn number facts as isolated bits of information. Rather they learn them as they repeatedly solve problems, so that they begin to see relationships between the various facts. Both word problems and symbolic problems are the vehicles through which students learn mathematical concepts and skills. Teachers choose problems so that they will enhance students' development, but in most cases do not provide explicit instruction on problem-solving strategies. Instead students develop and share their own problem-solving strategies, which become more efficient and abstract over time. Skills and number facts are learned in the process of problem solving and are thus learned with understanding rather than as isolated pieces of information.

Selecting and Posing Problems

The discussion in Chapters 2–4 of problem types and children's ways of solving them provides a framework for selecting problems that will be appropriate for getting started with your class. Young children can solve a variety of problems provided that they have appropriate tools to model the action in the problems and the problem contexts involve situations that children can easily imagine and relate to. The easiest problems are those that are easiest for children to directly model. Join (Result Unknown) and Separate (Result Unknown) are two of the easiest problem types. Multiplication, Measurement Division, and Partitive Division problems are also relatively easy. Join (Change Unknown) and Compare (Difference Unknown) are a little more challenging, but many kindergarten students can solve them once they have experience using Direct Modeling strategies with easier problem types. Some teachers start with relatively easy problems to give the students in their classes a successful beginning experience and to develop new ways of engaging together around mathematics. If you pose a problem and your students do not use a variety of strategies, it might be that you have chosen a problem that was too easy. You might try making the numbers larger or choosing a more challenging problem type so your students draw on their informal knowledge and engage in more complex problem solving. Choose contexts for problems that will be interesting, engaging, and understandable for your students. Teachers often relate the contexts to something the students are doing currently, such as a book they are reading, a social studies or science unit they are pursuing, or a field trip they are going to take.

Sharing Strategies

I have learned to listen to my students and how they think. Listening to and watching my students have given me the confidence and the knowledge to provide my students with the chance to solve many different types of problems and to use numbers based upon their understanding. I have learned many different strategies from the students that have helped me in solving problems. They have the strategies; we just need to provide the opportunity for them to apply their strategies and to build on these strategies.

—Susan Gehn, teacher

Finding ways for students to share their mathematical thinking with the teacher and with each other is key to students' learning. The sharing may happen as students are solving problems together in pairs, after students have solved a problem and a few share their ideas with the class, or even in the middle of solving a problem as students stop to share how they have gotten started. Sharing can happen in a variety of forms and at a number of different times in a math lesson. Sharing ideas and strategies allows students to make their own thinking explicit and notice new connections, learn from other students' ideas, and compare strategies to see underlying relationships across strategies.

For students to benefit from strategy sharing, they need the chance to explain the details of their thinking with each other. In asking students to share their strategies, you will learn from your students and your students will learn from and with each other. There are many ways to have your students share their thinking. One good question to start with is simply, "Could you explain how you solved that problem?" While the student explains the strategy, listen carefully to make sure you understand exactly what the student did.

The details are important. It is not sufficient for a student to say "I used the blocks" to explain his strategy. The blocks are the tool the student used in his strategy. They may have been used to directly model the quantities or to keep track of a count. So, to explain his strategy, the student needs to describe how he used the blocks in his strategy. Students need to expect that they are going to have to describe details such as how they used the blocks, what numbers they started with when they used a Counting strategy or how they used what they knew about doubles to use a Derived Fact strategy.

If a student does something you do not understand, ask about it when the student is finished. Your question could start with, "Can you tell me why you . . . ?" Even if you understand the strategy, it is important to ask specific questions about the strategy to help the other students make sense of it and to support the student who solved the problem learn to articulate her explanations and justify her thinking. Ask questions whether students' strategies are valid or invalid, complete or incomplete. With practice, you will notice which aspects are important for your students to explain in greater detail. The more you ask students to explain their thinking, the better you will be at asking questions to get students to explain the details of their strategies. Let your curiosity about children's strategies drive your questions, as children will appreciate your interest and enjoy being asked about their ideas.

BEGINNING THE JOURNEY

I saw children in my classroom who not only were able to do it, but understood what they were doing. Kids were seeing themselves as problem solvers, and doing phenomenal things.

—Mary Jo Yttri, teacher

If you have not posed some of the problems in this book to children, we encourage you to do so soon. All you need to get started with CGI is the ability to recognize and construct a variety of word problems and a beginning understanding of the common solution strategies used by children to solve these problems. Then you can ask students to solve one problem in any way that they wish, with the help of some tools and no preteaching of a strategy. As the students solve the problem, observe their work and ask questions about the solutions. After the students are done, encourage them to share how they have solved the problem. The more you pose problems and support your students in sharing their thinking, the more natural it will feel for you and your students. Our goal in sharing this information with you is to encourage you to start your journey toward becoming a CGI teacher. We know that you will learn more about word problems and more about children's mathematical thinking as you work with your students. The more you listen to students' mathematical thinking, the more you will be amazed by what students can do and what you can learn by listening to them describe how they solved problems.

> How I got started with CGI is simple: I just tried. I posed problems to see what kids would do. Sometimes it went well; sometimes it didn't go so well. I took risks and was willing to be wrong. I learned from each experience. Every day I grew along with the students. I talked to my colleagues. I asked questions, lots of questions. I kept track of what the students were doing and how they were changing. I reflected on my practice and learned to listen to the kids.
>
> —Kendra Bookout, teacher

QUESTIONS FOR FURTHER REFLECTION

Before moving on, we highly encourage you to try some of the problems in this book with your students. *If you have an idea about how you would like to try problems with children, there is no need to read questions 1–5.* It will probably work better for you and your students if you move forward with your own ideas about how to get started.

Some teachers like some direction about getting started, and the following steps may be helpful. Having another person to talk through this process with you would be extremely helpful. *These are guidelines for getting started. As you gain experience posing problems, you will modify this procedure to meet your teaching style and your students' needs.* Most teachers do not follow the same procedure every time they pose problems to their students.

1. Choose a problem. You can pick a problem from this book or write one of your own.

   a. Will your students understand the context and objects in this problem? If not, rewrite the problem with a different context or objects.

2. Choose the students you will work with. Many teachers start by posing problems to the whole class. Others prefer to start with a small group of students.

   a. Can these students count out sets as large as the numbers in the problem? If not, substitute smaller numbers.
   b. Will many of these students immediately know the answer to this problem? If so, substitute larger numbers or choose a different problem type with which they have had less experience.

3. Pose the problem to these students.

   a. Ensure that students have manipulatives available. If you are not used to providing manipulatives, distribute small blocks or cubes to each student. Make sure you give each student enough counters to model the problem you are posing. If your students are not used to having manipulatives, you may need to either explain to them that they are not playing right now or give them a few minutes to play with them before you begin.

   b. Before posing the problem, tell your students that you want them to solve the problem in a way that makes sense to them. They can use the manipulatives but they do not have to.

   c. Read the problem aloud. You can provide a written copy of the problem to each student or have the problem written on your board if that would be helpful. You may need to read the problem several times.

   d. You may or may not choose to have students produce a written representation of how they solved the problem. It is certainly not necessary to produce a written representation every time you solve a problem.

   e. If some students do not know how to get started solving the problem:
   - Check to ensure that they understand the story. Draw on what you do to assess comprehension when teaching reading to assess the student's comprehension of the story. For example, ask if they can tell the story back to you. Ask questions to determine if they understand what is happening in the story.
   - Give them some time to think. You could talk with another student and come back.
   - You could think about how to make the problem easier for the student— perhaps you could try using smaller numbers.

4. Observe your students solving this problem. Many teachers find it useful to just observe without saying anything as their students solve the problem during the first few problem-solving sessions.

5. After students are done solving the problem, you could be done for the day or you could try one or more of the following:

   a. Ask students to share how they solved the problem with a partner.
   b. Ask a few students to present to the class how they solved the problem.

c. Collect the students' written work (if there was any) and think about what questions you have for these students. Return to the students the next day and ask them these questions.

d. Collect students' written work (if there was any) and choose two or three students to present their strategies to the class the following day.

6. In the following video, a first-grade teacher poses a Multiplication problem to her students. The students solve the problem individually and then the teacher leads a sharing session. We suggest you watch this video twice, once to focus on the children's thinking and once to focus on how the teacher is supporting children to share their thinking with the class.

> **CLIP 5.1** Watch the first-graders in Ms. Hassay's classroom share their strategies for a Multiplication problem
> http://smarturl.it/CM5.1

a. What strategies did Ms. Hassay's students share with the class?

b. Why do you think Ms. Hassay chose these strategies to be shared?

c. What did Ms. Hassay do to support the students to explain their strategy? What did she do to help other students understand these strategies?

6

Base-Ten Number Concepts

In this chapter, we return to our analysis of the development of children's mathematical thinking. In particular, we discuss how the multiplication and division problems presented in Chapter 4 can be used to develop children's understanding of the base-ten number system. We present problems involving groups of tens, hundreds, thousands, and so forth and the strategies that children use to solve them that reflect their emerging understanding of base-ten numbers. For simplicity, we describe the development of basic grouping and naming principles for two-digit numbers before moving on to larger numbers.

The central principle that children must grasp to understand the base-ten number system is that collections of ten (or one hundred or one thousand and so on) can be counted. This means that we can talk about the number of tens just as we talk about the number of individual units. For example, a collection of thirty-six counters can be thought about as thirty-six individual counters or as three groups of ten counters and six additional counters. To find out how many objects are in a group, a child can count all of the objects by ones or put the objects in groups of ten and count the groups of ten and the leftover objects.

PROBLEM CONTEXTS FOR GROUPING BY TEN

The fundamental context for developing this notion of grouping by ten is found in the Multiplication and Measurement Division situations discussed in Chapter 4. When these types of problems involve situations with ten in a group, children have the opportunity to develop and use principles of the base-ten number system in their strategies. We give specific examples of Multiplication and Measurement Division problems in Figure 6.1.

Both Multiplication and Measurement Division problems provide contexts for introducing base-ten concepts that provide a link with the problems children have solved with

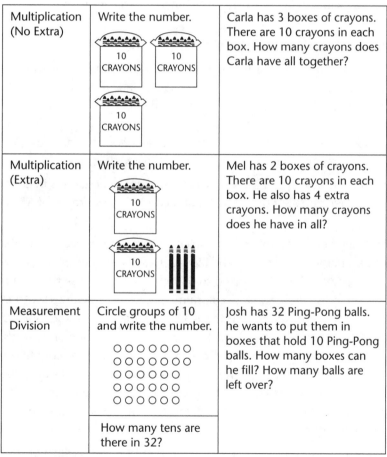

FIGURE 6.1 Multiplication and Division problems that develop base-ten number concepts

smaller numbers. Partitive Division problems, on the other hand, are not particularly good problems to introduce concepts of grouping by ten. For example, imagine how a child might use counters to direct model this Partitive Division problem:

Jae has 40 flowers. If she wants to put these flowers into 10 vases with the same number of flowers in each vase, how many flowers should she put in each vase?

Because the number of flowers in each group is unknown, a direct modeler would be likely to build up the number in each group by dealing the counters into 10 distinct groups. A direct modeler would not see how thinking of groups of 10 could help her solve this problem, because she is thinking in terms of 10 groups. The basic idea of place value involves grouping with ten in each group. The number in the group is given.

Posing Word Problems with Groups of Ten

As noted, Multiplication and Measurement Division word problems provide contexts for fundamental base-ten concepts involving grouping by ten. For example, consider children's responses to the following Multiplication problem:

Our class has 5 boxes of doughnuts. There are 10 doughnuts in each box. We also have 3 extra doughnuts. How many doughnuts do we have altogether?

Robin counts out 5 groups of individual counters with 10 counters in each group. He then adds 3 more counters and counts the entire set of 53 counters by ones.

Anna uses linking cubes to solve the problem. These are separate cubes that can be joined together. In this case, the teacher made sure that the cubes were always stored with 10 cubes linked so that children could use them when solving problems involving two-digit numbers. Anna has worked with the cubes previously and knows that there are 10 cubes in each rod. She puts out 5 ten-rods and then 3 loose cubes. She counts up along one of the rods, "1, 2, 3, 4, 5, 6, 7, 8, 9, 10 [picks up the next rod and continues counting the individual cubes], 11, 12 . . ." She continues counting the individual cubes in each rod. When she is finished counting all the individual cubes in the 5 rods, she continues the count with the loose cubes, "51, 52, 53. There are 53 cubes altogether."

Bob also puts out 5 ten-rods and 3 loose cubes, but he counts each of the ten-rods by 10 rather than by 1: "10, 20, 30, 40, 50, 51, 52, 53."

Tanya gives a response that is similar to Bob's, but she does not use any materials: "Let's see. That's 10, 20, 30, 40, 50 [putting up a finger with each count], 51, 52, 53 [again keeping track of the ones on her fingers]. We have 53."

Julio immediately answers, "53. Well, there's 5 boxes of 10 doughnuts. 5 tens is 50, and the 3 more doughnuts make 53."

Robin and Anna both counted by ones. Anna knew that there were 10 cubes in each rod, but she did not use this information to find the total number of cubes. Bob, on the other hand, was able to count the groups of 10. His response was similar to Tanya's except that Tanya did not have to actually construct the sets. Julio's response was different from the other children's in that he knew 5 groups of 10 was 50, without having to figure it out.

Measurement Division problems involving groups of ten provide another context for engaging in discussion of base-ten number concepts. Here are the same five children's responses to the following Measurement Division problem:

CLIP 6.1 Counting by Ones strategy to solve a base-ten Multiplication problem http://smarturl.it/CM6.1

CLIP 6.2 Counting by Tens strategy for a base-ten Multiplication problem http://smarturl.it/CM6.2

CLIP 6.3 Counting by Tens strategy for a base-ten Multiplication problem http://smarturl.it/CM6.3

CLIP 6.4 Counting by Tens strategy for base-ten Measurement Division http://smarturl.it/CM6.4

CLIP 6.5 Direct Place Value strategy for base-ten Measurement Division http://smarturl.it/CM6.5

Jim had 54 crayons. He put them into boxes with 10 crayons in each box. How many boxes did Jim fill?

Robin and Anna count out 54 counters. They make groups with 10 counters in each group and count the number of groups, "5."

Bob puts out 5 ten-rods to represent the 50 crayons and 4 counters to represent the 4 extra crayons. He looks at the collection for a moment, and then counts the ten-rods, "5."

Tanya counts by 10, "10, 20, 30, 40, 50." With each count, she extends a finger. When she reaches 50, she sees that she has raised 5 fingers and responds, "5."

Julio immediately responds, "5, because there are 5 tens in 54."

These responses demonstrate the same progression of understanding of base-ten numbers as the responses to the multiplication problems described above.

CLIP 6.6 Direct Place Value strategy for a base-ten Multiplication problem with follow-up questions http://smarturl.it/CM6.6

Problems in which there are more than 10 extra individual units require an additional measure of flexibility in thinking about multidigit numbers. Consider the following example:

> *The other first-grade class has 4 boxes of donuts with 10 donuts in each box, and they also have 17 individual donuts. How many donuts do they have altogether?*
>
> Bob puts out 4 ten-rods and 17 cubes. He counts the ten-rods and cubes, "10, 20, 30, 40, 41, 42, 43, . . . 55, 56, 57."
>
> Misha goes through the same counting sequence as Bob, but she does not use any counters. As she counts from 10 to 40 by 10, she puts up 4 fingers. When she reaches 40, she puts down her fingers so that she can use them to keep track as she counts on 17 from 40. As she counts from 40 to 50, she puts up a finger with each count. At 50, she puts them down again so that she can use them to keep track as she counts on 7 more from 50.
>
> Julio says, "Well, that's 40, and then 10 more is 50, then 7 is 57."

Bob and Misha did not recognize that 17 could be thought of as 10 and 7, or that the 10 could be combined with the other 4 tens. Julio understood that different groupings of 10 are possible. Fifty-seven can be thought of as 5 tens and 7 ones, as 4 tens and 17 ones, or even as 2 tens and 37 ones. This understanding represents an important milestone in the development of base-ten number concepts.

Measurement Division and Multiplication problems with ten in a group are fundamental for developing children's understanding of the base-ten number system. A child's strategies for solving these problems give the teacher a window into how the child understands base ten. We give a summary of children's strategies for problems that elicit basic concepts of grouping by ten in Figure 6.2. Note that these strategies are categorized based on what they indicate about a child's understanding of ten as a group that can be counted. This categorization differs from the one introduced for children's strategies for solving single-digit addition, subtraction, multiplication, and division problems because the focus is on a different aspect of children's thinking.

Grouping by Tens Strategies

Problem	Strategies		
	Counting by Ones	*Counting by Tens*	*Direct Place Value*
Multiplication *John has 6 pages of stickers. There are 10 stickers on each page. He also has 4 more stickers. How many stickers does he have in all?*	Makes 6 groups of counters with 10 counters in each group. Adds 4 additional counters and counts the set by ones.	Counts, "10, 20, 30, 40, 50, 60, 61, 62, 63, 64," keeping track on fingers.	Says, "64. 6 tens is 60 and 4 more is 64."
Measurement Division *Mary has 64 stickers. She pastes them in her sticker book so that there are 10 stickers on each page. How many pages can she fill?*	Counts out 64 counters and puts them into groups with 10 in each group. Counts the number of groups.	Counts, "10, 20, 30, 40, 50, 60," putting up a finger with each count. Counts fingers to get answer of 6.	Says, "6. There are 6 tens in 60."

FIGURE 6.2

Collections of More Than One Hundred Objects

When the total number of objects in a problem is more than one hundred, children may engage in more sophisticated reasoning. Consider the following Measurement Division problem with 10 in each group.

The high school band is going to sell donuts before the football game. If they want to sell 370 donuts and donuts come in boxes of 10, how many boxes of donuts should they get?

Emma constructs a set of 370 out of 3 hundreds flats and 7 tens sticks. She says, "10 donuts come in a box," and, pointing to the tens sticks, counts the boxes of donuts, "1, 2, 3, 4, 5, 6, 7." She continues counting boxes of donuts by

CLIP 6.7 Counting by Tens strategy for base-ten Measurement Division of more than 100 objects
http://smarturl.it/CM6.7

CLIP 6.8 Direct Place Value strategy for base-ten Measurement Division of more than 100 objects, in Spanish
http://smarturl.it/CM6.8

pointing to each row of 10 in one of the hundreds flats, "8, 9, 10, 11, 12, 13, 14, 15, 16, 17." In this way, she continues to count each row of 10 in the other 2 hundreds flats, ending with 37.

Eric solved the problem using the representation shown in Figure 6.3.

Nick simply says, "There are 10 tens in 100 so there would be 30 tens in 300. 70 has 7 tens so 37 boxes."

CLIP 6.9 Using a Direct Place Value strategy to solve base-ten Measurement Division of more than 100 objects http://smarturl.it/CM6.9

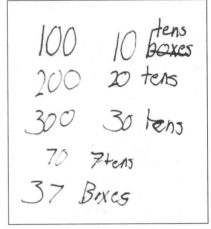

FIGURE 6.3 Eric's representation of his solution

These strategies are similar to the strategies children use when the total number of items is less than one hundred. Emma used a Counting by Tens strategy; she constructed a set of 370 and counted the number of tens in that set. Eric and Nick both used Direct Place Value understandings; Nick went directly from 10 tens in 100 to 30 tens in 300, whereas Eric figured the tens in each group of 100 separately.

Posing Word Problems with Groups of Hundreds, Thousands, and So On

Once children understand that collections of ten can be counted, they can start working with problems with collections of hundreds, thousands, and so on to further develop their understanding of base-ten number concepts. Here are some examples of such problems.

Owen's baking factory puts 100 donuts in each of their donut crates. If the university wants to sell 6,300 donuts at the football game, how many crates of donuts should they order from the baking factory?

If 734 people each donated $1,000 to the food pantry, how much money would the food pantry receive?

There are about 3,700,000 people in Wisconsin who want to receive the flu vaccine. If the lab that produces the vaccine for Wisconsin can produce 10,000 doses in 1 hour, how many hours would it take to produce enough flu vaccine for the people of Wisconsin?

It might be tempting to teach students procedures such as "add zeros to the end of the number," "take zeros off the end of the number," or "move the decimal point" to solve problems like these. Although it can seem efficient in the short run, these procedures do not help children develop an understanding of our base-ten number system. Children live in a world where they need to understand both very large and very small numbers. The strategies that children naturally develop to reason about Multiplication and Measurement Division problems with groups of ten, one hundred, one thousand, and so on help them develop this understanding.

NUMBER WORDS AND PLACE VALUE

In this chapter, we have focused on the principle that collections of tens (and hundreds, thousands, and so on) can be counted. This allows us to have a systematic and efficient method for naming numbers. Once we have more than ten objects to count, we group by tens and count the tens and the leftover ones. When we get 10 tens, we group into hundreds and count the hundreds. The process continues with thousands, ten thousands, hundred thousands, millions, and so on. To represent these numbers, we need some way of designating the groups of ten, one hundred, and so on that we are counting.

There is a major difference in how we designate these groups when we use spoken number words and when we use written numerals. With written numerals, we use a *place value* system to designate the groups of ten, hundred, and so forth. With only ten different digit symbols (0, 1, 2, 3, 4, 5, 6, 7, 8, 9), we can represent infinitely many numbers because the value of a digit in a numeral is determined by its position. Thus, 342 means 3 hundreds, 4 tens, and 2 ones. The numerals 342 and 234 represent different numbers, because the 2, 3, and 4 are in different places. We use zeros to maintain the place value when there are no ones, tens, hundreds, and so forth. Thus, 302 is represents 3 hundreds and 2 ones, and 302 represents a different number than 32 or 320.

Spoken number words are quite different. Although there is a conventional order to the way we say the number names (we start with the largest grouping: hundreds before tens, before ones), we literally name the groupings. The corresponding number word for 342 is not "three four two" as the numeral is written. Instead, we say "three hundred forty-two," specifically designating each of the groups of hundreds, tens, and ones. When there are no tens, we do not have to say zero tens to maintain the place as we do with written numerals. Because we name the groups, we can just say "three hundred two."

As adults, we have used number words and place value for so long that we no longer pause to think about the fact that there is a difference between spoken number words and written numerals or that the same symbol can have many different values depending on where it is placed in a numeral. We immediately see the 3 in 13 as 3 ones and the 3 in

347 as 3 hundreds and have an understanding of the relative size of these two quantities. This understanding takes time to develop. Young children need a variety of opportunities to reason about groupings of tens, hundreds, thousands, and so on in order to understand our number system. In fact, children continue to master these concepts as they devise strategies for adding, subtracting, multiplying, and dividing larger numbers.

QUESTIONS FOR FURTHER REFLECTION

1. Solve each of these problems as a child might solve it and identify the problem type:

   a. *Ramona has 9 bags of cookies with 10 cookies in each bag. How many cookies does Ramona have?*

   b. *10 friends are going to a play. Their tickets altogether cost $90. How much did each ticket cost?*

   c. *I am making word study books and I need 10 pieces of paper to make each book. If I have 97 pieces of paper, how many word study books could I make?*

   d. *Mr. Thomas made 97 word study books. If each word study book took 10 sheets of paper, how many pieces of paper did Mr. Thomas use?*

2. Which of the problems above are most likely to help students develop an understanding of base-ten number concepts? Why?

3. Here are some base-ten problems typically found in textbooks. For each problem, write a Multiplication or Measurement Division problem that would address the same concept. The first one is done for you.

Typical Problem	Multiplication or Measurement Division Problem
How much is 8 tens?	*I have 8 bags of potatoes with 10 potatoes in each bag. How many potatoes do I have?*
How many tens are in 52?	
How much is 97 tens?	

4. Write three Multiplication or Measurement Division problems that would help your students think about base-ten number concepts. You could choose the problems in question 3 if you wish. For each problem:

  a. Describe the strategies that students in general would use to solve each problem.
  b. Describe the strategies that your students might use to solve each problem.
  c. Choose one of these problems and pose it to your students.
  d. Did your students solve the problem the ways you anticipated that they would?
  e. Do you want to alter the other two problems after seeing how your students solved this problem? Perhaps you want to change the numbers or try a different problem type.

5. Figure 6.4 shows what a second-grader wrote on his paper to show how he solved this problem:

I have 85 toy cars. If I can put 10 toy cars in a storage box, how many boxes will I need?

What question would you ask Roger about his strategy?

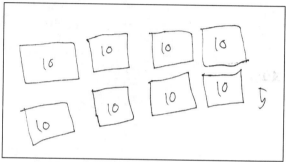

FIGURE 6.4 Roger's strategy

6. Figures 6.5 through 6.9 show some examples of how students solve this problem:

I have 74 crayons and 10 crayons fit in each box. How many boxes can I fill with my crayons?

Identify each strategy as Counting by Ones, Counting by Tens, or Direct Place Value.

For each strategy, write a question that would help the student explain the strategy. These questions can be either to help you understand the student's strategy, help her reflect on her strategy, or help her explain her strategy to other students.

FIGURE 6.5 Emily's strategy

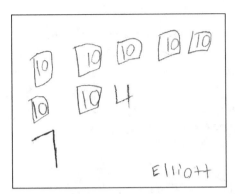

FIGURE 6.6 Elliott's strategy

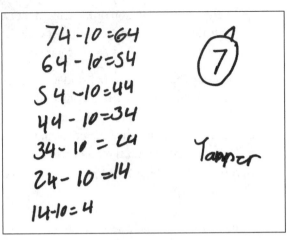

FIGURE 6.7 Tanner's strategy

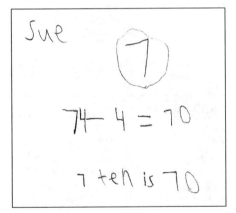

FIGURE 6.8 Sue's strategy

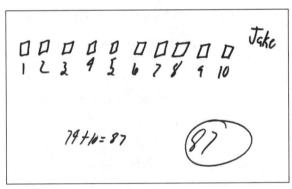

FIGURE 6.9 Jake's strategy

7. If your students were to produce the work shown in question 6, which students would you choose to explain their strategies to the class? In what order would you have them share their strategies? Why? What would be an alternative three to share? Why?

8. How would your students solve the following problems?

   a. *What is 10 more than 58?*
   b. *What is 10 less than 84?*
   c. *What is 20 more than 45?*
   d. *40 + 30 =* ☐

9. Watch Emma solve the following problem.

Ms. Green has 85 markers. If 10 markers fit in a box, how many boxes can Ms. Green fill?

Identify the strategy she used.

Once you have watched Emma solve the markers problem, predict how she would solve this problem.

There are 52 jelly beans in a bag. 10 children want to share them so that they each get the same amount. How many jelly beans would each child get?

CLIP 6.10 Watch Emma solve a base-ten Measurement Division problem
http://smarturl.it/CM6.10

CLIP 6.11 Now watch Emma solve a Partitive Division problem with similar numbers
http://smarturl.it/CM6.11

a. Identify the strategy she used for each problem.

b. How is her strategy for the jelly beans problem different from the strategy she used for the markers problem? What do you think accounts for this difference?

10. Watch Evan solve the following problem.

Mr. Cisco wants to figure out how many tortillas he has. There are 10 tortillas in a package. Mr. Cisco has 14 packages of tortillas and 5 extra tortillas. How many tortillas does he have?

CLIP 6.12 Evan solves a base-ten Multiplication with extras problem for the first time
http://smarturl.it/CM6.12

a. At first, Evan says he has never solved a problem like this one and does not know what to do. How does the teacher respond to his confusion?

b. What do you learn about Evan's understanding of base-ten number concepts?

7

Children's Strategies for Solving Multidigit Problems

In the past I thought children didn't understand subtraction with regrouping, when what they didn't understand was how to use the process that I was insisting that they use, rather than really understanding the concept of subtraction that might encompass regrouping.

—**Kerri Burkey, teacher**

It has been assumed children must develop base-ten number concepts before they can add, subtract, multiply, and divide multidigit numbers. That assumption has not proven valid. As long as children can count, they can solve problems involving multidigit numbers even when they have limited notions of grouping by ten. Problems with two- and three-digit numbers actually provide a context for children to develop an understanding of base-ten number concepts. As children solve and discuss these problems, their understanding of base-ten number concepts increases concurrently with an understanding of how to apply this knowledge to solve problems.

ADDITION AND SUBTRACTION

There are direct parallels between the strategies children use for problems with multi-digit numbers and the strategies they use for problems with smaller numbers. Children initially directly model the quantities and action or situation in problems, and proceed to inventing strategies that essentially are abstractions of these Direct Modeling strategies. Children develop and use increasingly sophisticated understanding of base-ten number concepts as their strategies become more abstract.

Direct Modeling and Counting with Ones

Before looking at strategies that use base-ten number concepts, consider the following example, which illustrates how children solve problems involving two-digit numbers without using base-ten number concepts.

> *Molly has 34 dollars. How many dollars does she have to earn to have 47 dollars?*
>
> Chris counts out a set of 34 counters. He continues counting out counters, "35, 36, 37, . . . ," until he has put out a total of 47 counters. He keeps the counters put out after the first 34 in a separate pile, which he now counts, "1, 2, 3, . . . 13. She needs 13 more."
>
> Fateen counts on from 34 to 47, "34 [pause], 35, 36, . . . 46, 47." With each count after 34, he extends a finger. When he has used up 10 fingers, he puts them all down and starts extending them again.
>
> **Fateen:** Thirteen dollars.
> *Ms. J: Can you tell me how you did that?*
> **Fateen:** I counted 34, 35, 36 . . .
> *Ms. J: Okay. But how did you know that it was 13?*
> **Fateen:** I kept track on my fingers.
> *Ms. J: But you don't have 13 fingers.*
> **Fateen:** No, but see after I put up 10, I started over again, there were 3 more: 11, 12, 13.

Chris' Direct Modeling with Ones solution was identical to a strategy that he might have used with small numbers. All that was required was the ability to count up to 47 objects.

Fateen's Counting On by Ones strategy was identical to a strategy he might use with smaller numbers. Because Fateen ran out of fingers to keep track with, his solution

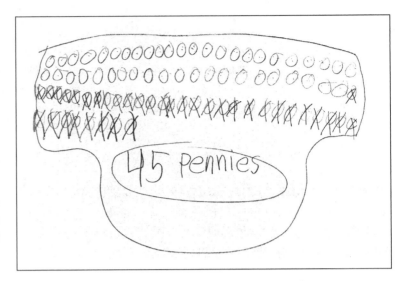

FIGURE 7.1 Representation of a Direct Modeling with Ones strategy for Separate (Result Unknown) problem

required a little more sophistication than Chris', but it made only limited use of base-ten number concepts.

Figure 7.1 shows an example of a child's representation of a Direct Modeling with Ones strategy for the following Separate (Result Unknown) problem:

Xaria had 82 pennies. She lost 37 of them. How many pennies does Xaria have now?

CLIP 7.1 Direct Modeling with Tens strategy for a Join (Result Unknown) problem http://smarturl.it/CM7.1

Direct Modeling with Tens

The following solutions illustrate how children use knowledge of base-ten numbers together with the Direct Modeling strategies they use for addition and subtraction problems. For these problems, the children had either a collection of base-ten blocks or linking cubes. The base-ten blocks consist of one-centimeter cubes and rods that are ten-centimeters long, with each centimeter marked off.

There were 28 girls and 35 boys on the playground at recess. How many children were there on the playground at recess?

Ralph uses the base-ten blocks. He puts out 2 ten-rods and 8 blocks. In another pile, he puts 3 ten-rods and 5 blocks. He pushes the bars and blocks together and counts all the individual blocks by one, "1, 2, 3, 4, 5, 6, 7, 8, 9, 10, 11, . . . 59, 60, 61, 62, 63."

Misha uses linking cubes with the cubes connected in groups of ten as shown in Figure 7.2. She puts out 2 ten-rods and 8 single cubes and 3 ten-rods and 5 cubes. To find the answer to the problem, she first counts the ten-rods, saying, "10, 20, 30, 40, 50." She then counts the rest of the cubes "51, 52, 53, 54, 55, 56, 57, 58, 59, 60, 61, 62, 63. There were 63 children."

FIGURE 7.2 Misha's solution to a Part-Part-Whole (Whole Unknown) problem using a Direct Modeling with Tens strategy

Ralph was just beginning to develop an understanding of base-ten concepts, and his knowledge appeared to be tenuous. He could construct sets using groups of ten, but when it came to finding how many there were altogether, he reverted to counting by ones. Misha, on the other hand, used groupings of ten both to construct the sets and to find the total.

Children also use Direct Modeling with Tens strategies to solve Separate (Result Unknown) problems.

There were 51 geese in the farmer's field. 28 of the geese flew away. How many geese were left in the field?

Misha uses the linking cubes again. She puts out 5 ten-rods and one extra cube. She takes away 2 ten-rods. Then she breaks 8 cubes off one of the ten-rods. She puts the remaining 2 cubes with the extra cube. She looks at the pile of ten-rods and cubes that are left and says, "23."

CLIP 7.2 Direct Modeling with Tens strategy for a Separate (Result Unknown) problem, with no trading http://smarturl.it/CM7.2

CLIP 7.3 Direct Modeling with Tens strategy for a Separate (Result Unknown) problem, with trading http://smarturl.it/CM7.3

Misha's solution was a relatively straightforward extension of the Separating From strategy used with smaller numbers, but because she used blocks in which the tens could be taken apart, her solution did not demonstrate knowledge of trading tens for ones. If she had used base-ten blocks, she would have had to find some way to deal with the fact that base-ten blocks cannot be physically broken apart as she did with the linking cubes. Consider the following examples of two students solving the same problem using base blocks:

Ralph makes a set of 5 ten-bars and 1 cube. He takes away 2 ten-bars, and looks at the remaining blocks for a long time.

Mr. B: *What's the matter?*
Ralph: I can't take away the 8.
Mr. B: *Is there anything you could do so that you could take away 8?*
Ralph: I can't think of anything . . . [Eventually he pushes the base-ten blocks back and uses single counters to solve the problem.]

Nora also uses base-ten blocks, but she successfully does the trading. She puts out 5 ten-bars and 1 extra cube. First she takes away 2 ten-bars. Then she takes away 1 ten-bar and replaces it with 10 cubes from the original pile. Now there are 11 cubes in the pile. She removes 8 of them. She counts the 2 ten-bars remaining and the 3 cubes and says, "23."

Although students may encounter earlier success with tens that can be broken apart, the use of base-ten blocks that cannot be taken apart may encourage children to trade a ten-bar for 10 ones, which corresponds more directly to what we do when we regroup (borrow from the ten). The use of base-ten blocks does not, however, force children to trade tens for ones. It is not necessary for children to physically trade a ten-bar for 10 ones to understand that 1 ten is the same as 10 ones and use that knowledge in solving the problem. Some children simply cover up some of the units on a ten-bar with one of their fingers or do the regrouping in their heads. What is important is not that students physically trade a ten-bar for 10 ones; it is that they understand the principle that 1 ten is equal to 10 ones and can use that principle in adding and subtracting. This is an important point. It is not children's manipulation of materials that is critical; it is their understanding of the principles involved in the manipulations.

Children can also use written representations to Direct Model with Tens as shown by Sally's solution in Figure 7.3 to the problem: *Xaria had 82 pennies. She lost 37 of them. How many pennies does Xaria have now?*

The knowledge explicitly demonstrated by Nora and Sally represents a substantial step in learning base-ten number concepts. Many children can construct and count sets using

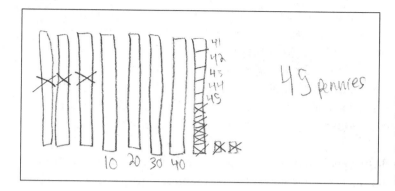

FIGURE 7.3 Sally's written representation of a Direct Modeling with Tens strategy for a Separate (Result Unknown) problem

knowledge of groupings of ten before they understand that within a particular representation of a number the tens can be broken apart. As a consequence, Join (Result Unknown) problems with regrouping may be somewhat easier for some children than Separate (Result Unknown) problems with regrouping.

Join (Change Unknown) problems can present additional difficulties when multidigit numbers are involved. The examples that follow illustrate one successful attempt and one unsuccessful attempt to model the action in a Join (Change Unknown) problem.

CLIP 7.4 Solving a Separate (Result Unknown) problem with an emergent understanding of ten as a unit http://smarturl.it/CM7.4

Elena has 37 dollars. How many more dollars does she have to earn to have 53 dollars?

Steve puts out 3 ten-rods and 7 cubes. He then puts a ten-rod in a separate pile and says, "That's 47." Then he puts loose cubes with the ten-rod, counting, "48, 49, 50, 51, 52, 53." Then he counts the loose cubes and says, "That's 6 and 10 more—that's 16."

James had 39 stickers. He got some more stickers for his birthday. Then he had 61 stickers. How many stickers did James get for his birthday?

Destiny puts out 3 ten-rods made of linking cubes. She takes another rod and breaks 1 cube off it and puts the nine-rod with the 3 ten-rods. She hesitates a moment and then puts 2 more ten-rods with the others, keeping them a little apart. Then she gets another cube and after a moment puts it on the nine-rod to make it a ten-rod. Then she adds another cube to the collection. Now she has 61 cubes altogether (6 ten-rods and 1 loose cube); but because she connected the loose cube to make a complete ten-rod, she cannot tell which cubes were in the original set of 39 and which cubes she added on to get to 61. She stares at the collection for a long time and is clearly confused. Ultimately, she says she does not know how to solve this problem.

Destiny had two conflicting goals in solving this problem. She wanted to join cubes together to make tens, and she needed to keep the cubes representing the stickers James got for his birthday separate from the original set of 39 cubes. This difficulty does not come up with Join (Result Unknown) or Separate (Result Unknown) problems or when children use Direct Modeling with Ones for Join (Change Unknown) problems.

The previous problems all involve two-digit numbers, but children's ability to use materials to solve problems is not limited to two-digit numbers. The following solution (Figure 7.4) illustrates how one first-grader solved the this problem:

FIGURE 7.4 Modeling a Separate (Result Unknown) problem with hundreds, tens, and ones

The elephant had 407 peanuts. She ate 129 of them. How many peanuts did the elephant have left?

Matteo draws 4 large squares representing the hundreds and next to them 7 small squares representing the ones. Then he crosses out 1 large square saying, "Okay, that's the hundred. Now I need to take away 20." He crosses out another big square and draws 10 small rectangles above the squares. Then he crosses out 2 of the rectangles and says, "Okay, now the 9." He crosses out the 7 small squares. He hesitates a moment, then crosses out another rectangle and draws 10 small squares to the left of the big squares. He crosses out 2 of those squares. Then he counts the rectangles and the small squares and says, "278."

For this problem, Matteo needed to represent ones, tens, and hundreds. He first drew large squares to represent hundreds and smaller squares to represent ones. When he traded one hundred for 10 tens, he used rectangles to represent tens. These figures and the way Matteo used them to solve the problem are essentially a paper and pencil representation of a solution using base-ten blocks in both form and structure.

INVENTED ALGORITHMS

When children solve addition and subtraction problems by Direct Modeling with Tens, they increase their understanding of base-ten number concepts along with their understanding of addition and subtraction. These understandings provide a foundation for children either individually or collectively to invent their own algorithms for addition and subtraction that are essentially abstractions of their Direct Modeling with Tens strategies. The Invented Algorithms share common elements with the Derived Fact solutions that children use with smaller numbers. In both cases, children demonstrate flexibility in thinking about numbers, as numbers are broken apart and put together in different ways.

We categorize three types of Invented Algorithms based on the how they build on and develop different understandings of how addition and subtraction work. Incrementing Invented Algorithms involve successively incrementing or decreasing partial sums or differences. In Combining the Same Units Invented Algorithms, the tens and ones are operated on separately, and the results subsequently combined. Combining the Same Units uses many of the same principles as the standard addition and subtraction algorithms. Compensating Invented Algorithms involve adjusting the numbers before calculating the answer. We distinguish between the different types of Invented Algorithms because each type of Invented Algorithm engages children in a different way of thinking about addition or subtraction.

Invented Algorithms for Addition Problems

The following examples illustrate the Incrementing Invented Algorithms that children use for Join (Result Unknown) and Part-Part-Whole (Whole Unknown) situations and for solving equations like $27 + 35 = n$.

There were 27 boys and 35 girls on the playground at recess. How many children were on the playground at recess?

Todd: Let's see. 20 and 30, that's 50, and 7 more is 57. Then the 5. 57 and 3 is 60, and the 2 more from the 5 is 62. There were 62.

Janika: 20 [pause], 30, 40, 50 [pause], 57, 58, 59, 60, 61, 62. There were 62.

Chico: 27 and 30 is 57 and then 5 more is 62.

CLIP 7.5 An Incrementing Invented Algorithm for addition http://smarturl.it/CM7.5

Todd, Janika, and Chico used an Incrementing Invented Algorithm in which they successively added on to the partial sum. Each of them used a different method of finding the partial sums. Both Todd and Janika started with 20. Chico, on the other hand, started with 27 and first added 30 and then 5.

Contrast these solutions with the following solutions based on a Combining the Same Units strategy:

There were 58 geese and 37 ducks in the marsh. How many birds were in the marsh?

Linda: 50 and 30, that's 80. Then 8 and 7, that's, ahh, 9, 10, 11, 12, 13, 14, 15. So it's 80 and 15 more. That's 90, 95. There were 95.

Carlos: 5 and 3 is 8, that's 80. Then the 8 and the 7 . . . um, 7 and 7 is 14, so 8 and 7 is 15. Okay, so now 15 and 80 is 95.

CLIP 7.6 Combining the Same Units Invented Algorithm for addition http://smarturl.it/CM7.6

CLIP 7.7 Combining the Same Units Invented Algorithm for addition, with an error that is addressed http://smarturl.it/CM7.7

CLIP 7.8 Combining the Same Units Invented Algorithm for addition, supported by student written notation http://smarturl.it/CM7.8

Notice that both children combined the tens and ones separately. They started with the tens and subsequently adjusted their answers to include the 10 from the ones' place. As shown in these examples, almost all children using Invented Algorithms start with the highest place value. Both children also thought about the numbers in the tens' place as multiples of 10 (50 and 30, not 5 and 3 as is done in the standard paper-and-pencil algorithm). Carlos added 5 and 3, but he immediately recognized that he had 80 rather than just 8.

Some children use a combination of Incrementing and Combining the Same Units, when they are combining two numbers greater than 100. Below is an example of how one child constructed a solution to a problem involving three digits:

There were 246 stalks of corn in a row. The farmer planted 178 more stalks of corn in the row. How many stalks of corn were there in the row then?

Elena: Well, 200 plus 100 is 300. And then you have to add the tens on. 40 plus 70 . . . well, um, if you started at 70, 80, 90, 100. And that's 400 because of the 300 I already have . . . But you've still got 1 more 10. Add 6 more onto 10, which is 16. And then 8 more—17, 18, 19, 20, 21, 22, 23, 24. So that's 424.

Elena used Combining the Same Units for working with the hundreds and the tens, but then used Incrementing to combine the remaining ones.

Invented Algorithms for Subtraction Problems

Using Invented Algorithms for Separate (Result Unknown) problems is generally more difficult than using Invented Algorithms for addition problems. As a consequence, many children use Invented Algorithms for addition problems before they use Invented Algorithms for subtraction problems. But children do invent algorithms for subtraction problems as illustrated by the following examples.

Gary had 73 dollars. He spent 55 dollars on a pet snake. How many dollars did Gary have left?

Janika: Mmm, 73 take away 50. That's 23. Now the 5. Take away 3. That's 20, and take away the other 2—that's 18. He had 18.

Todd: 70 take away 50 is 20, and 5 from the 20, that's 15. Then I have the 3 more from the 73, so that's 18.

CLIP 7.9 Incrementing Invented Algorithm for subtraction with student notation
http://smarturl.it/CM7.9

Both Janika and Todd used an Incrementing Invented Algorithm, similar to the Incrementing Invented Algorithm they used for the addition problems described on pages 103–4. A comparison of Todd's solutions to these problems illustrates why Separate (Result Unknown)

CLIP 7.10 Incrementing Invented Algorithm for subtraction with teacher notation of child's thinking
http://smarturl.it/CM7.10

problems are more difficult. For his solution to the Part-Part-Whole (Whole Unknown) problem, everything was added. For the Separate (Result Unknown) problem, the 3 from the 73 had to be added to the 20 and the 5 taken away. Because this makes more to keep track of when using an Incrementing Invented Algorithm for a Separate (Result Unknown) problem, children can get mixed up (e.g., take away the 3 also).

Children also use the Combining the Same Units Invented Algorithm for subtraction as is shown in the following example.

> *Gary had 73 dollars. He spent 57 dollars on a pet snake. How many dollars did Gary have left?*

Linda: 70 take away the 50, that's 20. Then 3 take away 7 is minus 4. So I need to take 4 from the 20. So that's 16.

CLIP 7.11 Combining the Same Units Invented Algorithm for subtraction http://smarturl.it/CM7.11

Linda subtracted the tens and then the ones. She recognized that she had to take 7 from 3, rather than 3 from 7, and that meant she had to take 4 more away. Children who understand subtraction do not make the common error of simply switching the order of the number when they find need to take a bigger number from a smaller number. Many children start to reason about negative numbers when they start Combining the Same Units for subtraction with regrouping or hear their classmates share these strategies.

Children who understand the relationships between addition and subtraction and are flexible in choosing strategies for different problems often recognize that they do not have to use a separating strategy for this problem. It can also be solved using an additive strategy that is usually used for Join (Change Unknown) problems. The following is another solution to the above problem:

Andy: Well, 57 and 10 more is 67, and 3 more than that is 70, and 3 more is 73. So I had 10 and 3 and 3, that's 16.

Invented Algorithms for Join (Change Unknown) Problems

Children most readily invent strategies for solving Join (Change Unknown) problems using some version of an Incrementing Invented Algorithm. Here are several variations of Incrementing Invented Algorithms for a Join (Change Unknown) problem:

Yoshi has 37 dollars. How many more dollars does she have to earn to have 61 dollars to adopt a dog?

Ricardo: Mmm, 37 [pause], 47, 57, 67. No, that's too much. 37 [pause], 47, 57. That's 20. Now, ahh, 58, 59, 60, 61 [extends a finger with each count from 58 to 61]. 24. She has to earn 24 dollars.

Megan: 37 plus 3 is 40, plus 20 is 60, then just one more is 61. I added 3, 20 and 1, that's 24; 24 dollars.

CLIP 7.12 Incrementing Invented Algorithm for Join (Change Unknown)
http://smarturl.it/CM7.12

CLIP 7.13 Incrementing Invented Algorithm for Join (Change Unknown), with a follow-up question
http://smarturl.it/CM7.13

Ricardo and Megan used slightly different ways to increment. Ricardo counted on by tens first and then counted on by ones to get the answer. Megan counted on by ones to get to a decade, counted by tens from the decade, and finished counting by ones.

Compensating Invented Algorithms

Children also invent algorithms for certain problems based on special characteristics of the number combinations in the problems. One number might be adjusted up or down to the nearest ten or hundred with corresponding adjustments made in the other number.

The lion cub weighs 98 pounds. How much will she weigh when she gains 56 more pounds?

Todd: 98 and 56. If I make 98 into 100, I need to take 2 from the 56. So this is like 100 plus 54. So it's 154.

These strategies, which are called *Compensating Invented Algorithms* because one number is adjusted to compensate for changes in the other number, are very similar to some Derived Fact strategies that children use for adding and subtracting small numbers. In both cases, the numbers are adjusted to make the calculation easier. Although all number combinations can lend themselves to Incremental or Combining the Same Units Invented Algorithms, Compensating Invented Algorithms are only useful for particular number combinations.

CLIP 7.14 Compensating Invented Algorithm for addition
http://smarturl.it/CM7.14

Examples of the three major types of Invented Algorithms for multidigit Addition and Subtraction are presented in Figure 7.5. When working with numbers over 100, children often use a combination of these Invented Algorithms. It is valuable for children to have opportunities to engage with the different types of Invented Algorithms because each type of strategy draws on different principles of addition and subtraction, and offers different advantages depending on the numbers involved in the calculation. Hearing other children's strategies can support children to be flexible and choose the strategy that is best for the numbers in a given problem.

Invented Algorithms

Problem	Incrementing	Combining the Same Units	Compensating
Join (Result Unknown) *Paul had 28 strawberries in his basket. He picked 35 more strawberries. How many strawberries did he have then?*	"20 and 30 is 50, and 8 more is 58. 2 more is 60, and 3 more than that is 63."	"20 and 30 is 50. 8 plus 5 is like 8 plus 2 and 3 more, so it's 13. 50 and 13 is 63."	"If I change 28 to 30, I have to take 2 from 35. 30 plus 33 is 63."
Separate (Result Unknown) *Paul had 83 strawberries in his basket. He gave 38 strawberries to his friend. How many strawberries did Paul have left?*	"83 take away 30 is 53, and take way 3 is 50. Then take away 5 more. That's 45."	"80 take away 30 is 50. 3 take away 8 makes 5 more to take away. 50 take away 5 is 45."	"83 take away 38 is the same as 85 take away 40. That's 45."
Join (Change Unknown) *Paul has 47 strawberries in his basket. How many more strawberries does he have to pick to have 75 altogether?*	"47 and 3 is 50 and 20 more is 70. So that's 23, but I need 5 more, so it's 28." "47 [pause], 57, 67. That's 20. 67 and 3 is 70, and 5 more is 75. So 8 and the 20, 28."	*Combining the Same Units is not commonly used for Join (Change Unknown).*	"If it were 45, it would be 30. But it's 47, so it's 2 less. 28."

FIGURE 7.5

Written Representations of Invented Algorithms

Figures 7.6 and 7.7 provide examples of two students' written representations of Invented Algorithms for a Separate (Result Unknown) Problem:

> *Xaria had 82 pennies. She lost 37 of them. How many pennies does Xaria have now?*

Note that this is the same problem for which Direct Modeling with Ones and Direct Modeling with Tens written representations strategies are provided in Figures 7.1 and 7.3. All four of these examples of student work come from the same class.

Figures 7.8 and 7.9 show two students' written representations for Invented Algorithms used to solve this Separate (Result Unknown) problem with three-digit numbers:

> *Enoch has 407 Lego pieces. He used 129 pieces to build a model spaceship. How many Lego pieces does Enoch have left?*

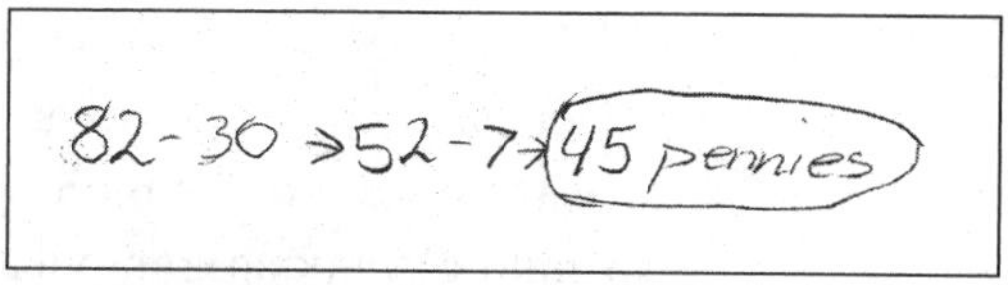

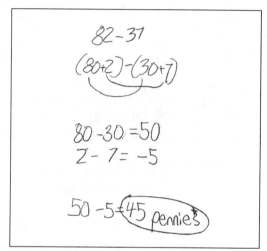

FIGURE 7.6 Student's written representation for an Incrementing Invented Algorithm for a Separate (Result Unknown) problem

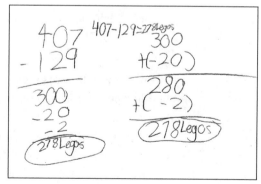

FIGURE 7.7 Student's written representation of a Combining the Same Units Invented Algorithms for a Separate (Result Unknown) problem

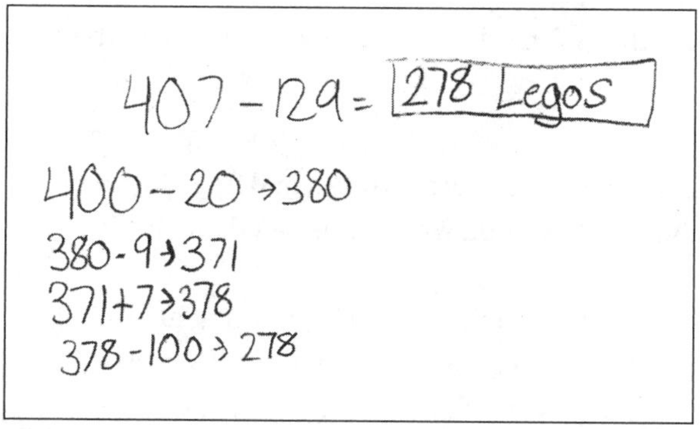

FIGURE 7.8 Student's written representation of an Incrementing Invented Algorithms for a Separate (Result Unknown) problem

FIGURE 7.9 Student's written representation of a Combining the Same Units Invented Algorithms for a Separate (Result Unknown) problem

Benefits of Inventing Algorithms

When children either individually or collectively invent their own algorithms, they usually avoid some of the more serious misconceptions that children exhibit when they try to imitate symbolic manipulations that someone else shows them. This is not to say that children's Invented Algorithms are always correct, but when children invent algorithms for themselves, they have a basis for understanding and correcting their errors.

The standard algorithms have evolved over centuries to be efficient methods for calculation. But the efficiency comes at a cost. Although base-ten number concepts and properties of operations drive all standard algorithms, their role in standard algorithms is not transparent. Most nine-year-olds do not understand number and operations sufficiently to understand why standard algorithms work. Children's Invented Algorithms are based directly on their understanding of operations and base-ten concepts. They are not isolated procedures. Because children develop these algorithms based on what they understand, the concepts and properties are explicit in the algorithm. Children talk about combining 50 and 30 or 5 tens and 3 tens, rather than adding numbers in the same column. They talk about still having more to add or being able to add numbers in any order. Although Invented Algorithms may initially be less efficient than the standard algorithms, this loss in efficiency is more than made up in the fact that Invented Algorithms are less likely to foster serious misconceptions and errors.

The following example illustrates how the flexibility afforded by Invented Algorithms can help children avoid some serious errors:

> *There were 302 animals at the zoo. 104 of the animals were monkeys. How many animals were not monkeys?*

> **Todd:** Well, if I take away the 100, that's 202. 4 less than that is like 2 less than 200. That's 198.

Problems with zeros are notoriously difficult for children using standard algorithms, but they pose no special problem for children like Todd who use and understand Invented Algorithms.

Furthermore, with experience children become quite proficient in using and notating Invented Algorithms, so there is not a huge difference in the time it takes children to use Invented Algorithms and the time it takes them to solve the same problem with a standard algorithm. With experience, children start to consolidate their Invented Algorithms.

Invented Algorithms actually can be more efficient than standard written algorithms. Todd's strategy to subtract 302 − 104 and most Compensating Invented Algorithms are both easier and more efficient than the standard algorithms applied to the same problems.

The use of Invented Algorithms also can contribute to the development of children's number sense and estimation abilities. Invented Algorithms require that children think about the size of numbers and that they break numbers apart in different ways. Because children generally start adding the larger digits first, estimation strategies are a natural extension of Invented Algorithms.

Finally, the use of Invented Algorithms contributes to children's understanding of base ten and properties of operations as these algorithms consistently require children to think about base-ten concepts and how operations work. Furthermore, listening to children describe their Invented Algorithms provides you with insight about what children actually understand about base ten and properties of operations (see Chapter 11).

MULTIPLICATION AND DIVISION

The development of multiplication and division strategies for multidigit numbers follows the same general pattern as the development of addition and subtraction strategies, with some added twists. Children may initially use individual counters to solve multidigit problems if the numbers are not too large. Direct Modeling with Tens for multiplication problems requires an understanding of base-ten concepts that is similar to the understanding required for Direct Modeling with Tens for addition problems. However, in order to use base-ten materials to solve most multidigit division problems, children need to be flexible in understanding that tens can be broken apart. For example, if children do not understand that 42 can be represented with 3 tens and 12 ones as well as with 4 tens and 2 ones, they will have difficulty using base-ten materials to solve a Partitive Division problem in which 42 objects are distributed among 3 groups. As is the case for addition and subtraction, children's Invented Algorithms for multiplication and division generally build on their Direct Modeling with Tens strategies. In this book, we address children's multidigit multiplication and division strategies for grouping problems where the number of groups is a single-digit number.

Direct Modeling with Tens

Multiplication
Children's use of Direct Modeling with Tens to solve Multiplication problems is a relatively straightforward extension of the grouping strategy they use for smaller numbers.

CLIP 7.15 Direct Modeling with Tens strategy for a Multiplication problem
http://smarturl.it/CM7.15

The school bought 6 boxes of markers. There are 24 markers in each box. How many markers are there altogether?

Maria makes 6 groups of markers with 2 ten-rods and 4 blocks in each group. She then counts all the ten-rods, "10, 20, 30 . . . 120." She continues counting the unit blocks, "121, 122, 123, . . . 144" and says, "144 markers."

As with problems involving smaller numbers, children tend to represent the number of groups and the number of objects in a group directly. Maria made 6 groups to represent the 6 boxes, and she put 24 in each group to represent the number of markers in each box. If the problem had stated that there were 24 boxes with 6 markers in each box, it is likely that she would have made 24 sets with 6 counters in each set. In this case, she probably would have just counted the total set of markers one by one and would not have used base-ten materials to solve the problem. Children tend to use base-ten materials to solve a multiplication problem only when more than ten objects are in the collections described in the problem.

Measurement Division

Children also use Direct Modeling with Tens when a problem calls for organizing objects into groups with more than ten objects in each group. For many Measurement and Partitive Division problems, it is necessary to break tens apart (or trade tens for ones) to form the groups. We illustrate how one child did this to solve the Measurement Division problem:

The class baked 84 cookies. We want to put them into boxes to sell at the school bake sale. If we put 12 cookies into each box, how many boxes can we fill?

Maria gets out 8 ten-rods and 4 blocks. She makes 2 groups with 1 ten-rod and 2 blocks in each group. She trades a ten-rod for 10 blocks and makes 5 more groups, with a ten-rod and 2 blocks in each group. She then counts the groups, "7."

Maria had to break up 1 ten-rod to put 12 in each group. If the problem had been about 48 cookies with 12 in each box, it would not have been necessary to trade tens for ones. It would have been a much easier problem, but it would not have challenged her knowledge of base-ten concepts to the same degree. As with the Multiplication problem, if there had been fewer than 10 cookies in each box, Maria would have had to trade all the tens for ones, which would have made the use of base-ten materials superfluous.

Partitive Division

Similar patterns are found in children's solutions of Partitive Division problems:

> There are 42 children in the second grade. If they are divided up into 3 teams with the same number of children on each team, how many children will there be on each team?

> Maria gets out 4 ten-rods and 2 blocks. She puts 3 of the ten-rods into 3 separate locations. She trades the remaining ten-rod for 10 blocks and deals the 12 blocks to the 3 ten-rods. Each pile now contains 1 ten-rod and 4 blocks. She counts the blocks and answers, "14."

Again Maria had to change one of the tens into ones so that the blocks could be distributed into 3 groups. If there had been 39 children in the second grade, trading would not have been necessary; and if there had been 6 teams, it would not have been productive to use base-ten materials at all.

Adding Strategies for Multiplication and Division Problems

After experience solving Multiplication and Division problems with Direct Modeling with Tens, children progress to Adding strategies to solve these problems. With Adding strategies, children represent each group with a numeral and make use of their Invented Algorithms for addition to add the amounts in each group. Children typically need to notate these strategies in order to keep track of their computation.

Multiplication

In Figure 7.10, Annie uses an Adding strategy to solve a Multiplication problem.

> Mrs. Kix is collecting cereal box tops. She has 4 bags of box tops with 12 box tops in each bag. How many box tops does Mrs. Kix have?

Annie drew 4 circles to represent each group and wrote "12" in each circle. She made the addition easier for herself by decomposing each 12 into 10 and 2. She then added all of the tens and all of the ones separately. For her final answer, she combined 40 + 8 = 48. Like most children who use Adding

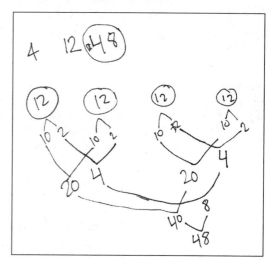

FIGURE 7.10 Annie's written representations of an Adding strategy for a Multiplication problem

CLIP 7.16 Adding strategy for Multiplication, in Spanish
http://smarturl.it/CM7.16

CLIP 7.17 Adding strategy for Multiplication
http://smarturl.it/CM7.17

strategies for multidigit Multiplication problems, Annie relied on Invented Algorithms for addition in the process of solving this problem.

Measurement Division
Annie also used an Adding strategy for solving the following Measurement Division problem:

> *The class baked 60 cookies. We want to put them into boxes to sell at the school bake sale. If we put 15 cookies into each box, how many boxes can we fill?*

Annie: 15 plus 15 is 30, that's 2 boxes, 30 plus 15 is 45, that's 3 boxes, 45 plus 15 is 60, that's 4 boxes.

Partitive Division
Children typically do not use Adding strategies to solve multidigit Partitive Division problems because the problem does not provide the amount in each group. Without knowing the amount in each group, children do not have an amount to add until they reach a total.

CLIP 7.18 Invented Algorithm for a Multiplication problem
http://smarturl.it/CM7.18

Children who use Adding strategies for multidigit Multiplication and Measurement Division tend to use Direct Modeling with Tens for multidigit Partitive Division problems.

CLIP 7.19 Invented Algorithm for a Multiplication problem, with follow-up questions
http://smarturl.it/CM7.19

Invented Multiplication and Division Algorithms

Children's multiplication and division Invented Algorithms build on their Direct Modeling with Tens strategies and their knowledge of multidigit addition.

Multiplication
In the following examples, DeWayne first multiplied the tens and then the ones, and Samantha multiplied by 6, by first multiplying by 3 and then multiplying the result by 2.

The school bought 6 boxes of markers. There are 24 markers in each box. How many markers are there altogether?

> **DeWayne:** 6 twenties is 120. 6 fours is 24. So it's 120 and 24, 144 [see Figure 7.11].
>
> **Samantha:** 3 groups of 24 is 72 because you have 60 and 12 more. 6 groups of 24 would just be double 72, 144 [see Figure 7.12].

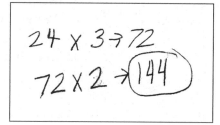

$6 \times 20 = 120$
$6 \times 4 = 24$
$6 \times 24 = 120 + 24 = 144$

FIGURE 7.11 DeWayne's Invented Algorithm for a Multiplication problem

Measurement and Partitive Division

Figure 7.13 is an example of an Invented Algorithm one student used to solve the following Measurement Division problem.

The class baked 84 cookies. We want to put them into boxes to sell at the school bake sale. If we put 12 cookies into each box, how many boxes can we fill?

> **Sebastian:** 12 and 12 is 24, that's 2 boxes. 24 and 24 is 48, that's 4 boxes. If I doubled 48, it would be more than 84, so I added just 1 more box instead. 48 and 12 is 60, 5 boxes. Then I added 2 more boxes and got 84, so it was 7 boxes.

$24 \times 3 \rightarrow 72$
$72 \times 2 \rightarrow 144$

FIGURE 7.12 Samantha's Invented Algorithm for a Multiplication problem

$$
\begin{array}{ccc}
1 & 1 & 2 \\
\end{array}
$$
$12 + 12 = 24$
$24 + 24 = 48$
$48 + 12 = 60$
$60 + 24 = 84$
7 boxes

FIGURE 7.13 Sebastian's Invented Algorithm for a Measurement Division problem

Figure 7.14 is an example of an Invented Algorithm one student used to solve the following Partitive Division problem.

There are 42 children in the second grade. If we divide up into 3 teams with the same number of children on each team, how many children will there be on each team?

Deon: If I put 10 in each group, that's 30 because 3 tens are 30. So there are 12 more. Oh, 3 fours is 12, so I can put 4 more with each 10. That's 14 on each team.

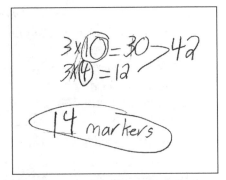

FIGURE 7.14 Deon's Invented Algorithm for a Partitive Division problem

Sebastian used a doubling strategy for the Measurement Division problem, and Deon multiplied the tens and then the ones for the Partitive Division problem. The doubling strategy lends itself to solving a Measurement Division problem, but is difficult to apply to a Partitive Division problem. For a Measurement Division problem, the number in each group is given, so it can be doubled. For the Partitive Division problem, the number in each group is the unknown, so there is nothing to double, which is why children do not generally use doubling for Partitive Division problems.

On the other hand, multiplying the tens and then the ones works well for Partitive Division problems but is difficult to apply to Measurement Division situations. In a Partitive Division problem, the number of groups is known. The number in each group can be built up by successively adding tens and ones to each group until the required number is used up. Multiplying the tens and then the ones for a Measurement Division problem would involve breaking the number in the group up into tens and ones, which would not be difficult, but deciding how to use that information to find the number of groups is a difficult problem.

THE DEVELOPMENT OF MULTIDIGIT STRATEGIES

Strategies for adding, subtracting, multiplying, and dividing multidigit numbers develop as natural extensions of the procedures that children use to solve problems involving single-digit numbers. Initially, children model problems involving two-digit numbers using individual counters in exactly the same way that they model problems with smaller numbers. Although the problems involve numbers greater than ten, children do not initially think of them any differently than problems that involve numbers less than ten. Their solutions make no use of base-ten concepts. When base-ten materials are first made available, children who use them to solve word problems often count by ones. The base-ten blocks simply serve as a convenient collection of counters that do not get all mixed up.

Modeling with Base-Ten Materials

Children come to recognize that they do not have to count all the blocks in the ten-rod each time they construct a set. At first, many children are relatively inflexible in constructing and counting sets using tens. They may solve an addition problem by making each of the addends by counting collections of ten but then find the sum by counting the total by ones. Even after children progress to counting both addends and sums using tens, their conceptions are rather tenuous. For example, to solve a problem that involves finding the sum 37 + 28, a child may put out 3 ten-rods and 7 cubes and 2 ten-rods and 8 cubes. Next, the child counts the tens (10, 20, 30, 40, 50) and continues counting the ones (51, 52, 53, . . . 64, 65). The child's knowledge is sufficient to solve this problem using some concepts of base-ten numbers, but the child might not recognize that 65 can be represented as 6 tens and 5 ones as well as 5 tens and 15 ones. The child simply generates an answer by counting by tens and then counting on by ones. The child is not confronted with the necessity of having to work out the relationship between alternative representations.

This same child might have more difficulty solving problems in which 1 ten has to be thought of as 10 ones. For example, in attempting to solve a subtraction problem that involves taking 38 from 52, a child who constructs 52 with 5 tens and 2 ones might not recognize that 1 of these tens can be thought of as 10 ones in order to remove the 3 tens and 8 ones. For the same reason, the child might also have difficulty with a Partitive Division problem in which 42 objects are to be divided into 3 groups.

Over time, children come to use base-ten materials flexibly and efficiently. They recognize that a given number can be represented by a variety of different combinations of tens and ones and readily trade tens for ones and ones for tens to solve problems. As children's use of base-ten materials becomes more automatic, they come to depend less on manipulations of the physical materials themselves. This sets the stage for their construction of Invented Algorithms.

Invented Algorithms

Children first use Invented Algorithms for problems in which it is relatively easy to keep track of the tens and ones. We present a sequences of problems for which it is increasingly difficult for children to use Invented Algorithms in Figures 7.15 and 7.16.

Problems involving multiples of ten (60 + 20) are the easiest problems for which children use Invented Algorithms. Once a child understands that tens can be combined, it is not a great deal more complicated to add or subtract multiples of ten than it is to add or subtract one-digit numbers.

> *Monday, Anna played video games for 20 minutes before school and for 60 minutes in the evening. How many minutes did she play video games on Monday?*

Julio: It's 80. It's like 2 and 6, only it's 2 tens and 6 tens, so that's 80.
Tanya: Mmm, 60 [pause], 70, 80. That's 80.

Problems in which one number is a multiple of 10 (60 + 25) are slightly more difficult than problems in which both numbers are multiples of 10, and problems that do

Development of Invented Addition Strategies

Problem Stem

_____ birds were sitting in a tree. _____ more birds joined them.
How many birds were in the tree then?

Numbers	Some Possible Strategies
60 + 20	"60 [pause], 70, 80" or "6 and 2 is 8, so 80."
60 + 25	"60 [pause], 70, 80, 85" or "60 and 20 is 80. 5 more is 85."
65 + 20	"65 [pause], 75, 85" or "60 and 20 is 80. 5 more is 85."
65 + 8	"65 and 5 is 70. 3 more is 73."
65 + 24	"60 and 20 is 80. 5 and 4 is 9. So 89."
65 + 28	"60 and 20 is 80. 5 more is 85, and 8 more is 90 and 3. 93." or "60 and 20 is 80. 5 and 8 is 13, so 93."

FIGURE 7.15

Development of Invented Subtraction Strategies

Problem Stem

_____ *ducks were sitting in a pond.* _____ *flew away.*
How many ducks were left in the pond?

Numbers	Some Possible Strategies
80 – 20	"80 take away 20 is 60" or "8 take away 2 is 6. So 60."
85 – 20	"80 take away 20 is 60. So 65."
85 – 7	"85 take away 5 is 80, and 2 more makes 78."
89 – 25	"80 take away 20 is 60. 9 take away 5 is 4. So 64."
80 – 25	"80 take away 20 is 60, take away 5 more is 55."
83 – 25	"80 take away 20 is 60. Take away 5 is 55. Put back the 3 from the 83. That's 58."

FIGURE 7.16

not involve regrouping (65 + 24) are quite a bit easier than problems that do (65 + 28). For problems involving multiples of 10 or 1 multiple of 10, it often is not possible to distinguish between an Incrementing strategy and a Combining the Same Units strategy because there are no ones to combine separately. Problems in which a one-digit number is added to or subtracted from a two-digit number tend to encourage an Incrementing strategy, and problems that do not involve regrouping tend to encourage a Combining the Same Units strategy.

A caution is in order in using these sequences of problems. Children should not be expected to master problems with one type of numbers before they are given more difficult problems. That can lead to misconceptions and errors. For example, when children only study computation exercises that do not involve regrouping for an extended period of time, they frequently form the misconception that numbers are simply added within columns. That can lead to the following error:

$$\begin{array}{r} 36 \\ + \ 47 \\ \hline 713 \end{array}$$

When presented with more difficult problems, children who use Invented Algorithms may revert to Direct Modeling with Tens. That does not mean that they have regressed. It suggests that they are trying to make sense of the problem and do not yet see how to extend their Invented Algorithm to more challenging numbers. Direct Modeling with Tens will help them consolidate the understanding of base ten that they need to generate Invented Algorithms for these problems.

Children generally have less difficulty inventing algorithms for addition than they do for subtraction, multiplication, or division; and, for most children, Invented Algorithms for subtraction, multiplication, and division appear to emerge considerably later than Invented Algorithms for addition.

LEARNING TO SOLVE PROBLEMS WITH MULTIDIGIT NUMBERS

Children can be encouraged to use more advanced strategies by solving problems where use of tens is encouraged. As they do this over time, they become increasingly flexible and efficient in thinking of ten as a unit. As they solve many problems, they come to depend less on the manipulations of physical materials and are able to abstract their solutions by inventing algorithms to add and subtract multidigit numbers without physical materials.

CLIP 7.20 Elijah uses a Direct Modeling by Tens strategy for a harder problem
http://smarturl.it/CM7.20

CLIP 7.21 Elijah uses an Invented Algorithm for an easier problem, with follow-up questions
http://smarturl.it/CM7.21

The transition to using more sophisticated strategies may be facilitated by teacher probes ("Is there an easier way to count those? Is there something you can do so that you can take away 8?"), by the selection of problem types and numbers in problems, and by having children listen to other children describe how they solved a given problem.

Consider how one first-grade teacher, starting on the first day of the school year, provided experiences that would lead to an understanding of base-ten concepts.

On the first day of the school year, Ms. Gehn asked the children to solve a variety of problems involving numbers in the teens or twenties. Various materials were available including counters, number lines, and fingers. As is typical in CGI classrooms, Ms. Gehn did not show her students how to solve the problems, but asked them to solve the problems in any way they wished. After solving the problems, children reported their solution strategies to their classmates. During the rest of the week, children solved a variety of addition, subtraction, multiplication, and division word problems and shared their solution strategies. Most children directly modeled the problems with counters or used the number line.

At the beginning of the second week, Ms. Gehn gave 10 ten-rods to each child and asked them to count the little cubes (units) that could be seen in the bars. After everyone agreed that each ten-rod was made up of 10 cubes, she asked how many little cubes there were in all 10 ten-rods. About half of the children counted the little cubes by ones and the others counted by tens. Children shared both strategies with the class, and a discussion ensued about which way was easier. To this point, Ms. Gehn provided the children with tools that would help them solve the problems using base-ten principles and gave them two-digit problems to solve. The teacher did not demonstrate how base-ten ideas would aid in problem solution. Although she drew the children's attention to the fact that there were 10 units in each ten-rod, she placed little emphasis on base-ten number concepts. Some children attempted to use base-ten ideas to solve problems, but all children's knowledge of these ideas appeared limited.

Throughout the year, Ms. Gehn continued to ask children to solve problems where base-ten ideas would be useful, asked them to report their solutions, and drew the children's attention to solutions that involved base-ten ideas. She often asked children to solve problems in at least two ways and would emphasize that combining tens or counting by tens was easier than counting by ones.

Development of multidigit concepts takes time. Children need time to explore the use of different representations and ways to think about numbers and to invent algorithms for solving problems. Even though some strategies may be inefficient, children cannot be rushed to use more efficient procedures without the potential loss of understanding. Children do not make the transition to more abstract and efficient strategies all at once. But they should be given problems and have the opportunity to engage in interactions that encourage them to use more abstract and efficient procedures. One ultimate goal of instruction is for all children to develop efficient procedures for adding, subtracting, multiplying, and dividing that are connected to an understanding of each of these operations. That goal is consistent with and is supported by the kinds of interactions we have portrayed in this chapter that provide an opportunity for children to invent and make sense of the mathematics they are learning.

QUESTIONS FOR FURTHER REFLECTION

1. Solve each of these problems with Direct Modeling with Ones, Counting with Ones, Direct Modeling with Tens, and an Invented Algorithm. You may wish to produce a written representation of each strategy in a table such as the following:

Problem	Direct Modeling with Ones	Counting with Ones	Direct Modeling with Tens	Invented Algorithm
A. *Miguel had 23 buttons. Chloe gave him 14 more buttons. How many buttons does Miguel have now?*				
B. *Angelina has 23 buttons. How many more buttons would she need to get to have 37 buttons?*				

2. Produce a written representation of a Direct Modeling with Tens and an Invented Algorithm for each of these problems.

Problem	Direct Modeling with Tens	Invented Algorithm
C. *Destiny had 27 crayons. Her dad gave her some more crayons and now she has 61 crayons. How many crayons did her dad give her?*		
D. *Alejandro had 60 crayons. He lost 32 of them. How many crayons does Alejandro have now?*		

Problem	Direct Modeling with Tens	Invented Algorithm
E. *Mr. Chang's class had a box with 214 crayons in it. Mr. Chang bought 327 more crayons and put them in the box. How many crayons are in the box now?*		

3. Choose one of the problems A–E above.

   a. Anticipate the strategies that your students might use to solve this problem.

   b. Pose the problem to the students in your class. Describe the students' strategies in enough detail that someone reading your description could solve the problem the same ways the students did.

   c. Were the strategies your students used different in any way from the ones you predicted they would use? How were they different?

4. Produce a written representation of a Combining the Same Units Invented Algorithm and Incremental Invented Algorithm for each of these problems.

Problem	Combining the Same Units Invented Algorithm	Incremental Invented Algorithm
A. *Vincent has 34 Popsicle sticks. If he got 52 more Popsicle sticks, how many Popsicle sticks would he have?*		
B. *Arianna has 36 pieces of gum. If she got 58 more pieces of gum, how many pieces of gum would she have?*		

(continues)

Problem	Combining the Same Units Invented Algorithm	Incremental Invented Algorithm
C. *Hector has 546 pebbles. If he got 327 more pebbles, how many pebbles would he have?*		
D. *Kaylee had 85 jelly beans. Over the weekend, she and her friends ate 43 jelly beans. How many jelly beans does Kaylee have now?*		
E. *The donut shop has 632 donuts. They sold 378 donuts. How many donuts does the donut shop have now?*		

5. See Figures 7.17, 7.18, and 7.19 for three written representations of how children solved this problem:

   Avi and his sister frosted all the cookies that their mom made for the party. Avi frosted 20 cookies. His sister frosted 13 cookies. How many cookies will there be at the party?

   a. Write a question that you would ask each student about his or her strategy. These questions can be either to help you understand her strategy, to help the student reflect on her strategy, or to help her explain her strategy to other students.
   b. Think of a question you could ask each of these students about one of the other strategies.

33

I kand the kyoons to figr at

And win I adid all fo them it matte 33!

FIGURE 7.17 Margie

Avl 20

O OOOOO OOOOO OOOOO OOO

20 + 13 = 33

OOO OO OOOOOOOO sister 13

FIGURE 7.18 Bob

32 I Used my fingers
20 2122 2324 25
26 27 28 29 30 31

FIGURE 7.19 Carrie

6. Suppose you read this problem to a student:

Destiny had 27 crayons. Her dad gave her some more crayons and now she has 61 crayons. How many crayons did her dad give her?

and the problem was too hard. Describe two ways you could make the problem easier.

7. Suppose you posed this problem to a group of five students:

Mr. Chang's class had a box with 214 crayons in it. Mr. Chang bought 327 more crayons and put them in the box. How many crayons are in the box now?

All of them used the traditional algorithm to solve the problem. You were pretty sure they did not completely understand the traditional algorithm. What might you do next with these students? If you chose to pose a different problem to them, what problem might you pose?

8. Figures 7.20 to 7.24 are some examples of what students wrote on their paper after solving the following problem:

Sashi had 213 mini-erasers. Her brother gave her 49 mini-erasers. How many mini-erasers does Sashi have now?

Identify each strategy as Direct Models with Ones, Counts with Ones, Direct Models with Tens, or Invented Algorithm. For each strategy, write a question that would help the student explain the strategy. These questions

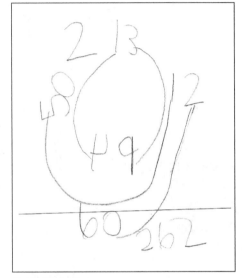

FIGURE 7.20 Anna

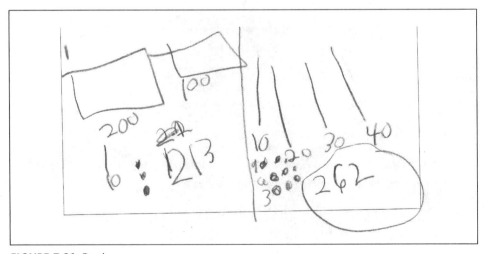

FIGURE 7.21 Brad

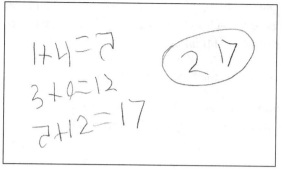

1+4=5
3+9=12
5+12=17
217

FIGURE 7.22 Carl

10+40=50 3+9=12
200+12=212
212+50=262

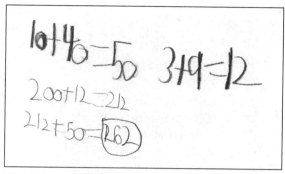

FIGURE 7.23 Evelyn

213+49=
10+40=50
3+9=12
50+12=62
62+200=262

FIGURE 7.24 Fred

can be either to help you understand the strategy, to help the student reflect on his strategy, or to help the student explain the strategy to other students.

9. If your students were to produce the work shown in question 8, which students would you choose to explain their strategies to the class? In what order would you have them share their strategies?

10. Watch two children solve a multidigit multiplication problem. In each case, the teacher asks some questions that help the child extend her thinking in some way. For each episode, describe the child's thinking and the teacher questioning. What does the teacher questioning reveal about the child's understanding that was not apparent

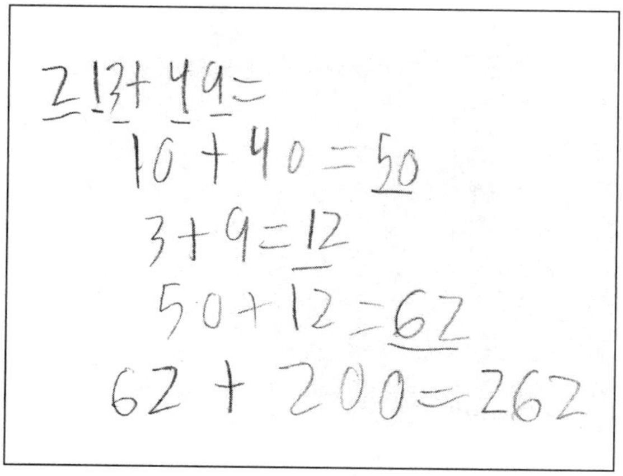

CLIP 7.22 Zakyla solves a multidigit Multiplication problem, and her thinking is extended
http://smarturl.it/CM7.22

CLIP 7.23 Emma solves a multidigit Multiplication problem, and her thinking is extended
http://smarturl.it/CM7.23

in the initial strategy? What is a follow-up problem you might pose to each child to encourage her to use these emergent ways of thinking?

a. Zakyla solves the following problem.

> ***Multiplication:*** *Grandma has 5 plates, with 27 cookies on every plate. How many cookies does Grandma have?*

b. Emma solves 6×32.

8

Problem Solving as Modeling

The framework we have discussed so far provides a basis for understanding the development of children's mathematical thinking. Although the framework appears complex at first, its coherence becomes more and more visible through experience talking to children about their mathematical thinking. The framework provides a basis for understanding why a child is able to solve certain problems and not able to solve others. The path of development of ideas becomes visible, so it is possible to predict how children's thinking will grow.

The unifying theme underlying this framework is that children naturally attempt to model the action or relationships in problems. They first directly model the situations or relationships with physical objects. They then move on to various Counting strategies in which the actions or relationships are at first somewhat visible but become less visible as children's thinking matures. Thus, children's solution strategies are first fairly exact models of problem action or relationships. As thinking progresses to using more Counting strategies, their representation becomes more abstract. Counting and Direct Modeling strategies are simply specific instances of the fundamental principle of modeling, and it is helpful to think of them as attempts to model problems rather than as a collection of distinct strategies. Over time, children begin to use fact-based strategies that are even more abstract and do not necessarily reflect problem context.

The solution of problems with larger numbers is a natural extension of the strategies that children use to solve problems with single-digit numbers and follows the same general pattern. Children initially model problems with large numbers using the same Direct Modeling strategies they used with smaller numbers. These strategies are replaced by similar strategies using physical objects grouped by tens and hundreds. Over time these physical models give way to Invented Algorithms that replace the manipulation of physical representations with symbolic representations.

MODELING AND THE PROBLEM-SOLVING PROCESS

The conception of problem solving as modeling not only serves as a basis for understanding children's strategies for solving addition, subtraction, multiplication, and division problems; it also can provide a unifying framework for thinking about problem solving. Students who struggle with problem solving are often taught problem-solving strategies such as looking for key words. These are superficial strategies that do not always work, and they have little application outside of school. Attending to the critical features of a problem and constructing a model of the situation specified in a problem is at the heart of real problem solving. It is a process that can be widely applied and extended to increasingly complex problems. Virtually all children start school with this basic sense-making strategy, but many students eventually abandon this fundamentally sound and powerful general problem-solving approach for the mechanical application of arithmetic skills.

If older children simply applied some of the intuitive, analytic modeling skills exhibited by young children to analyze problem situations, it appears that they would avoid some of their most glaring problem-solving errors. A fundamental issue is how to help children build upon and extend the intuitive modeling skills that they apply to basic problems as young children. That is a primary goal of CGI.

Generating intuitive models to solve problems involves complex reasoning and may be seen as appropriate for only the children who learn quickly and easily. This is simply not true. Virtually all children can construct models to solve problems. Children who are progressing more slowly than their classmates are better served by being supported in generating their own models to solve problems than by being taught problem-solving strategies that have no inherent meaning for them and simply become procedures to follow.

Modeling in More Complex Problem Situations

Although the foregoing analysis focuses on basic addition, subtraction, multiplication, and division situations, the general principle that children model the action and relations in problems applies to more complex problem situations as well. Many problem situations that are appropriate for elementary school children involve combinations of the problems described in the preceding chapters, and children's methods for solving them can be understood in light of the strategies that children use to solve one-step problems. For example, consider the following problem:

Maggie had 3 packages of cupcakes. There were 4 cupcakes in each package. She ate 5 cupcakes. How many cupcakes were left?

This problem is a combination of Multiplication and Separate (Result Unknown) problems, and young children readily solve it using a combination of the strategies used to solve these two types of problems. A typical solution would be first to count out 3 groups of counters with 4 counters in each group and then remove 5 counters.

Children can solve a variety of other problems by modeling, such as this example:

19 children are taking a minibus to the zoo. They will have to sit either 2 or 3 to a seat. The bus has 7 seats. How many children will have to sit 3 to a seat and how many can sit 2 to a seat?

To solve this problem, young children typically set out 19 counters and attempt to place them in 7 groups of either 2 or 3 to a group until the counters are used up. (See the photo at the beginning of the chapter.) Some children use a Trial and Error strategy to place the counters in groups, and others systematically deal the counters into 7 groups until the counters are used up. Note that even though the groups the children create to solve this problem will not have the same number of counters and the answer is not the number of counters in a given group, the strategies used are similar to those used to solve a Partitive Division problem. The key to understanding children's solutions to these problems lies in noting that children model the problem situations directly.

> **CLIP 8.1** A kindergartner uses Direct Modeling to solve a variety of problems
> http://smarturl.it/CM8.1

Determining Problem Difficulty

Thinking of children's problem solving as modeling also provides some perspective on whether a given problem might be difficult for children. When children have difficulty, even with a problem that appears relatively simple to us (e.g., a one-step Join [Start Unknown] problem), it is often because they cannot figure out how to model it. The previous examples illustrate that children can solve even seemingly complex problems as long as the action or relationships in a problem can be modeled in a reasonably straightforward fashion. Because modeling provides a framework in which problem solving becomes a meaning-making activity, a focus on problem solving as modeling may do more than just provide children with a general strategy for solving problems. Such a focus can also have an impact on children's conceptions of problem solving and of themselves as problem solvers. If from an early age children are taught to approach problem solving as a way of making sense out of problem situations, they may come to believe that learning and doing mathematics involves solving problems in meaningful ways.

MODELING, PROBLEM SOLVING, AND LEARNING SKILLS

This conception of problem solving provides a foundation for integrating instruction in problem solving with instruction in fundamental mathematical concepts and skills. Problem solving becomes a basis for learning symbols and formal procedures. Rather than learning a procedure (such as adding or subtracting) and then applying it to solve problems, children begin with intuitive problem solving that makes sense to them and then learn mathematical symbols as tools for representing ideas that they already understand.

This connection is reflected in the strategies that children use to calculate and solve equations. At first children solve equations using counters or pictures in the same way they do for a corresponding word problem. As with word problems, these Direct Modeling strategies are eventually replaced by Counting strategies and ultimately by Number Fact strategies. To find the answer to $15 - 8 = \Box$, children generally use the same strategies that they use to solve a Separate (Result Unknown) problem. To solve the equation $7 + \Box = 13$, children use the same strategies they use to solve a Join (Change Unknown) problem.

Thus, not only are symbols and procedures presented as ways of representing problem situations, but the construction of procedures for calculating answers is treated as a problem-solving task. As a result, the procedures can be used flexibly and adapted to new situations. The consequence of this flexibility is illustrated by the results of a study of the strategies fourth-grade students in CGI classes and sixth-grade students in traditional classes used to solve

$$\begin{array}{r} 300 \\ -299 \\ \hline \end{array}$$

Of fourth-graders in CGI classes, 76 percent immediately recognized that $300 - 299$ was 1, versus only 28 percent of the sixth-graders in traditional classes. The remaining children either used the standard subtraction algorithm with all borrowing notation included and/or got the wrong answer.

The theme of this chapter is that children intuitively construct models of the structure they see in problems they are solving. There is more to problem solving than modeling, but modeling plays a central role in problem solving at all levels, and the focus on modeling in CGI classes provides coherence to problem solving in the elementary grades. Another unifying feature of our analysis of children's mathematical strategies is that the strategies that children construct are grounded in fundamental properties of operations and in the relations among the four operations. This theme is the subject of Chapter 11.

9

Developing Classroom Practice: Posing Problems and Eliciting Thinking

Teachers regularly ask, "What does a CGI classroom look like?" "What do I do to make my classroom a CGI classroom?" There is no "one way" to organize your classroom for CGI. However, we have observed that instruction in CGI classrooms can be characterized by a set of classroom practices that are powerful for engaging children's mathematical thinking. In this chapter and the next, we describe some research-based classroom practices and the principled ideas that inform them. We draw on examples from a number of CGI teachers working in a variety of contexts, at different points in their CGI journey. This chapter elaborates the practices of posing problems and eliciting student thinking.

When you see CGI teachers engaging children in problem solving, the work may seem effortless. However, those teachers have prepared the way for students' engagement by choosing problem contexts that are accessible, ensuring students have tools available to support their thinking, encouraging students to do what makes sense to them, and making sure all students have a way to get started. Thus, CGI teachers work at creating an environment where students see that a range of strategies are expected and celebrated. This work begins with posing problems.

POSING PROBLEMS

Prior to posing a problem, CGI teachers select a problem type and numbers that allow students to engage with the mathematical goals they have in mind. Choosing which problem to pose depends on understanding the details of your students' mathematical thinking; understanding your students' thinking requires posing problems and listening to and watching the strategies your students use. In getting started, posing a problem that can easily be directly modeled offers the greatest possibility that students will be successful. The more you learn about your students' thinking, the easier it will be for you to choose problems and numbers to meet students' learning needs.

Problem posing starts with the teacher reading the problem to students, the class reading it together, or students reading it on their own. During this initial reading, check for understanding of the context and watch and listen to see if students can get started. As students begin to engage in problem solving, pay special attention to making sure the students know what the story is about, because students' understanding of the story drives their strategies. Engaging the class in discussion of the problem context before reading the problem, while reading it, or after the students have heard the problem can support students in making sense of the problem.

> If you are looking for support in deciding what problem to pose, try some of the questions for reflection in Chapters 3 (question 2), 4 (questions 3 and 4), 6 (question 4), and 7 (question 3).

If the problem context makes sense to students and they know what they might do to start on a solution, they will be able to engage in problem solving. When posing the problem, it can be helpful to unpack the problem with students. We use the term *unpack* to refer to engaging students in making sense of the context and the action or situation of the problem to ensure that all students understand the problem. When or how much to unpack depends on the context, the students' experiences, and what the students understand about the mathematics. With younger students, it may be necessary to spend more time making sure that they understand the context of the problem, particularly the consequences of the action on the number of objects in the story. Teachers in dual language classes or classes where English is not some students' primary language may choose to unpack in ways that ensure students have the opportunity to use their native language as a resource in making sense of the context. When posing a particular problem type for the first time, you might spend more time making sure students understand what is happening in the story as it relates to the mathematics involved. Or you might choose not to unpack as a way to assess students' abilities to make sense of the context on their own. Most important, when considering when and how to unpack a problem, remember that the goal of unpacking is to provide opportunity for students to make sense of the problem context, not to walk them through how to solve the problem.

CLIP 9.1 Unpacking
the problem context in
Ms. Scott's class
http://smarturl.it/CM9.1

Unpacking the Problem

In the following episode, Ms. Scott posed a problem to her second-graders by unpacking the problem context and having a discussion with students about what was happening:

Estabán has 71 marbles. On his way to school 39 marbles fell out of his backpack. How many marbles does Estabán have left?

Ms. Scott asked if her students were all ready for math today, and they responded with a "Yes!" She then asked, "I wonder who is in the story today?" and looking at her clipboard, said, "Oh, it's Estabán."

> *Ms. S:* Estabán, do you have marbles at home?
> **Estabán:** Yes.
> *Ms. S:* I had a feeling. How many do you have—a bunch, a little bit?
> **Estabán:** I have 100.
> *Ms. S:* [with eyes wide] Really? Do you ever bring your marbles to school?
> **Estabán:** My mom told me if I take them to school, my teacher might take them away.
> *Ms. S:* Well, you have a smart mom. Well, today we are going to be pretending that you brought your marbles to school. Can you all pretend with Estabán about that?
> **Students:** Yes.
> *Ms. S:* I am going to tell you the story and then we are going to say it together. Estabán had 71 marbles, and on his way to school, 39 marbles fell out of his backpack.
> **Estabán:** Oh, man.
> *Ms. S:* You had a hole in your backpack.
> **Estabán:** No, I don't.
> *Ms. S:* Well, let's all pretend you did. We want to know how many marbles Estabán had left. So I am going to say it again. [Rereads entire problem.]

The students repeated the problem, along with Ms. Scott, two more times. Ms. Scott then asked the students if they had a way they might figure it out. When the students responded that they did, Ms. Scott sent them to their tables to solve the problem.

The Separate (Result Unknown) problem Ms. Scott created for her students to solve involved a student in the class and a situation she thought would make sense to her students. The power of the context in a word problem is that it draws on relationships that students can reason about in ways that enable them to understand the mathematics of the problem. The context of Ms. Scott's problem told a story about marbles getting lost, a situation that was familiar to students and one that they could see as involving a separating action.

The key to unpacking a problem with students is supporting students to understand the context in relation to the mathematics of the problem. In unpacking the problem, Ms. Scott did not focus on "key words," the question at the end of the word problem, or what operation students should use. She also did not discuss how the problem could be solved. Instead, as she posed the problem, she focused on what the story was about. She checked with Estabán about his marble collection and highlighted the hole in Estabán's backpack to explain how he lost the marbles. Similar to what a teacher might do during a literacy activity, Ms. Scott engaged the students in comprehending the story.

CLIP 9.2 Unpacking the problem context to personalize the problem for a student
http://smarturl.it/CM9.2

CLIP 9.3 Unpacking the problem context to help a student get started
http://smarturl.it/CM9.3

Students Share Ideas About a Familiar Context

In the preceding example, Ms. Scott unpacked the problem as she posed it to the class by asking students questions along the way. Some teachers unpack a problem by having students talk to each other about the context. As we see in the next example, Mr. Torres has his first-graders pair share around what the story is about and then engages the students together in a whole-group conversation. The pair share allows more students the chance to verbalize their understanding of the context, and it can uncover aspects of students' personal experiences that the teacher needs to address, as the following example shows.

Before reading the problem, Mr. Torres asked his students about the breakfast items served in the cafeteria. He called on a number of different students to share their ideas. Mr. Torres then told the class they were going to solve a problem about breakfast in the cafeteria. On the board he had written a Compare (Difference Unknown) problem:

At breakfast in the cafeteria, 12 children ate cereal. 7 children ate eggs. How many more children ate cereal than eggs?

He read the problem to the students and had the students read the problem to him. He asked the students to turn to their partner and discuss what the problem is about. Mr. Torres moved around listening to the students' discussions. He then called them back together.

Mr. T: *So who can tell me one thing about the story?*

Senica: It is about cereal.

Mr. T: *Okay, what do we know about the cereal? Jesus?*

Jesus: 12 children ate it.

Mr. T: *Yes. [to the class] How many children were eating cereal for breakfast at the cafeteria?*

Students: 12!

Mr. T: *What else can you tell me, someone tell me one other thing about the story. Yvette?*

Yvette: 7 had eggs.

Aaron: But Mister, I had eggs and there were more people having eggs.

Mr. T: *Yvette, you are correct, the problem says 7 children ate eggs. Aaron is saying that today he had eggs and he thinks more than 7 people had eggs. That is good noticing. But today the problem we are solving is about 7 children eating eggs so we want to pay attention to those 7 people having eggs. So, Aaron, let's make sure we know what is going on in this problem. Jesus and Yvette told us we know that in this story, 12 children had cereal and 7 children had eggs. Do you agree with that, Aaron? [Aaron agrees.] So what are we trying to find out? Arleta?*

Arleta: How many.

Mr. T: *How many what?*

Arleta: How many more people had cereal.

Mr. T: *How many more people ate cereal than ate eggs. Do you agree with Arleta?*

Students: Yes.

Mr. T: *So are there more children eating cereal or eggs? [Students call out, "Cereal."] If we are trying to find out how many more people ate cereal than eggs, do you think it could be that 20 more people ate cereal than eggs? [Students call out, "No."]*

Brian: No, 'cause that would be too many.

Mr. T: *Okay, Caro?*

Caro: Only 12 have cereal. So that is too many.

Mr. T: Okay, raise your hand if you have a way to get started. If you still want to talk more about it, stay here with me for a minute.

Mr. Torres not only asked his students to pair share about the context; he also asked them to take the lead in describing the context. He supported Aaron to see that while he had particular knowledge of egg eating in the cafeteria, the problem being posed was about a different situation. Sometimes students draw on their experiences in ways that can confuse them; at other times students do not understand the context well enough to make sense of what is going on. In closing his problem posing, Mr. Torres posed a question to support students to think about the relationship between the action and the quantities: Could it be that 20 more people ate cereal than eggs? Students' responses to this question provided insight into their understanding of the mathematical relationships in the problem.

Making Sense of Problems

One of the biggest challenges in unpacking a problem with students is that you can end up doing all of the mathematical work. It is easy to lead students through the problem in a way that provides the students a strategy to use so that students already have the answer before you are finished unpacking the problem. The goal of unpacking the problem is to support sense making around the context, not to help students come up with a strategy or an answer. By focusing unpacking on having the students explain what the story is about, you can avoid doing too much of the work for the students.

CLIP 9.4 Ms. Byron, Ms. Hassay, and Ms. Grace begin by posing the problem http://smarturl.it/CM9.4

CGI teachers have found that students gradually learn to make sense of the context on their own. Students learn that whether the problem is about monkeys or squids or about a student in the class or about a stranger does not make a difference in the strategy they choose. Rather, students learn to look for the mathematical relationships that are a part of the story and use them to get started on a solution.

While the details of unpacking problems can vary, a set of principles underlies the unpacking in all of these instances (see Figure 9.1).

Principles for Unpacking Problems
Focus on story comprehension.
Attend to the connection between the story and the mathematics.
Support each student's participation and access.
Support students to learn how to unpack problems on their own.
Avoid doing the mathematical work of solving the problem.

FIGURE 9.1

ELICITING STUDENT THINKING

Asking students, "Can you tell me how you solved that?" is a central feature of CGI classrooms. The wording of the question may vary, but the underlying idea that students make explicit their mathematical thinking is common to all CGI classrooms. This general question, along with variations such as "What did you do?" or "Tell me about your strategy," is a productive way to start engaging students in explaining the strategies they used to solve a problem. More specific follow-up questions support students to elaborate the details of their strategy. Having a student share more details of her thinking engages the student in articulating, explaining, and justifying her thinking and enables the teacher and other students to understand the strategy the student used. Research shows that when students are expected to describe their strategies in detail with the teacher and with each other, they demonstrate higher mathematical achievement (see Webb et al. 2008 and 2009). Both the general initial question and the specific follow-up questions that teachers ask support students in explaining their strategies.

You can elicit student thinking throughout problem solving in ways that seek out how students solved problems or support students to complete or correct a strategy or extend students' mathematical thinking. There is no perfect sequence of questions nor can questions all be preplanned because supporting students to explain the details of their ideas requires listening and responding to what students share. The first examples that follow focus on eliciting student thinking after the students have solved the problem; the next section examines eliciting thinking when students' solutions are incomplete or incorrect and when teachers draw from student written work. The final section looks at eliciting where teachers work to extend students' mathematical thinking.

> Y*our best learning comes from your students so really listen to them and be open to the many ways they will teach you.*
>
> —Shernice Lazare, teacher

Eliciting Student Thinking After Students Have Solved the Problem

Teachers often search for the "best" question to ask in eliciting a student's thinking. However, it turns out there is no best question. Rather, the most productive questions following the initial general "Tell me what you did" are those questions that refer specifically to what a student shared in talk or writing. Your job is to listen and observe the details of the student's strategy, and then ask him a question about something you noticed.

For example, consider the interaction between Liz and her teacher about the following problem:

Kevin has 7 dollars. He wants to save up 11 dollars to buy a toy. How much more money does Kevin need?

Liz: I got 4.
Ms. T: *How did you figure that out, Liz?*
Liz: I put 4 with 7 and got 11.
Ms. T: *Tell me about the 4. What do you mean that you put it with the 7?*
Liz: I knew that 7 and 3 is 10 and 1 more is 11 and 3 and 1 is 4.

Liz's initial explanation let Ms. Thompson see that Liz had arrived at a correct answer and she was thinking about putting the 4 with the 7. Ms. Thompson's follow-up question prompted Liz to focus specifically on the 4 and describe the remainder of her strategy. The question supported Liz to detail her strategy so the teacher and class could see the specific derived fact she used.

Asking a Series of Follow-up Questions

Often one follow-up question is not enough to support the student to describe her entire strategy. Sometimes you need to ask a series of questions as illustrated by the following example. Kirta is solving the problem:

> Joshua had 8 buckets of sand for his sand castle. His brother brought him 11 more buckets of sand. How many buckets of sand does Joshua have now?

Ms. N: *Kirta, how did you solve the problem?*
Kirta: I made 8 and 11.
Ms. N: *Okay, you made 8 and 11. Can you tell me how you made the 8?*
Kirta: I used my cubes and counted 1, 2, 3, 4, 5, 6, 7, 8 and then I counted 1, 2, 3, 4, 5, 6, 7, 8, 9, 10, 11 and I got 19.
Ms. N: *So you counted out 8 cubes and then 11 cubes. How did you use that to get 19?*
Kirta: I counted 8 [sweeping her hand over the set of 8 cubes], 9, 10, 11, 12, 13, 14, 15, 16, 17, 18, 19 [pointing to each cube in the set of 11].

With each follow-up question, Ms. Navarro picked up a detail from Kirta's explanation and used that to ask her another question. Ms. Navarro asked about the 8, and how Kirta counted to get to 19. Kirta could have counted her cubes in several different ways. Kirta might have counted all 19 cubes in the combined set starting with 1. Or she might have taken advantage of the fact that she already knew that there were 8 cubes in one of the collections and started counting on at 9 to count the remaining cubes. Ms. Navarro learned that Kirta started counting from the 8 in the initial group and counted the second group. The follow-up questions allowed Kirta to work through explaining the details of her strategy and let Ms. Navarro and the class hear Kirta describe each step of her Direct Modeling strategy, which showed that she was beginning to transition to a Counting strategy.

Following up on student explanations not only helps the teacher and other students learn more about a student's thinking, it also helps the student doing the sharing in two important ways. First, sharing helps the student enhance his understanding because as he verbalizes he can make and deepen connections among mathematical ideas. Second, sharing allows the student and the class to learn what counts as a complete mathematical explanation.

Eliciting Student Thinking When Student Solutions Are Incomplete or Incorrect

As you observe students solving problems, you will see students who are unsure about how to proceed. Sometimes these students are on the right track, and sometimes they are not. In both cases, eliciting the student's thinking is an important way to support the student to engage in problem solving. How then do you apply the same principles about attending to the details of the student's strategy? You can start with what the student *has done* or on *what the student is thinking*. Christi Byron encountered this issue as her students solved a Join (Result Unknown) problem:

CLIP 9.5 Ms. Byron works with a student who has a partially correct strategy
http://smarturl.it/CM9.5

Natalie has 30 jelly beans. Her mom gives her 23 more jelly beans. How many jelly beans does Natalie have now?

Ms. Byron was checking in with students while they solved the problem. Samuel had finished solving the problem and arrived at the answer 33 (circled on his paper). Ms. Byron asked him to tell her about his thinking. (See Figure 9.2.)

Ms. B: *Will you tell me your thinking on here, Samuel?*
Samuel: [points to the circled tens on his paper] 10.

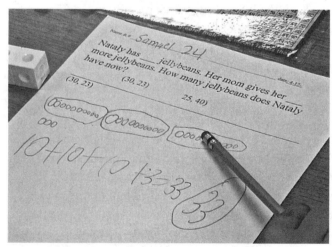

FIGURE 9.2 Samuel's solution

Ms. B: *10, okay.*

Samuel: Plus 10, plus 10, plus 3, equals 33.

Ms. B: *Equals 33, all right, let's read the story together.*

Ms. B and Samuel together: *Natalie has 30 jelly beans, her mom gives her 23 more jelly beans. How many jelly beans does Natalie have now?*

Ms. B: *All right. So can you show me the 30 jelly beans that Natalie had?*

Samuel: [points to his paper with his pencil where he has 3 groups of 10].

Ms. B: *Let's count them.*

Samuel: [with Ms. B] 10, 20, 30.

Ms. B: *Oh, so how many more jelly beans did her mom give her?*

Samuel: These [points to the 3 smaller circles under the 3 tens on his paper].

Ms. B: *Let's read that number. How many jellybeans did her mom give her?*

Samuel: 23.

Ms. B: *Where is the 23 in your picture?*

Samuel: [points to the 3 circles].

Ms. B: *Can you count those for me?*

Samuel: 10, 20, 21 [Counts 2 circles as tens and 1one as a one. It is not clear how Samuel solved the problem but Ms. B did notice that he was sometimes counting his circles as tens and sometimes as ones.]

Ms. B: *[points to his 3 circles] Right here is 21? Or is that, how much is this?*

[Ms. Byron picks up some base-ten blocks and asks Samuel to make 23 with the tens and ones. She sees he is having trouble thinking about the tens in 23. So she then goes on to ask him to build the 23 using just ones blocks. She leaves Samuel as he is making the 23 and checks in later to see if he counted all of his initial 30 and the 23 he counted out with the ones blocks.]

Ms. Byron followed the same principles as Ms. Navarro in eliciting the details of Samuel's thinking. She asked Samuel to show her what he was doing. She listened to him and watched him explain his strategy, asking very specific questions and asking him to be specific in his responses. When Ms. Byron was unsure about what Samuel had on his paper and how he was thinking about the problem, she asked him to reread the problem with her. She asked him to be specific about where he had shown the 30 from the problem and then the 23. She saw he was having trouble making his 23 using tens and ones, and recognized that when he made the 30, he made all 30 circles in groups of 10, so she gave him ones blocks and left him to see if he could finish. In summary, she asked specific questions about what he did and what he was thinking, and she referred back to the problem and provided appropriate tools to support him to move forward in his solution.

> I ask questions of all students (right or wrong) and encourage students to give more than one explanation. I also ensure (through record keeping and checklists) that over time all students have an opportunity to share their thinking and their strategies.
>
> —Darlene Fish, teacher

Eliciting Student Thinking from Student Written Work

This same principle of asking students questions about the details of their explanations also applies to students' written work. In Ms. Reid's second-grade class, the students had solved a Join (Change Unknown) problem. Ms. Reid noticed that Katie had finished and so she asked her about her work (see Figure 9.3.).

Ms. R: *Katie what did you find out about the Pokémon cards?*
Katie: Her mom got her 33 more.
Ms. R: *I see you have 28, 38, 48, 58 here [points to paper]. Can you tell me about that?*
Katie: I counted up from the 28.
Ms. R: *Okay, what about these tens that you wrote?*
Katie: [points to the 28] 28 to 38 is 10 and 38 to 48 is 10 and 48 to 58 is 10 and then I went 59, 60, 61 and that is 3.

1. Maria has 28 Pokemon cards in her collection. Her mom gives her some more cards for her birthday. Now Maria has 61 cards. How many cards did her mom give her for her birthday?

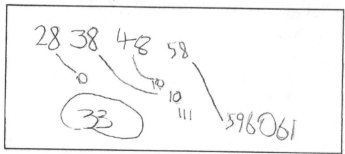

FIGURE 9.3 Katie's written work

Ms. R: So I see how you got the 3. Where did the 30 come from?

Katie: 10 and 10 and 10 is 30.

Ms. R: Nice.

Alex solved the same problem, but his answer was incorrect (Figure 9.4). Ms. Reid stops by Alex's desk to check in with him.

Ms. R: [points to the 28 on Alex's paper] I see you have a 28 written here. Can you tell me about what you were doing with the 28?

Alex: I counted from 28.

Ms. R: Okay, you counted from 28. Can you tell me what numbers you were counting?

Alex: I did 29, 30, 31 . . . 61 [pointing to the tallies on his paper].

Ms. R: I see. How did you get 34?

Alex: [points to his tallies and counts] 5, 10, 15, 20, 25, 30, 31, 32, 33, oh, 33.

Ms. R: So her mom gave her 33. I see you made tallies, how many groups of 5 did you have?

Alex: [points to the tallies of 5 one at a time] 1, 2, 3, 4, 5, 6. 6.

Ms. R: 6 groups of 5. How many groups of 10 are there?

Alex: [points to 2 groups of 5] 1, [points to 2 groups of 5] 2, [points to 2 groups of 5] 3.

As Ms. Reid questioned Alex, he was able to fix his miscount. He also worked through the details of his strategy and explained in words what he had done on paper. Alex had counted on by ones, but he had grouped the ones in groups of 5, which made them easier to count. He could count by fives, but when Ms. Reid asked a specific question about

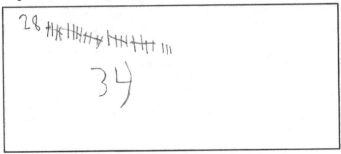

1. Maria has 28 Pokemon cards in her collection. Her mom gives her some more cards for her birthday. Now Maria has 61 cards. How many cards did her mom give her for her birthday?

FIGURE 9.4 Alex's written work

groups of 10, he showed that he was able to count by tens. In asking him about tens, Ms. Reid was able to gauge his understanding of tens and get Alex to think about the use of tens in his solution. The use of tens is a goal Ms. Reid has for Alex. Ms. Reid's questioning gave Alex a chance to reflect on his strategy and his representation and begin to extend his ideas.

In each of these examples, the teachers listened to students' mathematical explanations and used what they heard or saw to ask a specific follow-up question to elicit more of the details of the student's strategy. Sometimes the additional student explanation that resulted from the teacher's questioning allowed the teacher to know what strategy the student used, and other times it provided more detail about a mathematical idea central to the strategy. Working through the explanations also gave students the opportunity to work through their mathematical ideas verbally and in written form, allowing them to synthesize and connect ideas and make sense of new mathematical ideas.

While the students in these examples responded to the teachers' questions, there can be times when students do not respond. When you first begin to ask students to share their strategies, your questions may be met with silence. A student's lack of response does not necessarily mean that the student does not have a strategy to share or that the student is unable to share. Sometimes students do not know what you want to hear. Other times, students are worried about saying something wrong.

CLIP 9.6 Ms. Dominguez works with a student who has an error
http://smarturl.it/CM9.6

CLIP 9.7 Ms. Byron elicits a student's thinking about an invented algorithm
http://smarturl.it/CM9.7

If students do not answer your questions at first, consider a different approach to eliciting their thinking. If the student has written something or used some tools, one option is to ask him if he can show you what he did. Another option is to ask the student to show you what she is doing while she is still solving the problem. As students show you how they solved the problem, you can talk about what you notice them doing to help them learn what it means to explain their strategy. For example, if a student starts solving a Join (Result Unknown) problem with 40 and 25 by placing 4 ten-rods in front of her, you could say, "I see that you started with 4 tens. Did you start with 4 tens?" Depending on the student, you could ask, "Why did you start with 4 tens?" You can also ask more specific questions, such as, "What did you do first when you were solving the problem?" "Did you use any tools, your fingers, the cubes, the pencil and paper? Can you tell me what you did with those?"

Some students are able to use strategies that they can not yet explain. This may be because a student's verbal abilities are not yet developed in a way that supports their mathematical explanation or because their understanding of the strategy is not solid enough for them to produce an explanation. In supporting students to explain their strategies, it is wise to be particularly careful not to encourage students to use less sophisticated strategies just because they are easier to explain. You can support students to develop their abilities to explain using the approaches shown above, and in the beginning, allow students to explain a piece of their strategy and to use language that makes sense to them.

Eliciting Student Thinking to Extend Mathematical Ideas

In eliciting students' thinking, CGI teachers also support students to extend their mathematical ideas by inviting them to go beyond what they have shared in some way. To extend or build on a student's mathematical thinking, you can ask questions, provide tools, and suggest different representations to encourage the student to try a new strategy or explore a new idea. Extending student thinking requires that the teacher know what strategies could come next in the development of students' mathematical thinking. In the earlier example, Ms. Reid asked Alex about tens in his solution. His written work showed that he could count on by ones and group them by fives to count the number of tallies he made. Ms. Reid knew that developing tens would advance his strategy use and that he had the beginnings of the idea in his written solution to this problem.

Although it is productive to support students to extend their thinking, it is not all up to you as the teacher. Students extend their ideas on their own, as they explain, use different tools, talk to other students, engage with other students as they share, and so on. It is also important to realize that supporting students to extend their ideas is not the goal of each interaction. You want to support students to extend their ideas when you see evidence that they clearly understand the strategy they are using and are starting to move toward using strategies at the next level. Supporting students to extend their thinking works best when students see themselves in charge of deciding if and when to take up a new idea. This also enables them to develop productive skills and identities as learners of mathematics.

CLIP 9.8 Ms. Grace works with a student to extend a mathematical idea
http://smarturl.it/CM9.8

CLIP 9.9 Ms. Barron works with students to extend a mathematical idea
http://smarturl.it/CM9.9

Eliciting student thinking starts with regularly asking students to explain their thinking. Consistently asking students to share their thinking, expecting each student to do so, and accepting whatever ideas students can provide will help students come to understand how to do math in your class, what it means to explain their mathematical ideas, and that everyone is capable of explaining mathematics.

As you work on developing your ability to elicit student thinking, consider the principles in Figure 9.5.

Principles for Eliciting Student Thinking

Consistently ask students to share their thinking.

Find ways for each student to explain his thinking to you or other students.

Follow up with specific questions drawing from what the student shared or did.

Support students to work all the way through the details of their strategies.

Ask about correct, incorrect, and incomplete strategies.

Watch for students to tell or show you that they are ready to be supported to adapt their strategy or try a new one.

Listen, observe. Try to not impose your ideas on students.

FIGURE 9.5

Several years ago, I went through my first summer session of CGI. I can vividly remember being slightly overwhelmed and wondering how long it would take for me to be able to slip this to the side and reinstitute "real teaching" in my classroom. While teaching for understanding and not memorization made sense to me, I didn't understand how an eight-year-old's thinking was supposed to guide the direction of an entire lesson. I remember the first day of school that year. It was about 2:30 in the afternoon and amazingly enough, I had run out of all those cutesy, first-of-the-year, "get to know you"–type activities. I had a room full of second-graders ready to pounce and I had to act fast. Out of desperation, I gathered all my little darlings in a circle on the floor, dusted off the Unifix cubes, and passed them around. While I don't remember the problems I gave the students, nor the strategies they used, I do remember their engagement—and I was surprised. Surprised that they had so much to say about exactly how they got their correct or incorrect *answers and shocked that they were so eager to share their ways of solving with their peers. Even after this experience, CGI was by no means cemented in my mind as one of the greatest teaching philosophies of all time, like it is now. I was busy "teaching" so CGI wasn't practiced on a daily or even weekly basis at first. In the beginning, I only "did CGI" when our [math] specialist was coming for a visit or when we were supposed to take student work to our next CGI meeting. However, over time, the more and more I practiced CGI with my students, the less generic and more authentic and genuinely probing my questions became. Because of this, slowly, my students' thinking became deeper and more advanced. While powerful, the change was so subtle, I'm not sure I realized it until the end of the year.*

[The] math specialist asked me to give a specific problem to my students to see what they would do. When I saw the problem, I was more than a little worried.

> *Rachel and her brother are making gift bags for 6 friends. Each bag has 3 pencils and 2 erasers in it. How many total items are there in 1 bag? How many total items are in 6 bags?*

"Oh, come ON!" I remember thinking. This problem involves two different operations, one being multiplication, and is a two-step problem at that. All I could think about was how embarrassed I was going to be when my students bombed this question. The numbers weren't all that large, but I thought that the overall complexity of the problem would surely do them in. Well, you know what? It didn't. In fact, they did amazing. When I got back together with the specialist to look at the student strategies, we were thrilled with the results. That's when she informed me that my students had just solved a fifth-grade problem. A fifth-grade benchmark released item.

It was then that I realized how powerful the work we had been doing with CGI had been. The countless questions and strategies and the hours of understanding the problems and listening to student thinking had paid off, and this was only a piece of the evidence. I then began reflecting on the work we had done that year and thinking about those first days in a circle on the carpet with the Unifix cubes. I began to realize that because the progress my students had made was so subtle and slow, that it was twice as meaningful as all the fast and furious "learning" and intensive remediation we had done in years passed. Since then, and the years that have passed, I find myself thinking every day of how thankful I am for CGI. It not only changed my students, but it changed me, as a teacher, as well.

—**Tara Sanders, teacher**

USING KNOWLEDGE OF CHILDREN'S THINKING TO GUIDE INSTRUCTION

All of the teaching practices described in this chapter and throughout the book are based on knowledge of children's mathematical thinking, including both knowledge of the research frameworks for how children typically progress and knowledge of the thinking of individual children in your classroom. Decisions about what problem to pose, what numbers to use, what questions to ask, who to ask, whose idea to share, whose idea could be connected to the strategy shared all can be supported by your knowledge of the development of children's mathematical thinking. Each of the teaching examples in this chapter involved teachers considering what they knew about students' mathematical thinking in general and what they knew about their own students' thinking in relation to those general ideas. Ms. Scott described why she posed the problem about Estebán and his marbles. Her rationale was linked to the two kinds of Invented Algorithms she had seen her students use for joining problems and wanting to support the use of similar strategies in a separating context (shown in the following video). Ms. Byron purposefully stopped to check on Samuel as she had noticed that he was still working to make sense of tens and use them to solve problems even though he might not have developed enough understanding to do so. The framework detailed in earlier chapters can help you know what to listen for and how to think about where to go next. We know from our research that even teachers new to CGI can readily listen to their students' mathematical thinking and, as they make sense of this thinking in relation to the framework, they get better and better at using what they hear from their students to make instructional decisions.

CLIP 9.10 Ms. Scott explains how she decided to pose the marbles problem http://smarturl.it/CM9.10

I need a framework. I definitely think there's a framework with CGI that's made a big difference for me. Strategies have been identified, there's definitely a hierarchy. That's helped. . . . I mean, a lot of curriculum materials have problem solving. A lot of them do. But you don't know what to do with it. I mean, how do you decide why problems would be more difficult than others for children to solve? You know, what makes this problem difficult? And with CGI, that has been researched, and I think accurately researched, and it enables me to know why certain kids are struggling, what I can do to facilitate that. So I think a framework is critical. For a person like me, especially. I want to know where I'm going and where I'm taking them. So I need that framework.

—Sue Berthouex, teacher

10

Developing Classroom Practice: Engaging Students with Each Other's Ideas

If you are asking students to share their strategies with a partner or the class, you have taken an essential step in engaging students with each other's mathematical ideas. You have probably noticed that sharing ideas is helpful for the student doing the sharing, but you might worry that it is not as helpful for those not sharing their thinking. However, our research shows that engaging with the details of another student's thinking is productive for both the student sharing and for the students listening (see Webb et al. 2013 and Appendix A). Engaging with other students' mathematical ideas is one of the best ways to support students to generate insights into mathematical relationships and develop more sophisticated strategies. In this chapter, we provide a series of examples and a set of principles that show how you can productively support students to not only explain their ideas but also engage with others' ideas.

LEVELS OF ENGAGEMENT

Engaging students in each other's mathematical ideas involves more than asking students to listen while other students share. Engagement in each other's mathematical ideas requires students to notice, understand, and evaluate another student's strategy; this kind of engagement often initially requires teacher support. We categorize students' engagement in each other's ideas into three levels to help direct attention to student learning:

- comparing an idea to another student's idea
- attending to the details of another's idea
- building on another's idea.

Each level represents valid and mathematically important ways for students to engage. Research shows that students who participate in all three levels of engagement have the highest levels of mathematical achievement.

Comparing an Idea to Another Student's Idea

Creating an environment where students solve problems using different strategies provides students with the opportunity to notice whether someone else solved the problem the same way they did. If a student decides a strategy is not the same, she can then evaluate the strategy to determine if she agrees or disagrees with the reasoning. Sometimes this level of engagement occurs as students use the "thumbs up" signal to note their agreement with a shared strategy; other times students individually or chorally call out whether they did it the same way. This form of engagement asks students to look at another student's strategy in relation to their own ideas and make a judgment. This approach gives students a reason to attend to what is being shared, and it is a productive way to introduce students to the concept of attending to each other's ideas.

Attending to the Details of Another Student's Ideas

With support, students can move beyond deciding that another student's strategy is the same or different from their own and attend to the details of the strategy that was shared. This occurs, for instance, when students repeat or explain what they heard someone share, explain a representation that was displayed by another student, explain specifically how a strategy they heard is similar to another strategy, or ask a question about an aspect of someone's strategy.

Building on or Adding to Another Student's Ideas

When students engage with the details of someone else's strategy, it opens the possibility of building on that student's ideas. A student can, for instance, add further detail, correct a part of the strategy that was inaccurate, make a strategy more efficient, propose an alternative strategy, explain how the alternative strategy was different than the strategy that was shared, justify why a strategy works and how it could be used on other problems, or even co-construct a solution with another student. In each of these cases, the student has to make sense of another student's idea in a way that enables him to engage with the details and build on them.

> *O*ne *of the challenges for me was not being in the position of "I am in charge" and telling them what to do. Having the confidence in them to step back and let them struggle, and to allow other students through discussions talk about it and show their thinking, because with everybody thinking differently, they may not think about it the way I do but seeing how their friends do it might help.*
>
> **—Christy Byron, teacher**

SUPPORTING STUDENTS TO ENGAGE IN EACH OTHER'S IDEAS

CGI teachers have found a range of ways to structure and support student engagement in each other's mathematical ideas. Some of these approaches may be familiar to you because you have tried them, you have seen other teachers use them, or you use them when teaching in other content areas. As with posing problems and eliciting students' strategies, there is no one way or even one best way to support students' engagement with each other's ideas. There is also no one classroom configuration that best supports students to engage with one another's ideas; we have seen teachers step in and engage with one pair of students, orchestrate a small-group sharing, or involve students in each other's ideas in the context of a whole-class conversation. However, we do know that the teacher sets the tone, invites students to engage with each other, and supports them to figure out how to engage in a way that moves beyond agreeing or disagreeing that the strategy is correct.

Fostering Students' Engagement in One Third-Grade Class

We start with an example of students engaging with each other's ideas during the portion of the lesson where the teacher asked students to share their strategies. The example involves a number of students engaging with one student's strategy, contributing their own ideas about the strategy, and talking about these ideas with each other. The students are engaged with each other at all levels. The teacher makes many moves to support students' engagement with each other's ideas. We start with this complex example to provide you with a sense of how these moves are orchestrated in relation to each other with many students trying to participate. Following this example, we break the work of supporting

CLIP 10.1 Students in Ms. Grace's class share and compare strategies http://smarturl.it/CM10.1

students' engagement down into some smaller segments so you can attend to the different types of teacher moves that can support student engagement with each other's ideas.

Stacie Grace posed the following problem to her third-grade class.

> *Yesterday I went to the store, and I bought 8 boxes of candy. There were 23 pieces of candy in each box. How many pieces of candy do I have altogether?*

The students solved the problem at their tables. Most students worked independently. Ms. Grace interacted with students individually while they were solving the problem, and some students briefly consulted with each other during the problem-solving process. Ms. Grace asked four students to write their strategies on the whiteboard at the front of the room while the rest of the students either finished solving the problem or solved the problem using a different strategy.

We join this example at the point where the students are gathered on the carpet in front of the whiteboard and looking over the strategies students have shared. Students can be overheard saying, "I did it that way," or "I didn't write it like that." Ms. Grace asks Addison to share how he solved the problem. Before he starts, Ms. Grace asks the class to "remind us about the problem we are working on," and with student input they agree on "We had 8 boxes with 23 pieces of candy in each box." Addison used a Direct Modeling with Tens strategy (see Figure 10.1, Addison is on the far right). Ms. Grace turns to

FIGURE 10.1 Students sharing their strategies

Caden and says, "Addison has put his up here and I want us to look at it for a minute, and Caden, I am going to have you talk, and Addison, I want you to look and be the person who thinks, 'Is this what I really did?'" As you read through this example, notice how students were engaging with both Addison's strategy and other students' ideas about Addison's strategy.

Ms. G: *So here is Addison's strategy [points to his strategy on the board; see Figure 10.2a].*

Caden: I see.

Ms. G: *[looks at Caden] Did you notice something?*

Caden: Yes, I know what he did.

Ms. G: *You know what he did? What did he do?*

Caden: Well first he did . . .

Ms. G: *Come up, come up and talk to us.*

Caden: [comes to the board and points to the base-ten blocks] First he did 10, 20, and then 20, 21, 22, 23, and that equals 23.

Ms. G: *Where did that come from?*

Caden: You have, like, you have 23 of them.

Ms. G: *23 what?*

Caden: Candies.

Ms. G: *Addison, did you do that? [counts them out loud just as Caden did] Then what is this [pointing to the second group of 2 tens and 3 ones]?*

Students: The same thing.

Ms. G: *The same thing? So this is 1 box and this is another box, is this the second box and how many pieces are in here?*

Students: 10, 20, 21, 22, 23. 23.

Ms. G: *How many boxes did he do altogether?*

Students: 8.

Ms. G: *8 boxes, and how much in each box?*

Students: 23.

Drake: Ms. G, I did mine different. I counted by tens and did the ones later.

Ms. G: *Oh, okay, Addison, is this what you have done so far?*

Addison: Yes.

Ms. G: *Okay, I want you to listen to Drake and see if that is what you did.*

Drake: I counted 10, 20, 30 . . .

Ms. G: *Come show us.*

Drake: [comes to the board and counts the ten strips and then the ones] 10, 20 . . .160. Then I said 161, 162, . . .184.

Ms. G: *Addison, is this how you did that?*

Addison: Yes.

Ms. G: *So how did you [to Addison] write this on your paper?*

Addison: [draws boxes, and puts 10 + 10 + 3 = 23 in each box; see Figure 10.2b].

Ms. G: *Katie, what did he do?*

Katie: Wrote 10 plus 10 plus 3.

Ms. G: *Why did he do that, why did he break the 23 up into 10 and a 10 and a 3?*

Katie: It equals 23.

Students: I think we could do it easier.

Ms. G: *[to whole class] What do you think, is there another way to write these? [long pause]*

Patty: Twenties.

Ms. G: *Twenties, yes.*

Patty: You could do 20 + 20 + 20 + 20 + 20 + 20 + 20 + 20.

Ms. G: *How is that the same as Addison? Or different?*

Sam: Instead of tens you can write twenties 'cause you can count by 20.

Ms. G: *Okay.*

Patty: And 20 is 10 and 10.

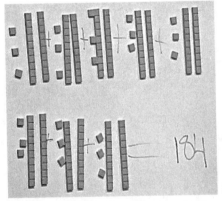

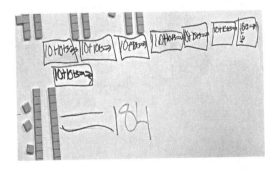

(a)   (b)

FIGURE 10.2 Addison's strategy with boxes

The class continued. Addison described how he counted the tens and then the ones to figure out that Ms. Grace bought 184 pieces of candy. He showed how his expressions 10 + 10 + 3 could be counted just like the base-ten blocks. Other students shared their strategies, while the class, Addison included, reflected on how each shared strategy related back to Addison's Direct Modeling with Tens strategy.

Ms. Grace supported the students to engage with each other's ideas in a number of different ways. She started by making sure everyone was clear about the problem they were solving; this put everyone in a position to engage. She called on Caden, who said he already knew what Addison had done before he shared. She asked Addison to listen to Caden and decide if that is what he actually did to solve the problem, since he was the authority on his solution. As Caden started to share, Ms. Grace interrupted him and called him to the board so he could point to what he was talking about. This move supported other students to reflect on the details of the strategy because now they could see exactly what parts of Addison's representation Caden was referring to.

Throughout the interchange, Ms. Grace called on several students in the class to participate in building on the details of the strategy. She called on Drake and Katie to add to what had been said. She pressed the students for details and asked them to relate what they were saying back to the problem. For example, she asked, "Where did that come from?" "23 what?" She came back to Addison to ask how he wrote his strategy on the paper and he added to his own strategy on the board with a new representation (boxes with 10 + 10 + 3). Ms. Grace supported Patty to add on to Addison's strategy with another idea of how to write his strategy down. Ms. Grace related Patty's adding of twenties back to Addison's strategy. She regularly returned to Addison to find out if he thought what was being discussed was the same or different from what he had done, allowing Addison to own his ideas throughout the exchange.

A particularly striking aspect of this example is that before Addison even began to share his strategy, students sitting on the rug were commenting on the strategies on the board and relating them to their own. Ms. Grace had established a routine during sharing in which students compared strategies on the board to what they had done to solve the problem, so explicitly asking them to do so was no longer required. Ms. Grace spent considerable time at the beginning of the year prompting students to examine the strategies written at the board to see if they did it the same way and to assess whether or not they agreed with the strategies. The students knew what was expected.

While this example highlights a number of productive moves for engaging students in each other's mathematical ideas, Ms. Grace's teaching was driven by the mathematical goals she had for her students. These goals were determined by her knowledge of children's mathematical development, her knowledge of each of her students' mathematical development, and the mathematical standards for her grade level. She chose a problem to support that set of goals. She watched for opportunities throughout the lesson to address her goals, and she used the goals to guide who shared and how she engaged students with each other's ideas. As Ms. Grace told us, "Caden, for instance, when I was walking around he was counting by ones and he really needed to see what Addison was doing because Addison was counting by tens, so I asked him a lot of questions. I wanted Caden to see 10 as a useful unit. I had Caden and I had Katie, Katie did not have a valid strategy. I knew that if she saw Addison sharing and just looked at his thinking and not even hearing what he did, she and Caden, they could reason and say, 'I know what, I think I know what he did' and explain it, because if you explain it, you can understand it better. This was a big deal for Caden. He often does not have a valid strategy and he really felt a part of this today."

I always notate on a clipboard what strategies I have seen, so that when I am doing discussion I can refer to that, and I know who I need to call on, who needs to tune into what.

—Stacie Grace, teacher

Teaching Moves for Supporting Students to Engage in Each Other's Strategies

Next we look at some shorter interactions in other classes to illustrate some options for supporting students to engage with each other's ideas. We provide short interchanges among students, mediated by the teacher, that represent common approaches to encouraging students to engage with each other's ideas: asking students if their way is the same or different than another, asking students to explain someone else's strategy, and inviting questions of a student who has described a strategy. The intention is not for you to make sure you use all of these approaches or make the exact same moves, but rather to provide a range of examples that enable you to make sense of what might work in your classroom and to have a range of ideas to draw upon in different situations to support your students in engaging with each other's ideas.

Is Your Way the Same or Different?
CGI teachers often begin to engage students in each other's ideas by inviting students to indicate if the way they solved the problem was the same or different than the one that another student shared.

Example 1: Comparison with One Student's Strategy

Students in Ms. Contreras' class had just solved a Join (Result Unknown) problem and were sharing their strategies. One student, Angela, showed her Direct Modeling with Tens strategy. Before asking any other students to share, Ms. Contreras asked the class: "So, we have seen Angela's strategy. Thumbs up if you think your way is like Angela's. I see a number of you used the same strategy. Did anyone solve it differently than Angela? David, you think you did it differently? [David nods yes.] Can you tell us what you did?"

Example 2: Comparison with Two Students' Strategies

In another class, Ms. Lara had two students share their strategies before asking the rest of the students to indicate which strategy they used. After both strategies had been presented, Ms. Lara said to the class: "Look up here [pointing to solutions on the board]. I noticed when I was checking in that some people have done it Gavin's way, some people have done it Allie's way, maybe some people have solved it in a way that is different from both Gavin and Allie. If you solved the problem like Allie or Gavin can you point to the one that is like yours? Tyson, you are pointing to Allie's way. Can you tell me one way yours is like Allie's?"

Both Ms. Contreras and Ms. Lara engaged students in each other's ideas. Both started at a comparing level; the students were asked to note if their strategy was like someone else's but not detail the ways in which that might be the case. Asking students to give a thumbs up or point to the strategy that was like theirs supported students to attend to the strategy that was shared and perhaps begin to compare it to their own. The teachers then continued to support students to engage with each other's strategies. Ms. Contreras asked a student to share a different strategy. If she wanted to engage David in Angela's idea, she might have asked David (after he shared) how he saw his as different than Angela's. Ms. Lara did this when she asked Tyson one way his strategy was the same as Allie's. To answer Ms. Lara's question, Tyson needed to attend to the details of Allie's strategy.

Explaining Another Student's Strategy

When a student shares her strategy on the board or a projector, it provides an opening for the teacher to invite students to figure out what the student did to solve the problem before asking the student who generated the strategy to explain it. Here are some examples of how teachers helped students engage with explaining another student's written work.

Example 1: Asking Students to Provide Details

In Ms. Jee's class, the students had solved a Separate (Result Unknown) problem: *Matthew had 12 boxes of cereal. He gave 5 boxes to his cousins. How many boxes of cereal does Matthew have left?* As is the regular practice, two students shared their strategies on the board while the rest of the students sat at their desks examining the strategies on the board. George drew a Direct Modeling strategy on the board. Ms. Jee noted that Stella had used a Direct Modeling strategy just as George had.

> **Ms. J:** *Stella, do you want to come up to explain George's way?*
>
> **Stella:** I did exactly the same thing. George did, um, he made 12 boxes, and then he took 5 boxes away.
>
> **Ms. J:** *Okay, great. Can you show me the boxes he took away?*
>
> **Stella:** [goes to the board] See here are the 12 boxes, and there are *x*'s on these 5. Those are the ones he took away, and he got 7 just like me.

Example 2: Tell Me One Thing

Ms. Lloyd uses the document camera when she wants students to look closely at one student's work. Ms. Lloyd shared Jacob's solution to a Compare problem: *Jamaal read 17 books. His sister read 9 books. How many more books did Jamaal read than his sister?*

Jacob had used a Counting strategy. Jacob drew two people. He put a 17 under one to note Jamaal's books and a 9 under his sister. He wrote 10, 11, 12, 13, 14, 15, 16, 17 and under these numbers he wrote the numbers 1 to 8 (see Figure 10.3).

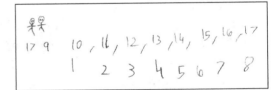

FIGURE 10.3 Jacob's strategy

> **Ms. L:** *Okay, so here is Jacob's strategy. Everyone take a minute to look at what he has here. See if you can figure out what he was doing. [pauses for 30 seconds] Can someone tell me one thing that you notice? Kim?*
>
> **Kim:** I noticed that he made numbers for Jamaal's and his sister's books.
>
> **Ms. L:** *What numbers?*
>
> **Kim:** 17 and 9.
>
> **Ms. L:** *Okay. Can other people see that? Someone else, what one thing do you notice? Carl?*
>
> **Carl:** Next to the 9, he put numbers 10, 11, 12, 13, 14, 15, 16, 17.
>
> **Ms. L:** *Who can tell us more about the numbers Carl is talking about?*

[The students continue to talk about what they notice and Ms. Lloyd gets them to be explicit about the details of the Counting strategy.]

Example 3: What Is Next?

Ms. Moore asked Sunanda to share her strategy for a Part-Part-Whole (Whole Unknown) problem: *There are 14 boys and 9 girls working in the garden. How many children are working in the garden?* Ms. Moore wanted to have the students follow along with Sunanda's strategy as many students had tried using the same strategy.

[Sunanda is at the board and is writing down her strategy.]

Ms. M: *Sunanda, can you stop where you are, even though you are not finished? Who can tell us what Sunanda has done so far? Maria.*

Maria: She made 14 lines.

Ms. M: *Okay, let's count her lines together and see if there are 14. Sunanda, will you point to them while we count. [Class counts aloud the marks to 14.] So who knows why she made 14 lines? Lilia?*

Lilia: Because there are 14 boys.

Ms. M: *Okay, who has an idea of what Sunanda might do next? Don't call it out, just think about it, and if you have an idea, give me a thumbs up. [pause] Sunanda, what did you do next, can you show us?*

Inviting a student to make sense of someone else's written strategy requires students to engage with the details of that student's strategy. Students new to this process may describe generalities such as, "She drew a picture," or "We both used the blue blocks." Follow-up questions can help students focus on the relevant details. In Ms. Jee's class, Stella explained that she did it the same and told briefly what that meant to her. Ms. Jee followed up by asking her to provide more details of George's strategy. Ms. Lloyd asked students to only tell her one thing about Jacob's strategy, not repeat the entire strategy, so that she could both engage more students and get them to attend to the details of Jacob's strategy. Ms. Moore stopped Sunanda at key places in her sharing and asked students to predict what Sunanda might do next. This focused students on particular details and provided something for students to watch for as Sunanda continued her sharing.

Do You Want to Ask a Question?

In establishing norms for sharing, it can be productive to invite students to ask questions or make comments about another student's shared idea. This requires regularly inviting students to make a comment or ask questions of another student about her strategy so they learn about the kinds of questions that may be productive. Initially students' questions often are not related to mathematically relevant details of the strategy shared.

Teacher follow-up questions can support students to attend to the details that are important for solving the problem. Ms. Hayward, Mr. McMillan, and Ms. Kern's examples show three different ways to support question asking as a way to engage in each other's ideas.

Example 1: Talk to a Partner

Ms. Hayward posed a Measurement Division problem: *Annette bought 18 donuts. She wants to put the donuts in boxes. She can put 6 donuts in each box. How many boxes will she need?* She invited her students to ask questions of Morgan who had just shared his Direct Modeling strategy with the class.

> **Ms. H:** *Do you all understand how Morgan did this? [Students nod and say yes.] Great. Turn and talk to your partner and see if you can come up with a question you could ask Morgan. [Students pair share for a minute; Ms. Hayward listens in.]*
>
> **Ms. H:** *Who has a question for Morgan? Rodrigo?*
>
> **Rodrigo:** Why did you do it that way?
>
> **Ms. H:** *Rodrigo, I like that you have a question about why he did it that way. Can you ask about one part of what he did and ask him why he did that part that way?*
>
> **Rodrigo:** Why did you make the boxes?
>
> **Ms. H:** *Rodrigo, how many boxes did Morgan make?*
>
> **Rodrigo:** [pause] 3.
>
> **Ms. H:** *Can you ask the question and this time talk about the three boxes?*
>
> **Rodrigo:** Why did you make 3 boxes?

Ms. Hayward provided students with time to talk to a partner before asking a question in the whole group. This created an opportunity for more students to participate and for students to figure out together a question to ask. She then followed up on Rodrigo's initial question, starting with what he asked and supporting him to attend to something specific in Morgan's strategy.

Example 2: Focus on the Details

Mr. McMillan posed a Join (Result Unknown) problem about one of the students in the class: *Sophie has 5 red balloons. Her friends gave her 11 more balloons. How many balloons does Sophie have now?* He called on Sophie, who solved the problem by counting on her fingers: "12, 13, 14, 15, 16," holding up a finger with each count. Mr. McMillan repeated Sophie's solution and then asked another student what he thought about it.

> **Mike:** I don't get why you didn't count from 5.
> **Sophie:** I knew I had 5 red balloons and then I got 11 more and 11 is faster.
> **Mr. M:** *Can you tell him why you think 11 is faster? Do other people have an idea about that?*
> **Sophie:** Because you don't have to count as many; you can start with the bigger one and it is the same.

Mr. McMillan started by restating Sophie's strategy and then turned to Mike to see how he was thinking about what Sophie said. Mike asked a specific question that Sophie then responded to. Mike was able to engage with the details of Sophie's strategy, and Sophie had a chance to engage with Mike's question and further elaborate her own ideas.

Example 3: Students at Different Levels

A group of first-graders in Ms. Kern's class were solving a Part-Part-Whole (Whole Unknown) problem: *John had 8 trucks and 7 airplanes. How many vehicles did John have?* When Cassie solved the problem, she used a Direct Modeling strategy by drawing a box with the 8 circles for the trucks and another box with 7 circles for the airplanes and counted each circle to get 15. She shared her strategy with the class, and Ms. Kern asked if there were any questions for Cassie.

> **Travis:** Wouldn't it be easier if you just moved 2 of the airplanes over with the box of 8 cause that would give you 10 and then you can easily add the other 5 left to have 15?
> **Ms. K:** *Cassie, do you understand what Travis is saying?*
> **Cassie:** But you, you can't move them. These [first box] are trucks and these [second box] are airplanes. You can't mix them. You can't put the airplanes with the trucks. It said 8 trucks.
> **Ms. K:** *What do other people think?*

Travis could think beyond trucks and airplanes and move airplanes to the "truck box," while Cassie was adamant that one group was trucks and the other was airplanes and the vehicles needed to stay in the right group. Even so, Travis had a chance to make sense of Cassie's idea in relation to his own, Cassie got to hear his argument and say why she

CLIP 10.2 Ms. Byron supports students to engage with each other's ideas http://smarturl.it/CM10.2

disagreed, and the class was able to hear more about the details underlying how the students were thinking about their strategies.

In this example, we see that students do not always understand the mathematical ideas in the same ways even though they may benefit from hearing them. So while a student can add to another student's strategy, the original student may not be able to make sense of the contribution or question that gets asked.

Discussing How Shared Strategies Are the Same or Different: An Extended Example

Another way to engage students in each other's ideas is to ask students to look across a set of shared strategies and discuss how the strategies are the same or different. To illustrate the teacher moves that can support productive engagement across levels when discussing similarities and differences across strategies, we again turn to an extended classroom example. This is not the only way to carry out such discussions and it is quite complex given the large number of students who share, but it serves as a way for you to see the particular moves a teacher can make to support the conversation. These same interactions can occur even if only two or three students share.

CLIP 10.3 Ms. Barron's class discusses a student's Invented Algorithm http://smarturl.it/CM10.3

Heather Barron's third-grade class solved this Join (Change Unknown) problem:

> *Gilberto had 81 stickers. Then he bought some more and now he has 312 stickers. How many did he buy?*

Ms. Barron asked five students to share their strategies on the board. As they were putting their strategies up, the other students cleared their areas of counters and papers and came to the floor in front of the board. Ms. Barron reminded the students that while they were waiting they should be looking at the strategies being put up on the board (Figure 10.4).

Before getting started on individual student sharing, Ms. Barron told the students to find their partners, look at the strategies, and talk to each other about what they noticed. You could hear students say things like, "I think the most efficient one is . . ." or, "I did it like she did." Ms. Barron moved around, listened in, and asked questions. In response to a student saying all the strategies are subtraction, she asked the student what she noticed about the subtraction. Ms. Barron asked the students to share what they noticed, and they

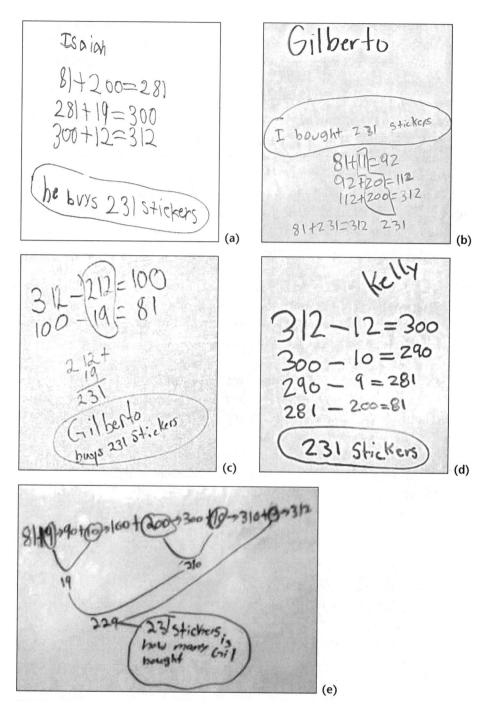

FIGURE 10.4 Five srategies shared at the board in Ms. Barron's class

then spent about four minutes in whole-class conversation about what students noticed across strategies. Ms. Barron invited the first student to share her strategy. Ms. Barron asked other students to comment and ask questions and they did. She did this for each of the sharers. At this point in the year, the students were quite skilled at engaging in the mathematically relevant details of each other's strategies.

We drop into the lesson for a conversation students were having about Kelly's strategy. Each of the students before Kelly shared an Incrementing Invented Algorithm that modeled the action in the Join (Change Unknown) problem; they all started with 81 and added on in increments until they reached 312. In contrast, Kelly used a Subtraction Incrementing Invented Algorithm that started with 312 and took away in increments until she reached 81. Ms. Barron asked questions to help the students analyze how Kelly's Subtraction Invented Algorithm was similar to another student's Addition Invented Algorithm (see Figure 10.4d).

Ms. B: Okay, now we are going to have Kelly come up here and share. Ready, Kelly?

Kelly: Well, I first, I started with 312, I took away 12 and equaled 300, I took away 10 and it equaled 290, I took away 9 and it equaled 281, I took away 200 and it equaled 81. [Kelly does not yet explain where her answer of 231 comes from.]

Ms. B: Wow, I am really confused. I thought the story said something about how about Gilberto had 81 stickers and then he bought some more and after that he had 312 stickers. I am not seeing that in Kelly's. Can someone help me with that? David, what are you thinking?

David: You can just switch the number sentence.

Ms. B: What do you mean I can switch the number sentence?

David: In the last one [Kelly's] you can say 281 – 200 = 81, you could say 81 + 200 = 281.

Ms. B: Oh, I can say 81 plus 200 would get me 281, then what [pointing to the pieces of Kelly's notation]?

Students: 281 plus 9 is 290.

Students: That is the same as Isaiah's [see Figure 10.4].

Ms. B: Okay, one at a time, can you keep going what were you thinking [to David]?

David: [picks up from the 281 plus 9] 281 plus 9 equals 290, 290 plus 10 is 300, plus 12 is 312.

Ms. B: Okay, so what are you all thinking?

Gissel: It is the same as mine and Isaiah's.

Students: Kelly has a 200, 19, 12 just like Isaiah.

Ms. B: Is that true, so you are saying I could subtract or I could . . .

Students: Add.

Student: You have to put the 10 and the 9 together [pointing to Kelly's work].

Ms. B: [circles Kelly's take away 10 and take away 9] So I have to put these two together to get the 19? So where would this be in Isaiah's? Who can show us? Who can find it in Isaiah's work? Marlene [she comes up to the board]. Okay, so David said he would start here [points to the 281 in the bottom line of Kelly's picture].

David: No, the 81.

Ms. B: Okay, Marlene can you show us this, the 281 – 200 is 81, in Isaiah's picture? Draw a line or an arrow.

Marlene: [draws a line on the board under the 200 in Isaiah's first line, 81 + 200 = 281; see Figure 10.5].

Ms. B: Okay, so this would be like . . . ? Can I draw a line from there to Kelly's? [draws a line across the board to the corresponding lines in their solutions—Isaiah's first and Kelly's last; see Figure 10.6].

Ms. B: So are they the same? [Students call out yes, but subtracting.] Well, what about this, can we find the next step? Nancy? [They continued connecting each piece of the two solutions to each other with different students taking on each piece. They go on to talk about why subtraction worked.]

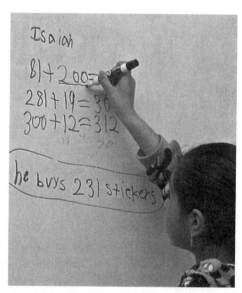

FIGURE 10.5 Marlene underlining Isaiah's strategy

Ms. Barron supported her students to engage with each other's ideas. She started by asking them to take a quick look across strategies before any sharing started. This oriented them to the strategies and had them thinking about how they might be the same or different before sharing started. It also communicated to the students that making sense of others' strategies was their responsibility and part of doing math in this classroom. She then chose five students to share. Three of the students used a similar Addition

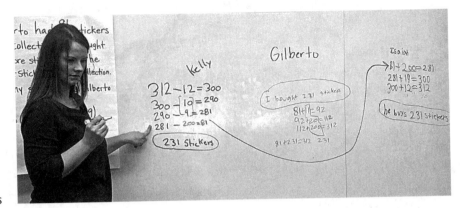

FIGURE 10.6
Ms. Barron connecting Isaiah's and Kelly's strategies

Incrementing Invented Algorithm but added in different increments. This required students to examine the nuanced differences between the strategies. The fourth student, Kelly, had a different approach to solving the problem, one that raised the issue of the relationships between addition and subtraction.

Ms. Barron invited the students to make sense of Kelly's strategy by explicitly raising the issue that Kelly was taking away and the problem said that Gilberto bought more. Ms. Barron asked students to make sense of this, and in doing so, they connected Kelly's ideas to Isaiah's strategy. Ms. Barron required students to attend carefully to the details of the representation on the board and the strategies they represented. She made sure David worked all the way through his idea. She marked on the board how students wanted to combine Kelly's 10 and 9 to match the 19 in Isaiah's. She let the students do the mathematical work. She could have stepped in to explain how the separating approach Kelly took and the joining approach Isaiah took were the same and how they were different. But instead she supported the students to struggle together and attend to the details of each of the strategies to compare them to each other. The students' discussion moved beyond a single solution and involved a discussion of mathematical ideas that may not have arisen in examining or describing a single strategy.

Ms. Barron's decisions about how and when to engage students in each other's ideas were based on her goals and her knowledge of her students' mathematical thinking. Her mathematical goals included working on place value through multidigit problem solving and developing understanding of the relationship between the addition and subtraction Incrementing Invented Algorithms. Ms. Barron wrote a problem that she felt would support these goals and meet the needs of the range of her students. When she decided on who to have share, she thought about these goals, her students' knowledge and dispositions, and how to engage the range of students in her class. "I chose Gissel because she incremented and was following the structure of the problem, when she incremented she was doing it in smaller chunks, she was trying to get to benchmark numbers. I wanted to compare that to…Gilberto, who was very specific about the numbers he was using in relation to the 312 . . . I chose Isaiah because . . . I wanted them to see the efficiency in adding bigger chunks to start . . . And then I chose Kelly because she did not follow the structure of the problem, she actually subtracted, but she subtracted using small chunks to get to benchmark numbers and I wanted to compare and contrast that with Karen, who subtracted also but used bigger numbers to make hers more efficient."

CLIP 10.4 Ms. Dominguez's class engages with each other's ideas
http://smarturl.it/CM10.4

CLIP 10.5 Ms. Scott engages her class in a student's shared strategy
http://smarturl.it/CM10.5

PRINCIPLES FOR SUPPORTING STUDENT ENGAGEMENT

As we've seen, supporting students to engage with each other's mathematical ideas creates opportunities for students to reflect on their strategy in relation to others' strategies, explain and justify strategies that are similar and different than their own, recognize key elements of strategies, make sense of representations that are the same and different from their own, engage in discussion across mathematical ideas, and discuss key mathematical ideas that emerge. These types of engagement can support students as they develop in their strategy use, and their understanding of the operations.

This type of learning does not occur because the teacher enacted a "right" move to engage students; rather, the teacher used what she knew about the development of children's thinking coupled with her knowledge of her students' mathematical thinking and the standards and curricula to create her mathematical goals for students, and she used those goals to drive how she made in-the-moment decisions about engaging students.

You can create a classroom environment that supports this type of learning by attending to the principles in Figure 10.7.

Supporting students to engage with each other's ideas can start as simply asking students if they solved the problem the same way as someone who just shared and can become as complex as discussing across strategies the relationship between addition and subtraction. It will take some time to establish routines that support student engagement

Principles for Supporting Student Engagement in Each Other's Mathematical Thinking
Develop a set of routines that support students to consistently engage in some way with each other's ideas.
Attend to the different levels at which particular students are engaging with each other's ideas.
Follow up with students as they engage with each other's ideas to support students' engagement with the details of the strategy.
Provide as many students as possible opportunities to engage with a student's idea or to have other students engage with theirs.
Position students as the experts about their strategies and as capable of engaging with other students about their strategies.
Position students to engage with each other's ideas on their own without your participation.

FIGURE 10.7

with each other's ideas. Students will need some guidance from you to get started. Use some of the strategies you already have for engaging students in critical thinking in other subject areas. You can start by asking students to compare their idea to others' ideas, but students will benefit the most if they engage with the details of another student's ideas either within or across strategies or add on to another student's ideas.

11

Mathematical Principles Underlying Children's Mathematics

This chapter provides insight into the mathematical principles underlying children's mathematics. When children generate their own increasingly efficient and flexible strategies for solving problems, they naturally engage in a process we call *relational thinking,* in which they explicitly or implicitly use fundamental properties of number and operations in their intuitive strategies. The purpose of the chapter is to describe how children's strategies depend on and contribute to their understanding of the fundamental properties of number and operations. Relational thinking and the role of fundamental properties of number and operations in integrating the learning of arithmetic and algebra are discussed in more detail in *Thinking Mathematically* (Carpenter, Franke, and Levi 2003).

FUNDAMENTAL PROPERTIES IN CHILDREN'S STRATEGIES

One of the earliest uses of a fundamental property is seen in children's Counting On from Larger strategy for addition. In the following example, a child implicitly draws on the commutative property of addition when solving a Join (Result Unknown) problem.

Owen had 3 rocks. He got 12 more rocks for his birthday. How many rocks does Owen have now?

> **Karen:** 3, 4 [holds up a finger when she says, "4" and then holds up another finger for each count after that] 5, 6, 7, 8, 9, 10, 11, 12, 13, that's 10, how many rocks did he get?
>
> **Ms. F:** *He got 12 more rocks.*
>
> **Karen:** What did I do?
>
> **Ms. F:** *Why don't you start again?*
>
> **Karen:** 3, 4 [holds up a finger when she says, "4" and then holds up another finger for each count after that] 5, 6, 7, 8 9, 10, 11, 12, 13, that's 10, but he got 12 and I don't have any more fingers. [long pause] Oh I have an idea! I can do 12 and 3 more, 12, 13, 14, 15. 15 rocks!
>
> **Ms. F:** *Are you sure that works?*
>
> **Karen:** Yes. Because when you are putting things together it doesn't matter which you count first, 3 and 12 more is the same as 12 and 3 more.
>
> **Ms. F:** *Karen, that is really important. When we share our ideas with the class, maybe you could share that idea.*

In this example, Ms. F noticed Karen used the idea that when you are adding numbers, you can change the order and still get the same amount ($3 + 12 = 12 + 3$). Ms. F wanted to ensure that Karen shared this beginning awareness of the *commutative property of addition* ($a + b = b + a$) with the class so that students could discuss it as a group, giving other students the opportunity to share their perspectives on this property.

In the following example, Leon generated a Derived Fact using another fundamental property of addition, the associative property of addition.

> *8 birds were sitting on a wire. 5 more birds joined them. How many birds were there then?*

> **Leon:** 8 and 2 is 10 and then 3 more is 13.
>
> **Mr. P:** *Rather than adding 5 all at once, what did you do?*
>
> **Leon:** I first added 2 and then I added 3, 2 plus 3 is the same as 5.
>
> **Mr. P:** *Does that always work?*
>
> **Leon:** Yes, when you are adding, you can add part of the number and then the rest of the number.

Leon's statement, "When you are adding, you can add part of the number and then the rest of the number," indicates that he is implicitly using the *associative property of addition* $(a + b) + c = a + (b + c)$. His strategy can be written as:

$$8 + 5 = \boxed{8 + (2 + 3) = (8 + 2) + 3} = 10 + 3 = 13$$

The highlighted section shows where his strategy draws on the associative property of addition.

All Derived Fact strategies involve relational thinking in that they depend on properties of operations and/or relationships between operations. A property that plays a central role in deriving multiplication number facts, understanding base-ten number concepts, and using Invented Algorithms is the *distributive property of multiplication over addition*, $a \times (b + c) = (a \times b) + (a \times c)$ (often just called the *distributive property*). The use of the distributive property in multiplication Derived Facts is illustrated by the following strategy for finding 4×7:

> **Rico:** 2 groups of 7 is 14. Another 2 groups of 7 would also be 14, 14 plus 14 is 28 so 4 groups of 7 is 28.

In his solution, Rico implicitly uses the distributive property of multiplication over addition in his discussion of adding 2 groups of 7 to 2 groups of 7 to get 4 groups of 7. He did not know the answer to 4×7, so starting with the fact that $4 = 2 + 2$, he used the distributive property to transform the problem (4×7) into problems ($2 \times 7 = 14$ and $14 + 14 = 28$) that he did know the answer for. Rico's strategy can be written as:

$$4 \times 7 = \boxed{(2 + 2) \times 7 = (2 \times 7) + (2 \times 7)} = 14 + 14 = 28$$

where the highlighted section represents his use of the distributive property.

The distributive property comes into play in most calculations involving multidigit numbers that make use of base-ten number concepts. For example, in adding 40 + 30, older children typically use their knowledge of 4 + 3 to combine 4 tens and 3 tens to get 7 tens or 70. This strategy relies on the distributive property and can be written as:

$$40 + 30 = \boxed{(4 \times 10) + (3 \times 10) = (4 + 3) \times 10} = 7 \times 10 = 70$$

Most strategies for multiplying multidigit numbers rely on the distributive property of multiplication over addition. For example:

$$6\times24 = \boxed{6\times(20 + 4) = (6\times20) + (6\times4)} = 120 + 24 = 144$$

Another fundamental property of multiplication is the *associative property of multiplication*, $a\times(b\times c) = (a\times b)\times c$. In the following example, Tom uses the associative property of multiplication to solve a Multiplication problem with groups of 10.

> *It costs 10 dollars for 1 person to go the movies. The math club is going to raise money so that all 40 people in the club can go see a movie. How much money do they need to raise?*

Tom: 10 tens is 100 so 40 tens would be 4 times as much, 400. They need to raise 400 dollars.

Tom's thinking can be represented as,

$$40\times10 = \boxed{(4\times10)\times10 = 4\times(10\times10)} = 4\times100 = 400$$

All of these examples as well as all the Derived Facts and Invented Algorithms described in Chapters 3, 4, and 7 are examples of relational thinking. When children use relational thinking, properties of operations are used to transform a computation for which students do not have a ready answer into a series of simpler calculations that generally just require repeated use of number facts and base-ten number concepts. Essentially, this is what is involved in any calculation with large numbers.

Surprisingly, virtually everything we do in arithmetic and algebra can be justified in terms of a relatively short list of basic properties. A subset of that list that includes properties that are commonly involved in the strategies children invent is given in Figure 11.1.[1]

---

1. We provide a more complete list of the basic properties of number and operations and their role in developing algebraic thinking in *Thinking Mathematically: Integrating Arithmetic and Algebra in Elementary School* (Carpenter, Franke, and Levi 2003).

Selected Properties of Addition and Multiplication

	Symbolic Representation	Example of Property in Use
Properties of Addition		
Commutative	$a + b = b + a$	$2 + 98 = 98 + 2$
Associative	$a + (b + c) = (a + b) + c$	$7 + 4 = 7 + (3 + 1) = (7 + 3) + 1$
Properties of Multiplication		
Commutative	$a{\times}b = b{\times}a$	$10{\times}8 = 8{\times}10$
Associative	$a{\times}(b{\times}c) = (a{\times}b){\times}c$	$30{\times}10 = (3{\times}10){\times}10 = 3{\times}(10{\times}10)$
Distributive Property of Multiplication over Addition		
	$a{\times}(b + c) = (a{\times}b) + (a{\times}c)$	$8{\times}12 = (8{\times}10) + (8{\times}2)$

FIGURE 11.1

THE RELATIONSHIP BETWEEN OPERATIONS: SUBTRACTION AND DIVISION

Subtraction and division are notably absent from the list of properties in Figure 11.1, and the properties in this list do not all generalize to subtraction or division. A distributive property of multiplication over subtraction is a valid property, $a{\times}(b - c) = (a{\times}b) - (a{\times}c)$. But neither subtraction nor division is commutative or associative. This distinction is important because not all young children recognize that properties that hold for addition or multiplication do not hold for subtraction or division. For example, many young children do not realize there is a difference between $8 - 5$ and $5 - 8$. Some of them make the mistake of thinking $5 - 8 = 3$.

Some properties that can be used to transform addition and multiplication problems are not available for subtraction and division. However, children often use relational thinking for subtraction and division by drawing on the relationship between subtraction and addition or the relationship between multiplication and division as is shown in the following examples:

> *Elizabeth had 63 dollars. She spent 59 dollars on books. How much money does Elizabeth have now?*

> **Zach:** 59 plus 1 is 60. Add 3 more. That's 4. Elizabeth has 4 dollars.

> *If 4 children are sharing 24 cookies, how many cookies would each child get?*

> **Bettina:** I know that 4 sixes is 24, so each friend would get 6 cookies.

Children also use other relational thinking strategies for subtraction and division as shown in the following example:

> *Tyrone had 22 cookies. He gave 7 cookies to his friend. How many cookies does he have now?*

> **Kayla:** 22 minus 2 is 20 then minus 5 more is 15.
> **Mr. A:** *Tell me more about what you did, Tyrone gave away 7 cookies.*
> **Kayla:** I took away 2 and then 5. That is the same as taking away 7. When you subtract a number, you can take away part of the number and then the rest of the number.

HELPING TO MAKE RELATIONAL THINKING EXPLICIT

Children implicitly engage with the fundamental properties of operations as they develop addition, subtraction, multiplication, and division concepts and procedures. A long-term goal is for children to grow in their awareness of the properties they are using in their relational thinking strategies. One way of making these properties more explicit is to introduce notation to record relational thinking strategies so that there is a written record that can be used to discuss a given strategy, highlight the properties used in that strategy, and compare it to other strategies. In the following example, Ms. Thomas used an equation to highlight and discuss a child's use of the commutative property of addition.

$$4 + 19 = m$$

Sally: 23.

Ms. T: How did you figure that out?

Sally: I went 19, 20, 21, 22, 23.

Ms. T: Does anyone notice anything about Sally's strategy? [After a variety of responses, Simon says, "She did 19 + 4 not 4 + 19."] Is that the same?

Students: Yes.

Ms. T: I hear a lot of yeses, but I am not sure everyone said yes. Before we talk more, let me write what I think you are saying.

$$4 + 19 = 19 + 4$$

The class goes on to discuss whether they think this equation is true and whether they can always change the order of the numbers when they add.

In the next example, Mr. Carter uses equations to highlight a child's implicit use of the distributive property of multiplication over addition. Many of his third-grade students had been using derived multiplication facts for several months, and he decided to record this strategy to engage children in discussing the distributive property.

Antonio has 6 bags with 7 rocks in each bag. How many rocks does Antonio have?

Alisha: I knew that 4 groups of 7 would be 28 and then another 2 groups of 7 is 14, so 6 bags of 7 would be 28 plus 14, which is 42.

Mr. C: I am going to write an equation that I think shows what you did.

$$6 \times 7 = 4 \times 7 + 2 \times 7$$

Mr. C: Alisha, does that show what you did?

Alisha: 6 times 7 is the same as 4 times 7 plus 2 times 7, yes, that is what I did.

Mr. C: What do the rest of you think about this strategy? Alisha figured out 6 groups of 7 [points to 6×7] by finding 4 groups of 7 [points to 4×7] and adding it to 2 groups of 7 [points to 2×7].

We are not proposing that it is always necessary to introduce equations or use names of properties with children. What is important is that children meaningfully engage with these properties and that they begin to explicitly recognize how the mathematics they are using depends on them.

SUMMARY

The fundamental properties of operations are an important part of understanding addition, subtraction, multiplication, and division that provide coherence to students' understanding of these operations. Children's relational thinking strategies show a beginning understanding of these properties. This understanding can serve as a foundation for a deeper understanding of relationships and properties when children work with larger numbers, fractions, positive and negative numbers as well as abstract quantities in algebra. Standard algorithms for computation are grounded in the very same properties, but it is difficult to unpack standard algorithms to see how the properties apply. Typically, what is learned by memorizing the steps of standard algorithms is limited to the algorithms themselves. One of the benefits of engaging children in using fundamental properties of operations to generate Derived Facts and Invented Algorithms is that the thinking involved in this activity is generative and provides a foundation for learning algebra.

Almost everything we want children to understand about whole number computation depends on the properties of operations, relationships between operations, and base-ten number concepts. Children naturally engage with these properties, relationships, and concepts when they use relational thinking to generate strategies for solving a variety of problems. Becoming familiar with these properties, relationships, and concepts can help teachers decide what to focus on when discussing strategies with students. Although the development of a comprehensive understanding of these properties should extend through a student's K–12 math experiences, children in the primary grades can begin to build the foundation for that understanding.

QUESTIONS FOR FURTHER REFLECTION

1. Look at the examples in Figures 11.2 through 11.5 of student work already presented in this book.

   For each example:

   a. Identify where a student might have used a property of an operation.
   b. Identify the property the student might be using. (Figure 11.1 might be helpful in identifying these properties.)
   c. Write a question you might ask each student about his strategies to help him verbalize this idea.

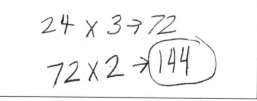

$6 + 7 = \square$

Colette

$$6+4 \longrightarrow 10+3 \longrightarrow \boxed{13}$$
$$7$$

FIGURE 11.2 Figure 3.9, Solution to 6 + 7

$$3 \times 7 = 21 \searrow 42 \searrow 56$$
$$3 \times 7 = 21$$
$$2 \times 7 = 14$$

$$3 + 3 + 2 = \boxed{8}$$

FIGURE 11.3 Figure 4.10, Solution to 8×7

$$6 \times 20 = 120$$
$$6 \times 4 = 24$$
$$6 \times 24 = 120 + 24 = 144$$

FIGURE 11.4 Figure 7.11, Solution to 6 groups of 24

$$24 \times 3 \rightarrow 72$$
$$72 \times 2 \rightarrow \boxed{144}$$

FIGURE 11.5 Figure 7.12, Solution to 6 groups of 24

2. Consider a student's solution to the following problem:

I have 6 boxes of donuts with 13 donuts in each box. How many donuts do I have?

The student responded, "6 groups of 10 is 60 and 6 groups of 3 is 18. Add them together, 60 plus 18 is 78."

What equation might you write to help make this relational thinking explicit to the rest of the students in the class?

3. Consider a student's solution to the following problem:

I had 60 colored pencils. I went to the store and bought a package of 48 colored pencils. How many colored pencils do I have now?

The students responded, "60 and 40 is 100, 8 more is 108."

What equation might you write to help make this relational thinking explicit to the rest of the students in the class?

4. Consider a student's solution to the following problem:

Natalia had 600 dollars. She spent 250 dollars on a bike. How many dollars does Natalia have now?

The students responded, "600 minus 200 is 400, take away 50 more, that's 350."

What equation or equations might you write to help make this relational thinking explicit to the rest of the students in the class?

5. Use the associative property of multiplication and the distributive property of multiplication over addition to show how the property might be used implicitly in a solution a student might use to solve each of these problems. The first one is done for you. What a student might say and an equation to represent the relationship are provided.

Problem	Associative Property of Multiplication	Distributive Property of Multiplication Over Addition
$6 \times 7 = \square$	"3 sevens are 21. If I double that, I will get 6 sevens, so 6 times 7 is 42." $6 \times 7 = 2 \times (3 \times 7)$	"6 fives are 30, 6 twos are 12, so 6 sevens is 42." $6 \times 7 = 6 \times 5 + 6 \times 2$
$8 \times 7 = \square$		
$4 \times 6 = \square$		

6. Watch Juliet solve the following problem and listen to her explanation:

Jayden had 17 flowers. She picked 20 more flowers. How many flowers does Jayden have now?

CLIP 11.1 Juliet uses a fundamental property of addition in her strategy
http://smarturl.it/CM11.1

a. What is an equation you could write to represent the fundamental property that Juliet used implicitly in her strategy?

7. Watch Roger solve the following problem and how the teacher asks a series of follow-up questions to elicit further understanding:

Ms. Rojo is getting ready for the school year and wants to figure out how many markers she has. 10 markers can fit in each box. She has 9 boxes of markers and 2 extra markers. How many markers does she have?

CLIP 11.2 The teacher extends Roger's thinking about multiplication and elicits the use of a fundamental property
http://smarturl.it/CM11.2

a. What questions does the teacher ask to extend Roger's understanding?
b. Roger's strategy for figuring 12 groups of 10 reveals the use relational thinking. What equation or equations might you use to represent this thinking?

12

The Conceptual Basis for Cognitively Guided Instruction

Cognitively Guided Instruction is a research-based professional development program that is grounded in a conceptual framework in which learning with understanding is central. The research upon which CGI is based is summarized in Appendix A. In this chapter, we briefly describe our conception of learning with understanding and how it is represented in CGI.

UNDERSTANDING UNDERSTANDING

Most recommendations for mathematics instruction highlight the importance of learning mathematics with understanding. But often, discussions of learning with understanding leave *understanding* undefined or use a circular definition that relates understanding and meaningful learning. CGI is based on a very specific definition of learning with understanding.[1] Four interconnected themes provide the basis for our conception of learning with understanding. In classrooms where students learn with understanding:

1. Knowledge is connected.
2. Knowledge is generative.
3. Students describe, explain, and justify their mathematical thinking.
4. Students identify themselves as mathematical thinkers who see that mathematics should make sense and that they have the power to make sense of it.

Knowledge Is Connected

Perhaps the central feature of learning with understanding is that knowledge is connected rather than consisting of bits of isolated information. When knowledge is connected, it can be accessed in a number of ways. A rich network of interconnections makes knowledge less subject to forgetting and better adapted for connecting new knowledge and for use in solving unfamiliar problems. But it is not enough to say that knowledge should be connected. We need some perspective on exactly how knowledge might be connected in ways that support learning. CGI explicitly provides that perspective.

In general, we make sense of new ideas by relating them to things we already know. Young children are no different. They learn best by relating the mathematics they are learning to ideas they already know. CGI provides a very specific picture of the informal mathematical knowledge and problem-solving abilities that children bring to school. We map out how children can build on that knowledge to learn the formal mathematics that is taught in school. We portray how knowledge continues to build on prior knowledge as children progressively abstract and extend their knowledge and the strategies they use to solve problems. The evolution of children's strategies from Direct Modeling, through Counting Strategies, to the use of Derived Facts and Invented Algorithms is a process of continuously building on knowledge that is understood. Connections to prior knowledge are not the only connections that are key to learning with understanding. Equally important is that the knowledge being acquired is rich in connections. In CGI classes, children solve a variety of problems. The CGI analysis of problem types provides a principled way of relating problems to one another. That structure helps teachers anticipate and keep track of the strategies that children are likely to use, but children in CGI classes do not learn to classify problems based on this taxonomy of problem types. For students, coherence comes from the common features of the strategies that they use to solve the

---

1. For additional discussion of learning with understanding see Carpenter and Lehrer (1999) and Hiebert and Carpenter (1992).

problems. Rather than keeping track of the variety of problems they solve and the differences in the strategies used for each problem, children essentially use the same process to solve all the problems, directly modeling the action and relations described in each problem. Initially children use Direct Modeling. Counting strategies are related to Direct Modeling strategies in that they are essentially abstractions of the corresponding Direct Modeling strategies.

Children learn number facts by noticing relations among number facts. To construct derived facts, children relate unknown to known number facts by implicitly drawing on fundamental properties of number operations such as the associative, commutative, and distributive properties. Children also implicitly apply these same properties to connect more complex calculations to simpler calculations that they have already learned. For children in CGI classes, learning how to perform calculations with an expanding range of numbers does not involve learning a new collection of unrelated procedures. They develop computational skills by connecting more abstract invented algorithms to manipulations of concrete representations of the problems. Both the manipulations of concrete representations and invented algorithms draw implicitly on an interconnected network of basic concepts that includes the meaning of operations, properties of operations, place value, and the like.

The communities that emerge in CGI classrooms support students to recognize and construct the relations described above. The interactions in Ms. Barron's class portrayed in Chapter 10 illustrate how sharing alternative strategies in CGI classrooms provides continuing opportunities for students to relate strategies and to discuss what makes different solutions equivalent. In Ms. Grace's classroom, also portrayed in Chapter 10, students connected a concrete Direct Modeling strategy for a multiplication problem to a more abstract Repeated Addition strategy highlighting the use of tens and ones.

Learning an integrated network of related ideas rather than a collection of isolated facts and procedures makes learning more efficient and easier. There is less to learn, and what is learned can be recalled because it is accessible in many different ways through the myriad of connections. Furthermore, this structure makes it possible to extend what is understood to acquire new knowledge and apply it to solve new problems. For example, children extend their strategies for solving single-digit addition and subtraction problems together with their knowledge of place value to construct invented algorithms for adding and subtracting with multidigit numbers. Children's application of a familiar strategy to an unfamiliar problem is illustrated by kindergarteners' success in applying Direct Modeling strategies to solve the problem discussed in Chapter 8 in which 19 children were riding in a minibus with 7 seats.

Knowledge Is Generative

The two examples at the end of the previous section illustrate the second defining feature of learning with understanding: that knowledge can be extended to learn new ideas and to solve problems. This outcome is so basic that we take it to be one benchmark in the definition of learning with understanding. But some caution is in order in applying this benchmark. Understanding is not an all-or-none phenomenon. Understanding can occur at multiple levels, and the fact that a child cannot apply her knowledge to a particular problem does not mean that she totally lacks understanding. With that caveat in mind, we characterize classrooms that promote learning with understanding as ones that provide opportunity for students to engage in extending knowledge to learn new ideas and solve problems. Clearly this benchmark is related to the first. Knowledge that is rich in connections has multiple entry points and as a consequence multiple ways that it can be related to new situations or problems.

On the other hand, students who learn procedures by rote have little flexibility in deciding when such procedures are appropriate and when a simpler, more efficient strategy would do. For example, subtraction with regrouping is an inefficient and error-prone procedure for solving $300 - 299$, yet students who have learned subtraction as a rote procedure often use a standard algorithm to figure this small difference.

In CGI classrooms, virtually all activity involves students in extending what they already understand to new situations. Students in CGI classes are not shown procedures to imitate and practice. The learning of new concepts and skills is treated as a problem-solving activity. Students are constantly extending their strategies by applying them to new number domains, developing strategies that are more efficient, and seeing connections across strategies. The understanding developed through this process provides the basis for developing skills. Skills are not mastered and then applied to solve problems. Skills are acquired in the context of and as means for solving problems and are a part of the rich network of connections students create.

Describing, Explaining, and Justifying Mathematical Thinking

Explaining and justifying mathematical ideas is an integral part of understanding mathematics at all levels. To understand a strategy, students need to know why it works, not just that it works. In order to extend strategies and apply them in new situations, students need to be able to reason why they can adapt the strategy to the problem they are trying to solve. Students at all levels of understanding are capable of explaining and justifying their mathematical reasoning and, just as importantly, students' engagement in explaining and justifying their reasoning expands their understanding.

Students in CGI classrooms are constantly describing, explaining, and justifying the strategies they use to solve a problem. They talk about their strategies with their teacher, with other students in small groups, and in whole-class discussions. Students not only describe, explain, and justify their own strategies, they also often are asked to explain or justify another student's strategy that has been shared with the class. They are asked to compare different strategies, to explain how they are equivalent, and to justify whether or not they all are valid solutions. Participation in these practices is just as much a part of learning with understanding as developing well-connected knowledge.

Children's Identity as Mathematical Thinkers

As students in CGI classrooms acquire knowledge and skills, they also develop a sense of themselves as mathematicians. Students learn to see themselves as capable; they know they can figure out how to solve problems, even problems that may seem challenging at first. They know that they can learn by solving problems and exchanging ideas with each other and that a problem that seems hard one day may seem just right in a month or two. They see that explaining their strategies, asking questions of others, and trying a new representation or tool will help them figure out a new strategy.

Seeing oneself as someone who can do mathematics successfully is a part of understanding. It is not just the students with the most efficient or sophisticated strategies who see themselves as capable. A primary goal of CGI is that each student, from those using strategies early in the trajectory to those using advanced strategies, see themselves as able to make sense of mathematics. This orientation is potentially one of the most enduring legacies of student participation in CGI classes in the elementary grades.

A question we are frequently asked is whether the focus on understanding in CGI classes will place students at a disadvantage if they are in classes in later grades that emphasize computational skills. You are never doing a disservice to students by helping them develop understanding. The understanding that students acquire in earlier grades will provide a foundation that can make learning skills in subsequent grades easier even if the emphasis is not on understanding. Furthermore, students believing that mathematics should make sense and that they are capable of making sense of it can support learning in any class.

UNDERSTANDING AND JUSTICE FOR ALL

All students benefit from and deserve to be in classes in which teaching for understanding is the norm. Opportunity to learn with understanding is first and foremost a matter of equity. There is no compelling evidence that there are large numbers of students who cannot learn with understanding, and denying any student opportunity to learn with understanding is an injustice. For virtually all students, teaching for understanding as we have defined it in this chapter makes sense.

All students are capable of and benefit from learning mathematics that:

- is organized in a rich network of connections
- provides a basis for ongoing learning
- they can describe, analyze, and justify
- provides support for them to develop an identity as being capable of making sense of mathematics.

Each student brings relevant knowledge to instruction. Some of what students know may be wrong, but often they know more than we give them credit for or even notice. It is our job as teachers to find out what our students do know so that we can build on what they know that is valid and useful. We have consistently found that virtually all young children have informal knowledge of number and problem-solving strategies that they can build upon to develop arithmetic concepts and skills.

We have documented young children's rich informal knowledge of number operations, which turns out to be remarkably consistent across different demographic groups within the United States and other countries as well as for children demonstrating different levels of achievement. That does not mean that all children have the same knowledge at any given age or grade, but the development of strategies for basic number concepts and skills follow pretty much the same general pattern for all learners. Teachers often find that students who have been identified or presumed to be achieving below grade level know more than anticipated. Building on this knowledge makes learning more efficient. There is less unfamiliar material to learn, and because new ideas are connected to what the students already know, they can make sense of the new ideas and integrate them into a coherent structure.

Students who are presumed to not be successful in mathematics may actually be more capable of learning meaningful networks of ideas than isolated concepts and skills. There is much more to learn when facts and skills are not connected, and what is learned is easily forgotten, subject to errors, and not generalizable to new ideas and solving unfamiliar problems. A great deal of the success of students who show an aptitude for mathematics is due to the fact that they organize their knowledge into rich networks. It is our obligation to make that kind of learning available to each student.

One of the benefits of acquiring knowledge rich in connections is that it can be applied to learn new content and to solve problems. It is not only easier to learn ideas that are interrelated; when knowledge is rich in connections, it is easier to learn new ideas that depend on it. If knowledge is limited to narrow contexts and cannot be applied outside those contexts, it is of little value. Thus, a clear goal of instruction for all students has to be to acquire knowledge that is generative.

The goal that students describe, explain, and justify their mathematical thinking is often presumed to be beyond the capabilities of many students. That has not been the case in our experience within CGI classrooms. We have consistently found that, with support, students can successfully participate in CGI classes in which students routinely describe, explain, and justify their mathematical thinking. When students participate in these ways, we can better understand their mathematical thinking, and we often are surprised by what we learn. Even though students often do not think about mathematics in the same way we might, they have knowledge on which to build.

I teach students with disabilities in a self-contained classroom. When asked, "Does CGI math work well with kids who have disabilities?" my answer is, "Yes!" As with any child, children with disabilities need opportunities to use concrete as well as Counting strategies. They often need a little extra thinking time to develop that understanding or to think about how to attack a problem. Through my own learning of how to probe and question my students, I'm able to allow them every opportunity to be successful. They need exposure to different problem types; they need be allowed to use tools. Many of my students are able to solve word problems better than equations—they do especially well when the story is all about them. So, I make the stories all about them. Some of my students solve word problems more efficiently than the general education students. Through this they come to understand numbers and what they truly represent. This understanding is something that stays with them and they are able to grow on that knowledge like any other child who doesn't have a disability.

—Remona Moore, teacher

A question that we initially struggled with was whether classes in which students describe, explain, and justify their mathematical thinking would place additional burdens on students who are English Language Learners. It has turned out that these students have benefited from the interactions that characterize CGI classes, and the benefits go beyond their success in learning mathematics. Teachers have consistently reported that participation in CGI actually helped their students develop their language skills.

By participating in the sense-making activity of CGI classrooms, students at all levels develop a perspective that mathematics should make sense and that they are capable of making sense of it. This attitude is particularly important for students who have not been seen as successful or who face challenges in learning mathematics.

A central theme of this chapter is that ideas that are learned with understanding are of higher quality than ideas that are not supported by understanding. The difference in quality is reflected in retention, transfer, solving problems, articulating ideas, persistence, seeing oneself as mathematically capable, and the like. Even though there may be differences in the levels of understanding that students attain at a given point in time, all students benefit from being in classes that emphasize learning with understanding.

Finally, we want to emphasize that providing opportunity for all students to learn with understanding is a necessary but not sufficient condition for addressing equity in the teaching and learning of mathematics. Working toward equity in mathematics learning requires attention to not only how a student thinks about mathematics but also all aspects of who the student is and the resources a student brings to learning as well as how school and societal structures shape a student's opportunities to learn.

*T*hree years ago, our school was identified among the bottom 5 percent of persistently low-achieving schools in the state based on state test scores. We were required to develop a transformation plan and called on University of Washington professors Elham Kazemi, Alison Hintz, and their team to help us.

Some people might suggest that the best approach to improving test scores is to focus on drill, practice, and test prep—that we didn't have the time or luxury of developing understanding. However, we knew that we couldn't afford not to develop understanding. Drills and test prep might have enabled us to improve test scores more quickly. However, it would have been like building a house over a sinkhole. Student performance on tests might have improved, but students would have been left with big holes in their conceptual understanding.

Educational equity is a central issue for us. Poverty has a significant impact on our school—almost 90 percent of our students qualify for free or reduced lunch. But equity isn't about raising test scores. It is about providing all children with equitable opportunities to learn. Math is about making sense of problems and explaining ideas, developing sound reasoning for evaluating solutions. While it is challenging to help children access the mathematical ideas described in the Common Core State Mathematics Standards, all children are able to learn and deserve the opportunity to develop the ability to think critically and be able to express mathematical ideas.

The test scores didn't tell us what the students did or didn't understand, so we assessed students using a CGI assessment that provided us a window into the students' thinking. We discovered significant gaps in number sense and problem solving. During the first two years, we focused on helping students making sense. We focused on improving our core math instruction through the principles of CGI.

The first test score gains we saw were on our spring CGI assessments. Kids who did not have strategies in the fall now had strategies for solving problems. Students who used Direct Modeling now used more advanced strategies. The next fall, our CGI assessments showed that students continued to make sense of problems. That told us that we were on the right track. Few summer learning losses meant that the students had a deep understanding.

We also saw gains on our state test scores. In the first year, our students who were well below standards—the children who would have been identified for intervention—benefited the most from problem solving, talking with each other, and learning to persevere. After two years, our third- and fifth-grade test scores were close to the state average. After three years, the percentage of students meeting standards increased in third grade from 30 percent to 60 percent, in fourth grade from 24 percent to 67 percent, and in fifth grade from 20 percent to 79 percent

Because our work with CGI principles guides professional learning and student learning from kindergarten through fifth grade, we are building stronger and stronger cohorts of students who can grapple with deep mathematical ideas as they move through the elementary grades. We have set the bar high for ourselves. We know the test scores tell a part of the story and have learned together how to attend to students' mathematical thinking in order to interpret the successes or challenges they face in solving mathematical problems accurately. This attention to student thinking guides our instructional foci and our professional learning opportunities.

—Teresa Lind, math coach

THEORY OF CHANGE IN COGNITIVELY GUIDED INSTRUCTION CLASSROOMS

Students in CGI classrooms participate in a community of inquiry in which the focus of inquiry is on the strategies that students use to solve problems. Students do not just passively apply strategies to solve a given problem; the strategies become objects of reflection by individuals and by the group. As students analyze and compare alternative strategies, they begin to lift out the essential mathematical features of the solutions. Over time, they start to abstract the solutions and no longer need to actually manipulate the physical tools that they initially used to solve a given problem. The progressive abstraction of strategies is a hallmark of learning in CGI classes. Rather than characterizing student achievement strictly in terms of the tasks students can successfully complete, progress is defined to a great degree by the increasingly sophisticated strategies that students can apply to the tasks.

When students are learning with understanding, the learning process becomes a genuine partnership between the students and teacher and among the students. The students feel empowered to share their ideas, ask questions, and contribute problems for the class to explore rather than sit back and be told what to do. When a student is sharing a strategy and other students ask, "Do you think that always works?" or "Why does that work?" then I know that not only are they thinking how to solve a given problem, but they also view themselves as able to generate their own knowledge for mathematical ideas. It is my job as their teacher to establish routines and provide problems to initiate them into this kind of learning process, but when students begin to assume responsibility for questioning and probing, then I know they are learning with understanding and, more important, they know they are capable of doing so and they know what to do to build that understanding. Learning math to them no longer means relying on the teacher to tell them what to do, but rather, it is dependent on their strategies, observations, questions, and explanations.

—Lesley Wagner, teacher

This progressive abstraction takes place over an extended period of time, and at any given point, students in any class are at very different places in this progression.

In other words, a range of strategies are almost always being used and discussed by the class. Students using more basic strategies are given the opportunity to hear and discuss the more advanced strategies used by their classmates. Although they may not completely understand the more advanced strategies at first, they generally can participate at some level in the discussion of these strategies. Over time this participation makes an important contribution to their learning more advanced strategies. On the other hand, the students who are using more advanced strategies have to articulate the basis for their strategies and relate them to the physical models used by other students. This tends to keep the abstractions grounded in the physical operations that give them meaning. One of the difficulties that teachers in traditional classes often encounter is that once students learn computational skills, the connections with physical representations that initially were used to give meaning to the skills are abandoned and forgotten. The time that is spent in CGI classes drawing connections between concrete strategies and more abstract strategies is time that is well spent for everybody. One of the biggest challenges faced by teachers at all levels is dealing with the range of abilities that are found in virtually every class. The emphasis on the discussion of alternative strategies turns this challenge into a virtue.

TEACHERS' LEARNING

Our stance on learning with understanding applies to teacher learning as well as the learning of their students. The four hallmarks of learning with understanding discussed throughout this chapter are as important for learning about teaching as they are for learning mathematics. In other words, teacher learning for understanding is characterized by the following principles: (1) knowledge of mathematics, teaching, and learning is organized in a rich network of connections; (2) knowledge is generative so that it provides a basis for ongoing learning; (3) teachers describe, analyze, and justify decisions about teaching; and (4) teachers develop an identity as learners capable of learning in their classrooms and making decisions based on what they learn.

Knowledge of Teaching Is Connected

Teachers have a great deal of informal knowledge about how children might solve different problems, and they have specific knowledge about the students in their class. As teachers read about the development of children's mathematical thinking, talk with other teachers, and work with students, they build on their prior knowledge and organize it into a coherent framework. The classification of problem types and our analysis of development of children's strategies based on that classification provide a structure for understanding the development of children's mathematical thinking. The structure of this model makes this information more accessible during the complex tasks of teaching. This allows CGI teachers to keep track of what each of their students knows at any given point of time. This model of children's thinking is extremely robust. When teachers try the problems with their own students, their students generally solve them in the predicted ways. This allows teachers to connect what they are learning in their professional development with what they are learning about their own students.

Teachers' Generative Growth and Problem Solving

Teaching in CGI classes is a form of problem solving. Although CGI provides teachers with a basic framework for understanding the evolution of student thinking, teachers are left with the essential work of elaborating the details and figuring out how it all applies to their students. Just as we know that explicitly telling students how to solve math problems does not result in increased mathematical understanding, explicitly telling teachers how to teach does not result in improvements in teaching math for understanding. CGI does not script teaching or specify how to organize a classroom to support learning. The coherent focus on student thinking positions teachers to engage in inquiry about how their students' knowledge is evolving, what problems may be most appropriate, what questions might provide the best window on student thinking or might encourage a student to think about a higher-level strategy, what class norms would support student engagement, and the like. An overarching goal of CGI is that classrooms become places for learning through problem solving for both students and teachers.

Describing, Analyzing, and Justifying Decisions About Teaching

Learning from inquiry requires reflection where teachers articulate reasons for their decisions and analyze how their decisions impacted student learning. Describing, analyzing, and justifying decisions occurs both privately and as teachers participate in a community of inquiry. Note that we are not using the term *justify* to mean that teachers need to be prepared to defend their decisions to someone they are accountable to. Rather, we intend it to refer to teachers examining their assumptions and reasons for making decisions so that they can learn from those decisions and apply that knowledge to future decisions. As teachers reflect on what happened when they posed a particular problem, the strategies students used, and whether they saw what they expected to see, they have the opportunity to think about why students responded in the way they did and consider what to try next. When teachers participate with colleagues in a community of inquiry, they have the opportunity to describe details of their instruction so that others in the group have the relevant information and then analyze and justify their responses collectively. Making this practice public provides teachers the space to consider options with justification for adapting and building their practice.

When teaching is grounded in the type of inquiry described above, teachers develop knowledge and practices to support their view of themselves as capable of designing opportunities for learning that build on the knowledge, skills, and dispositions of their students. Teachers become learners themselves, and see themselves as continually improving their practice, capable of making valid decisions about students, classroom practices, and norms.

> Every time you interact with a child, you're gaining more knowledge of how to interact with other children. Every time they show you, and tell you, what they're doing and thinking, you just learn more about what's going on in their head.
>
> —Barb Wiesner, teacher

Teachers as Learners

One of the most powerful findings from our research with CGI teachers is that their knowledge is generative. The key to teacher change both during and following the CGI professional development is that teachers learn from their students and their colleagues. Teachers who listen to and learn from their students continue to grow in their use of CGI long after the formal CGI professional development has ended. For teacher learning to become generative in this sense, teachers have to be able to attend to the details of children's thinking and see how they can adapt that knowledge. Knowing that generativity is the goal provides teachers a path to making their classes places for their own learning.

> Because I keep watching the kids, I learn from the kids a lot. I really do. I even stop and think a lot more conscientiously about my numbers. I think [my knowledge of children's thinking] can't help but change, because I think I am more able to understand and break things apart and build on kids' knowledge the longer I use this and see it developmentally. . . . I think definitely you cannot help but grow, because there is still more knowledge out there to be explored, and so I keep looking for that.

Particularly having [Annie and Barb] here, I mean, we really talk a lot about what we are doing. . . . I think it is increasing my knowledge base . . . I am just not sure where I would be without their support. I would not be as far along as I am. I am not sure I would be able to go back to the workbook kind of thing, even if I'd been alone, but I know I wouldn't be where I am without the support that I've had.

—Sue Berthouex, teacher

Teachers participate in multiple communities that afford ongoing learning. One is the community that teachers participate in with their students. Another is a community of colleagues sharing stories of children's mathematical thinking and working together to figure out how to support children's mathematical learning. Crossing the boundaries of these communities so that what is learned in one feeds into what is shared in the other provides teachers and their students particularly rich learning opportunities.

13

Conclusion:
Keep on Learning

I equate this with a journey. The children have been my teacher as well as people at the university and fellow teachers . . . When you're on this journey, there will be things that you as a teacher won't know, but you have to take a risk. You have to trust the kids. You do learn from the kids. You don't learn it in a week. You don't learn it in a workshop. You don't learn it in a month. You don't even learn it in a couple of years. You continually improve. I think good teachers always are learners . . . They have gotten hooked on how children learn and how they can best facilitate that learning, so they are always searching. That's what keeps teachers alive and vibrant, because they are always learning. You learn from kids, from fellow teachers, from the readings. You are always questioning. How can I be better? How can I be better, so my students are better? When you really start looking at kids, you see all the challenges.

—Mazie Jenkins, teacher

Teaching is complex. Almost every minute, a teacher makes a decision about what to teach, how to teach, whom to call on, how fast the lesson should move, how to respond to a child, and so on. These decisions depend on many things, but because of the intimate knowledge that teachers have about their own students, no one is in a better position than the teacher to make these decisions about what to do in the classroom. Because immediate teaching decisions cannot be made by anyone but the teacher, we have not attempted to provide explicit directions for how to organize a classroom, how to implement instruction, or when to teach specific topics.

Our goal in writing this book is to share what we have learned about the development of children's mathematical thinking and how that knowledge can have an impact on decisions about what to teach and how to teach it. Our purpose, however, is not to provide a static body of knowledge about teaching and learning for you to apply in your own classroom. We do not view learning of teachers or students as simply assimilating knowledge that is written in a book or presented in a class. Both students and teachers take an active role in generating their own knowledge and understanding. We hope that you will use what we have learned to help you construct a framework for analyzing students' mathematical thinking and that you will use this structure to listen to and learn from your students and colleagues. Our vision is that classrooms and schools become places of inquiry for both students and teachers.

Almost all CGI teachers find that listening to and understanding their students' thinking is one of the most rewarding things that has happened to them professionally. These teachers become strong advocates of the importance of understanding children's thinking, and they use that understanding to select problems that challenge children to engage in problem solving.

CGI teachers have found many ways to productively pose problems, elicit their children's mathematical thinking, and engage students with each other's mathematical ideas. Professional developers, teachers, and researchers have documented what teachers are doing to support student learning in CGI classrooms, and we have shared what they have learned. We want to emphasize that we have learned about teacher practice because teachers have innovated. They have found ways to make sense of the problem types and strategies and the development of children's mathematical thinking and have used their understandings to create classrooms that meet the needs of each of their students. Teachers have created opportunities and developed tools and pedagogies far beyond what we envisioned when we began. We look forward to CGI teachers continuing to generate new ways to support the development of children's mathematical thinking and adding to our understanding of what is possible.

APPENDIX A

The Research Base of Cognitively Guided Instruction

CGI (Carpenter et al. 1999, 2014) is a professional development program based on an integrated program of research focused on (a) the development of students' mathematical thinking; (b) instruction that supports that development; (c) teachers' knowledge and beliefs that influence their instructional practices; (d) the way that teachers' knowledge, beliefs, and practices are influenced by their understanding of students' mathematical thinking; and (e) how professional development impacts teachers' knowledge, beliefs, and practices and what they learn from interacting with their students.

Our research has been cyclic. We started with explicit knowledge about the development of children's mathematical thinking (Carpenter 1985), which we used as a context to study teachers' knowledge of students' mathematical thinking (Carpenter et al. 1988) and the way teachers might use knowledge of students' thinking in making instructional decisions (Carpenter et al. 1989). We found that although teachers had a great deal of intuitive knowledge about children's mathematical thinking, it was fragmented and, as a consequence, generally did not play an important role in most teachers' decision making (Carpenter et al. 1988). If teachers were expected to plan instruction based on their knowledge of students' thinking, they needed some coherent basis for making instructional decisions. To address this problem, we designed CGI to help teachers construct conceptual maps of the development of children's mathematical thinking in specific content domains (Carpenter, Fennema, and Franke 1996).

In a series of studies (Carpenter et al. 1989; Fennema et al. 1993, 1996), we found that learning to understand the development of children's mathematical thinking could lead to fundamental changes in teachers' beliefs and practices and that these changes were reflected in students' learning. The studies provided contexts for examining the development of children's mathematical thinking in situations in which their intuitive strategies for solving problems were a focus for reflection and discussion. Other studies (Carpenter et al. 1993, 1998; Carpenter, Ansell, and Levi 2001) provided new perspectives on the development of children's mathematical thinking and on the instructional contexts that support that development, which in turn has led to revisions in our approach to teacher professional development.

In the sections that follow, we describe the CGI professional development program and discuss the research base for CGI with respect to: (a) children's thinking; (b) teachers' knowledge and beliefs about children's thinking and the relation of teachers' knowledge and beliefs to their students' achievement; (c) the effect of the CGI Professional Development Program on teachers' knowledge, beliefs, and practice; and (d) the achievement of students in CGI classes. Note that this division does not represent a sequence in which the research was conducted. In fact, most of our studies have crossed several categories. This review also includes three new strands of research that have been initiated since the publication of the first edition: (a) research by Philipp, Jacobs, Lamb, and Schappelle and associates documenting the importance of sustaining professional development over years and introducing the construct of professional noticing of children's mathematical thinking (Jacobs, Lamb, and Philipp 2010; Jacobs et al. 2011; Philipp et al. 2013); (b) research by Turner, Celedón-Pattichis, Dominguez, Empson, and associates documenting how CGI teachers have supported English language learners to successfully participate in mathematics instruction (Turner and Celedón-Pattichis 2011; Turner, Celedón-Pattichis, and Marshall 2008; Turner et al. 2009; Turner, Dominquez, Empson, and Maldonado 2013; Turner, Dominquez, Maldonado, and Empson 2013); and (c) research by Franke, Webb, and associates identifying classroom practices that enhance student participation and learning (Franke et al. 2009, in press; Webb et al. 2008, 2009, 2013, in press).

THE COGNITIVELY GUIDED INSTRUCTION PROFESSIONAL DEVELOPMENT PROGRAM

The CGI professional development program (Carpenter et al. 1999, 2014) engages teachers in learning about the development of children's mathematical thinking within particular content domains. The theme that ties together our analysis of students' mathematical thinking is that children intuitively solve word problems by modeling the action and relations described in them. Through this theme, we portray how basic concepts of addition, subtraction, multiplication, and division develop in children and how they can construct concepts of place value and multidigit computational procedures based on their intuitive mathematical knowledge (for elaboration, see Carpenter, Fennema, and Franke. [1996]).

Our engagement with teachers is driven by two principles: (1) focus interactions with teachers on the principled ideas underlying the development of children's thinking about mathematics, and (2) build on the teachers' existing knowledge. We attempt to provide an environment for teacher learning that offers opportunities for teachers to build on their existing ideas to create continually evolving organizing frameworks of children's mathematical thinking.

Whenever we interact with teachers, be it in a group working session or in a one-on-one interaction, we focus on children's mathematical thinking. We have particular knowledge about the development of children's thinking that we would like teachers to come to understand. In coming to understand this thinking, the teachers create their own ways of organizing and framing the knowledge. They also think hard about the relationship between this knowledge and their teaching. We try to not direct the ways in which the teachers choose to implement their teaching practice. There does not exist one way of implementing CGI. Our intent is not to get teachers to adopt a set of teaching behaviors or moves. Rather, we provide a framework so teachers can think about their students' understandings of mathematics and then make instructional decisions based on the underlying principles. We strive to create inquiry about teaching so teachers are thinking about why they would do certain things and how that relates to the children's learning of mathematics.

RESEARCH ON CHILDREN'S THINKING

The model of children's thinking that is the basis for CGI is built on an extensive research base. The research support for our analysis of the development of addition/ subtraction concepts was synthesized in Carpenter (1985), Fuson (1992); Gutstein and Romberg (1995), and Verschaffel and De Corte (1993). The research support for our analysis of multiplication/division and the general notion of modeling was reported in Carpenter et al. (1993) and Greer (1992). The analysis of the development of multidigit concepts was supported by research reported in Carpenter et al. (1998) and Fuson et al. (1997).

The results of a study that we conducted with kindergarten children (Carpenter et al. 1993) are summarized in Figure A.1. In this study we found that, by the end of kindergarten, children in CGI classes could solve a variety of problems by modeling the action or relations described in the problems. Many teachers and curriculum developers considered the problems too difficult for young children, and the results provided compelling support that children as young as kindergarten can invent strategies to solve a variety of problems if they are given the opportunity to do so. In almost every case, the children used the Direct Modeling strategies predicted by our model of the development of children's mathematical thinking.

Kindergarten Children's Success in Solving Various Word Problems

Problem	Percent of Children Who Solved Each Problem Correctly Using the Expected Strategy
Carla has 7 dollars. How many more dollars does she have to earn so that she will have 11 dollars to buy a puppy?	74
James has 12 balloons. Amy has 7 balloons. How many more balloons does James have than Amy?	67
Tad had 15 guppies. He put 3 guppies in each jar. How many jars did Tad put guppies in?	71
19 children are going to the circus. 5 children can ride in each car. How many cars will be needed to get all 19 children to the circus?	64
Maria had 3 packages of cupcakes. There were 4 cupcakes in each package. She ate 5 cupcakes. How many are left?	64
19 children are taking a minibus to the zoo. The bus has 7 seats. How many children will have to sit 3 to a seat, and how many can sit 2 to a seat?	51

FIGURE A.1

TEACHERS' KNOWLEDGE AND BELIEFS ABOUT CHILDREN'S THINKING

In a study of teachers who had not participated in the CGI Professional Development Program, we found that teachers had a great deal of intuitive knowledge about children's mathematical thinking; however, because that knowledge was fragmented, it generally did not play an important role in most teachers' decision making (Carpenter et al. 1988). This study indicated that teachers have informal knowledge of children's thinking that can be built upon in the CGI Professional Development Program. In particular, teachers can identify differences between problem types, and they have some idea of many of the modeling and counting strategies that children often use. But most teachers' understanding of problems and strategies is not well connected, and most do not appreciate the critical role that Modeling and Counting strategies play in children's thinking or understand that more than a few students are capable of using more sophisticated strategies.

This study also showed that teachers' knowledge of their students' thinking was related to student achievement. Students of teachers who knew more about their students' thinking had higher levels of achievement in problem solving than students of teachers who had less knowledge of their students' thinking. In a related study (Peterson et al. 1989), we found that classes of teachers whose beliefs were more consistent with principles of CGI tended to have higher levels of achievement than classes of teachers whose beliefs were less consistent with principles of CGI.

THE EFFECT OF PARTICIPATING IN COGNITIVELY GUIDED INSTRUCTION PROFESSIONAL DEVELOPMENT PROGRAMS ON TEACHERS' KNOWLEDGE, BELIEFS, AND INSTRUCTION

In the first CGI study, which investigated the effect of CGI professional development on teachers, we focused entirely on addition and subtraction with first-grade teachers (Carpenter et al. 1989). This experimental study compared twenty CGI teachers with twenty control teachers. We found that CGI teachers placed greater emphasis on problem solving and less on computational skills, expected more multiple-solution strategies rather than a single method, listened to their children more, and knew more about their children's thinking than did control teachers.

Whereas the initial experimental study compared different groups of teachers, a three-year longitudinal study of twenty-one teachers (Fennema et al. 1996) explicitly examined the nature and pattern of change among teachers and the relation between beliefs and instruction. Several levels of beliefs and practice in becoming a CGI teacher were identified. *Level 1* teachers believe that children need to be explicitly taught how to do mathematics. Instruction in their classes is usually guided by an adopted text and focuses on the learning of specific skills. Teachers generally demonstrate the steps in a procedure as clearly as they can, and the children practice applying the procedures. Children are expected to solve problems using standard procedures, and there is little or no discussion of alternative solutions. *Level 2* teachers begin to question whether children need explicit instruction in order to solve problems, and the teachers alternately provide opportunities for children to solve problems using their own strategies and show the children specific methods.

Level 3 is a turning point. Level 3 teachers believe that children can solve problems without having a strategy provided for them, and they act accordingly. They do not show students specific procedures for solving problems. Children spend most of mathematics class solving and reporting their solutions to a variety of strategies and compare and contrast different strategies. In sum, Level 3 teachers epitomize the characteristics that distinguished CGI teachers from control teachers in the initial experimental study. Their classrooms are strongly influenced by their understanding of children's thinking, they know appropriate problems to pose and questions to ask to elicit children's thinking, and they understand and appreciate the variety of solutions that children construct to solve them.

What distinguishes Level 3 teachers from Level 4 teachers is their use of what they learn from listening to students in making instructional decisions. Whereas Level 3 teachers apply their understanding of children's thinking to select appropriate problems and accurately assess their own students' thinking by listening to the strategies they use, *Level 4* teachers conceptualize instruction in terms of the thinking of the students in their classes. They have a more fluid perspective of their students' thinking that they use to plan instruction, and they also regard their instruction as an opportunity for developing a deeper understanding of children's thinking in general. In the terms of Richardson (1994), teachers regard their knowledge as a basis for engaging in "practical inquiry." For these teachers, our research-based analyses of children's thinking are not conceived as fixed models to learn but as a focus for reflection on children's mathematical thinking, which helps them organize their knowledge and interpret their students' thinking. These teachers continually reflect back on, modify, adapt, and expand their models in light of what they hear from their students (Franke et al. 1998, 2001).

By the end of the study, nineteen of the twenty-one teachers in the longitudinal study were at Level 3 or higher (seven were at Level 4). Eighteen of the twenty-one teachers had changed at least one level in beliefs and practice, and twelve had changed at least two levels.

In a follow-up study conducted four years after the end of the professional development program, all of the teachers continued to implement principles of the program at some level. Five of the teachers had slipped one level, but ten of the teachers showed continued growth. Not only did they sustain their beliefs and practices, but their learning had become generative so that their classes became places for the teachers as well as the students to learn. What distinguished these ten teachers was that they (a) viewed children's mathematical thinking as central to their teaching, (b) possessed detailed knowledge about their students' mathematical thinking, (c) had a well-developed framework for thinking about children's mathematical thinking, (d) perceived themselves as creating and elaborating their knowledge about children's thinking, and (e) sought out colleagues for support in understanding children's mathematical thinking.

Case studies (Carpenter, Fennema, and Franke 1996; Fennema et al. 1992, 1993; Franke et al. 1998, 2001) supported the findings of the quantitative studies and provided rich descriptions of teacher change and of the ways teachers have implemented the principles of CGI in their classrooms. These studies confirmed the finding of the longitudinal study that change is difficult and takes place over an extended period of time. Developing an understanding of children's thinking provides a basis for change, but change occurs as teachers attempt to apply their knowledge to understand their own students. It is a slow process, with changes in knowledge and instruction building upon one another. But almost all teachers in our studies have changed in fundamental ways and have sustained their change after the formal professional development ends.

Philipp et al. (2013) provided additional evidence of the complexity of teaching that builds on children's thinking as well as the importance of sustaining professional development over years to help teachers gain this expertise. In their large-scale study of 129 K–3 prospective and practicing teachers, they investigated, through a cross-sectional design, teachers who differed in the amount of time they had been engaged in CGI professional development as well as the amount of time they had been teaching. In this study, multiple teacher competencies were explored, including *professional noticing of children's mathematical thinking*—a hidden skill of teaching that is essential for implementing the principles of CGI. When children offer verbal or written strategy explanations, teachers must make in-the-moment decisions about how to respond. This decision making requires complex noticing that consists of three distinct but related subskills: (a) attending to children's strategies, (b) interpreting children's understandings, and (c) deciding how to respond on the basis of children's understandings (Jacobs, Lamb, and Philipp 2010; Jacobs et al. 2011). By focusing on the hidden practice of noticing, Jacobs and colleagues highlighted and unpacked the important work that teachers do before they even make a move to respond to a student. Philipp et al. (2013) found that although most teachers did not gain this expertise from teaching experience alone, the expertise of professional noticing is learnable with sustained professional development, a result consistent with other findings in their large-scale study. Although important teacher growth occurred within the first two years of professional development, additional critical growth required professional development support beyond two years, underscoring the importance of sustained support for teacher learning.

Not only has this body of work shown how teachers can change by learning about children's thinking, it has also demonstrated how much can be accomplished by both teachers and students when children's thinking becomes a primary focus for instruction. The studies illustrate how teachers provide an environment in which children's thinking is the focus, children communicate about mathematics, children construct their own procedures for solving problems, and concepts are developed through problem solving. The case studies described exceptional teachers engaged in the kind of teaching that captures the spirit of current reform recommendations and documented how much children are capable of learning in such environments.

STUDENT ACHIEVEMENT

In the initial experimental study (Carpenter et al. 1989), we found that CGI classes had significantly higher levels of achievement in problem solving than control classes had. Although there was significantly less emphasis on number facts in CGI classes, there was no difference between the groups in achievement on the test of number facts. In fact, there was some evidence that CGI students actually had better recall of number facts than did students in the control classes. A traditional standardized achievement test of the kind typically used in the 1980s also was administered in this study, and no differences were found between CGI and control classes on this test.

In a related study using the same measures, Villasenor and Kepner (1993) found that urban students in CGI classes performed significantly higher than a matched sample of students in traditional classes. Similar results were found by Secada and Brendefur (2000). Further discussion of the effectiveness of CGI with students from typically underachieving groups can be found in Carey et al. (1995) and Peterson, Fennema, and Carpenter (1991).

The longitudinal study (Fennema et al. 1996) extended the findings of the initial experimental study. By the third year of the study, the concepts and the problem-solving performance of the classes of every teacher were substantially higher than they had been at the beginning of the study. Improved performance in concepts and problem solving appeared to be cumulative, with students having longer participation in CGI classes showing greater gains in the upper grades during the second and third years of the study. Changes in student achievement reflected changes in teacher practice. For each teacher in the study, substantial improvement in the performance in concepts and problem solving of the teacher's students followed directly a change in the level of the teacher's practice.

Thus, our studies consistently demonstrate that CGI students show significant gains in problem solving. These gains reflect the emphasis on problem solving in CGI classes. On the other hand, despite the decreased emphasis on drill and practice, there is no commensurate loss in skills.

COGNITIVELY GUIDED INSTRUCTION AND ENGLISH LEARNERS

Research on CGI and English learners documented how a focus on students' mathematical thinking can be enhanced by attention to students' cultural, linguistic, and community knowledge. For example, a series of reports on a yearlong study of three dual language kindergarten teachers using CGI examined how the teachers drew upon students' cultural and linguistic knowledge and experiences to support students' mathematics learning (Celedón-Pattichis and Turner 2012; Turner and Celedón-Pattichis 2011; Turner, Celedón-Pattichis and Marshall 2008; Turner, et al. 2008, 2009). The kindergarten students, who were predominantly low-income and Latino/a, including many English learners, demonstrated impressive advances in their capacity to solve word problems over the course of the year. This research contributed powerful evidence of the problem-solving capacity of young Latino students (an important counterpoint to research that has focused on perceived deficiencies of these students), and also identified specific instructional moves that teachers used to support students in solving problems and explaining their reasoning.

Case studies of English learners' participation in CGI classrooms focused on how instructional interactions supported English learners to solve and discuss problems (Maldonado et al. 2009; Turner, Dominguez, Empson, and Maldonado 2013). For example, research by Turner, Dominguez, Maldonado, and Empson (2013) examined seven Latino/a English learners' participation in discussions of mathematics word problems over a ten-week period and identified ways that English learners positioned themselves and were positioned by others, via discourse, to take on active problem-solving roles and develop positive identities.

COGNITIVELY GUIDED INSTRUCTION AND CLASSROOM PRACTICE

Through a series of studies in both CGI and non-CGI classrooms, Webb and Franke and their colleagues studied teachers' classroom practice and how and when that practice leads to student participation and learning. These studies focused on teacher-student(s) and student-student interactions. Students who had an opportunity to explain their strategies or ideas in fully detailed and complete ways had higher student achievement (Webb et al. 2008, 2009). This is true even when taking into account prior achievement. Franke, Webb, and colleagues then examined what teachers were doing to support students to explain more completely. Teachers' most productive support came as they probed student thinking and asked students about something they had said to support them to provide more mathematical detail (Franke et al. 2009).

These researchers also examined how students participated together around mathematical explanations and how students engaged in each other's ideas. Students often engaged with another's ideas in general ways—like agreeing or disagreeing with another's idea—and while this is an important way to begin to support students to attend to another's ideas, it was not related to student achievement. Engagement with the details of another student's ideas or having someone engage in the details of yours was related to student achievement (Webb et al. 2013, in press). Engaging at this level involved sharing some of the details of another's idea, asking a question about something within someone's strategy, comparing two or more strategies, constructing strategies together, or adding on to someone's idea. Teachers played a role in supporting students to engage with each other's ideas by inviting students to engage with each other in a variety of ways, following up to support students as they learned to engage with each other's mathematical ideas and positioning students as capable of engaging with each other (Franke et al., in press).

REVIEWS OF COGNITIVELY GUIDED INSTRUCTION BY OTHER RESEARCHERS

Extended reviews of CGI appear in several syntheses of research in mathematics education and research in professional development. See for example, Borko and Putnam (1996); De Corte, Greer, and Verschaffel (1996); Ginsburg, Klein, and Starkey (1998); and Wilson and Berne (1999).

APPENDIX B

Answers to Selected Questions for Reflection

Chapter 2

2. Identify each problem type
   a. Join (Result Unknown)
   b. Part-Part-Whole (Whole Unknown)
   c. Compare (Difference Unknown)
   d. Join (Change Unknown)
   e. Separate (Start Unknown)

3. Identify each problem type
   a. Separate (Change Unknown)
   b. Separate (Start Unknown)
   c. Separate (Result Unknown)
   d. Join (Change Unknown)
   e. Part-Part-Whole (Whole Unknown). Note that there are three parts rather than two in this word problem.
   f. Part-Part-Whole (Whole Unknown) and Separate (Result Unknown). Note that this is a two-step problem.

Chapter 3

1. The problem types are Join (Result Unknown), Separate (Result Unknown), and Join (Change Unknown).

5. Here are the strategies types
   a. Margie—Direct Modeling strategy (She represents each quantity. She most likely she meant to write 23 rather than 32.)
   b. Reiner—Counting strategy (He counts on from 20.)
   c. Bob—Number Fact strategy (He most likely also used an understanding of base-ten number concepts. See Chapters 6 and 7 for more information on children's understanding of base ten.)
   d. Carrie's strategy is invalid. She made 20 and crossed off 3. (See the x's on the first 3 cookies.)
   e. Jay—Direct Modeling strategy (His strategy is almost exactly like Margie's, although he writes 23 correctly.)

9. Aaliyah uses Direct Modeling on all of the problems.

10. Jordyn uses a Counting On from Larger strategy.

11. Melissa uses Number Fact strategies to solve both problems. Note that Melissa uses the equal sign in a nonstandard manner when she notates her strategy for the SRU problem. As students are learning to use mathematical notation, they are likely to use some symbols in a nonstandard manner. In this example, the teacher understood Melissa's notation and chose not to correct her use of the equal sign. The standard notation would be $10 - 7 \rightarrow 3 + 5 \rightarrow 8$ or $15 - 7 = 10 - 7 + 5$.

Chapter 4

1. Identify the problem types
   a. Multiplication
   b. Partitive Division
   c. Multiplication
   d. Measurement Division
   e. Measurement Division. Note that 8 cars are needed to get all children to the zoo.
   f. Partitive Division
   g. Partitive Division. Note that some students will say that each person gets 4 cookies and there will be 1 left over and that other students will divide the last cookie among the 4 friends.

3. The problem types are Multiplication, Measurement Division, and Partitive Division in that order.

Chapter 6

1. The problem types are
   a. Multiplication
   b. Partitive Division
   c. Measurement Division
   d. Multiplication

6. The strategies are
   a. Emily—Counting by Ones
   b. Elliot—Counting by Tens
   c. Tanner—Counting by Tens
   d. Sue—Direct Place Value
   e. Jake—incorrect strategy

Chapter 7

8. The strategies are:

    a. Anna—Invented Algorithm—Combining the Same Units

    b. Brad—Direct Models with Tens. How might he have counted to figure that the total was 262.

    c. Carl—incorrect strategy

    d. Evelyn—Invented Algorithm—Combines the Same Units for the tens and the ones and then incrementing to add the sum of the tens and the sum of the ones to 200.

    e. Fred—Invented Algorithm

Chapter 11

1. Properties of operations these students used (equations shown have bolded sections to show use of property)

Colette's solution for 6 + 7 used the associative property of addition

$$6 + 7 = 6 + (4 + 3) = (6 + 4) + 3 = 10 + 3 = 13$$

The solution for 8×7 used the distributive property of multiplication over addition

$$8\times7 = (3 + 3 + 2)\times7 = 3\times7 + 3\times7 + 2\times7 = 21 + 21 + 14 = 56$$

The first solution to 6×24 uses the distributive property of multiplication over addition

$$6\times24 = 6\times(20 + 4) = 6\times20 + 6\times4 = 120 + 24 = 144$$

The second solution to 6×24 uses the commutative and associative properties of multiplication

$6\times24 = 24\times6$ Commutative property of multiplication

$24\times6 = 24\times(3\times2) = (24\times3)\times2 = 72\times2 = 144$ Associative property of multiplication.

2. One equation that represents the relationship used in this strategy is

$$6\times13 = 6\times10 + 6\times3 = 60 + 18 = 78$$

3. One equation that represents the relationship used in this strategy is

$$60 + 48 = (60 + 40) + 8 = 100 + 8$$

4. A series of equations that represents the relationship used in this strategy is

$$600 - 250 = 600 - 200 - 50$$
$$600 - 200 = 400$$
$$400 - 50 = 350$$

REFERENCES

Borko, H., and R. Putnam. 1996. "Learning to Teach." In *Handbook of Educational Psychology*, edited by D. Berliner and R. C. Calfee, 673–708. New York: Macmillan.

Carey, D. A., E. Fennema, T. P. Carpenter, and M. L. Franke. 1995. "Equity and Mathematics Education." In *New Directions in Equity for Mathematics Education*, edited by W. Secada, E. Fennema, and L. Byrd. New York: Teachers College Press.

Carpenter, T. P. 1985. "Learning to Add and Subtract: An Exercise in Problem Solving." In *Teaching and Learning Mathematical Problem Solving: Multiple Research Perspectives*, edited by E. A. Silver. Hillsdale, NJ: Erlbaum.

Carpenter, T. P., E. Ansell, M. L. Franke, E. Fennema, and L. Weisbeck. 1993. "Models of Problem Solving: A Study of Kindergarten Children's Problem-Solving Processes." *Journal for Research in Mathematics Education,* 24 (5): 427–40.

Carpenter, T. P., E. Ansell, and L. Levi. 2001. "An Alternative Conception of Teaching for Understanding: Case Studies of Two First-Grade Mathematics Classes." In *Beyond Classical Pedagogy in Elementary Mathematics: The Nature of Facilitative Teaching*, edited by T. Wood, B. S. Nelson, and J. Warfield. 27–46. Mahwah, NJ: Erlbaum.

Carpenter, T. P., E. Fennema, and M. L. Franke. 1996. "Cognitively Guided Instruction: A Knowledge Base for Reform in Primary Mathematics Instruction." *The Elementary School Journal,* 97 (1): 3–20.

Carpenter, T. P., E. Fennema, M. L. Franke, S. B. Empson, and L. W. Levi. 1999. *Children's Mathematics: Cognitively Guided Instruction*. Portsmouth, NH: Heinemann.

Carpenter, T. P., E. Fennema, M. L. Franke, S. B. Empson, and L. W. Levi. 2014. *Children's Mathematics: Cognitively Guided Instruction. Second Edition* Portsmouth, NH: Heinemann.

Carpenter, T. P., E. Fennema, P. L. Peterson, and D. A. Carey. 1988. "Teachers' Pedagogical Content Knowledge of Student's Problem Solving in Elementary Arithmetic." *Journal for Research in Mathematics Education,* 19: 385–401.

Carpenter, T. P., E. Fennema, P. L. Peterson, C. P. Chiang, and M. Loef. 1989. "Using Knowledge of Children's Mathematics Thinking in Classroom Teaching: An Experimental Study." *American Educational Research Journal,* 26 (4): 499–531.

Carpenter, T. P., M. L. Franke, V. Jacobs, and E. Fennema. 1998. "A Longitudinal Study of Invention and Understanding in Children's Multidigit Addition and Subtraction." *Journal for Research in Mathematics Education,* 29: 3–20.

Carpenter, T. P., M. L. Franke, and L. Levi. 2003. *Thinking Mathematically: Integrating Arithmetic and Algebra in Elementary School.* Portsmouth, NH: Heinemann.

Carpenter, T. P., and R. Lehrer. 1999. "Teaching and Learning Mathematics with Understanding." *Classrooms That Promote Mathematical Understanding,* edited by E. Fennema and T. A. Romberg, 19–32. Mahwah, NJ: Erlbaum.

Carpenter, T. P., and J. M. Moser. 1984. "The Acquisition of the Addition and Subtraction Concepts in Grades One Through Three." *Journal for Research in Mathematics Education,* 15: 179–202.

Celedón-Pattichis, S., and E. Turner. 2012. "'Explícame qué tienes ahí': Supporting Mathematical Discourse in Emergent Bilingual Kindergarten Students." *Bilingual Research Journal,* 35 (2): 197–216.

De Corte, E., B. Greer, and L. Verschaffel, L. 1996. "Mathematics Teaching and Learning." In *Handbook of Educational Psychology,* edited by D. Berliner and R. C. Calfee, 491–549. New York: Macmillan.

Empson S. B., and L. Levi. 2011. *Extending Children's Mathematics: Fractions and Decimals.* Portsmouth, NH: Heinemann.

Fennema, E., T. P. Carpenter, M. L. Franke, and D. A. Carey. 1992. "Learning to Use Children's Mathematics Thinking: A Case Study." In *Schools, Mathematics, and the World of Reality,* edited by R. Davis and C. Maher. Needham Heights, MA: Allyn and Bacon.

Fennema, E., T. P. Carpenter, M. L. Franke, L. Levi, V. Jacobs, and S. Empson. 1996. "Learning to Use Children's Thinking in Mathematics Instruction: A Longitudinal Study." *Journal for Research in Mathematics Education,* 27 (4): 403–34.

Fennema, E., M. L. Franke, T. P. Carpenter, and D. A. Carey. 1993. "Using Children's Knowledge in Instruction." *American Educational Research Journal,* 30 (3): 555–83.

Franke, M. L., T. P. Carpenter, E. Fennema, E. Ansell, and J. Behrend. 1998. "Understanding Teachers' Self-Sustaining, Generative Change in the Context of Professional Development." *International Journal of Teaching and Teacher Education,* 14: 67–80.

Franke, M. L., T. P. Carpenter, L. Levi, and E. Fennema. 2001. "Capturing Teachers' Generative Growth: A Follow-up Study of Professional Development in Mathematics." *American Educational Research Journal,* 38: 653–89.

Franke, M., Turrou, A.C., Webb, N., Ing, M, Wong, J., Shim, N, Fernandez, C. In press. "Student Engagement in Each Other's Mathematical Ideas: The Role of Teacher Invitation and Support Moves." *Elementary School Journal.*

Franke, M. L., N. M. Webb, A. G. Chan, M. Ing, D. Freund, and D. Battey. 2009. "Teacher Questioning to Elicit Students' Thinking in Elementary Mathematics Classrooms." *Journal of Teacher Education,* 60: 380–392.

Fuson, K. C. 1992. "Research on Whole Number Addition and Subtraction." In *Handbook of Research on Mathematics Teaching and Learning*, edited by D. Grouws. New York: Macmillan.

Fuson, K. C., D. Wearne, J. C. Hiebert, H. G. Murray, P. G. Human, A. I. Olivier, T. P. Carpenter, and E. Fennema. 1997. "Children's Conceptual Structures for Multidigit Numbers and Methods of Multidigit Addition and Subtraction." *Journal for Research in Mathematics Education,* 38: 130–62.

Ginsburg, H. P., A. Klein, and P. Starkey. 1998. "The Development of Children's Mathematical Thinking: Connecting Research with Practice." In *Handbook of Child Psychology*, edited by I. E. Sigel and K. A. Renninger, 401–78. New York: Wiley.

Greer, B. 1992. "Multiplication and Division as Models of Situations." In *Handbook of Research on Mathematics Teaching and Learning*, edited by D. Grouws. New York: Macmillan.

Gutstein, E., and T. A. Romberg. 1995. "Teaching Children to Add and Subtract." The *Journal of Mathematical Behavior,* 14: 283–324.

Hiebert, J., and T. P. Carpenter. 1992. "Learning Mathematics with Understanding." In *Handbook of Research on Mathematics Teaching and Learning*, edited by D. Grouws. 65–97. New York: Macmillan.

Hiebert, J., T. P. Carpenter, E. Fennema, K. Fuson, P. Human, H. Murray, A. Olivier, and D. Wearne. 1997. *Making Sense: Teaching and Learning Mathematics with Understanding.* Portsmouth, NH: Heinemann.

Jacobs, V. R., L. L. C. Lamb, and R. A. Philipp. 2010. "Professional Noticing of Children's Mathematical Thinking." *Journal for Research in Mathematics Education,* 41 (2): 169–202.

Jacobs, V. R., L. L. C. Lamb, R. A. Philipp, and B. P. Schappelle. 2011. "Deciding How to Respond on the Basis of Children's Understandings." In *Mathematics Teacher Noticing: Seeing Through Teachers' Eyes*, edited by M. G. Sherin, V. R., Jacobs, and R. A. Philipp, 97–116. New York: Routledge.

Maldonado, L., E. Turner, H. Dominguez, and S. Empson. 2009. "English Language Learners Learning from and Contributing to Mathematical Discussion." In *Mathematics for Every Student: Responding to Diversity, Grades PreK–5*, edited by D. White and J. Spitzer, 7–22. Reston, VA: National Council of Teachers of Mathematics.

National Council of Teachers of Mathematics. 2000. *Principles and Standards for School Mathematics.* Reston, VA: NCTM.

National Council of Teachers of Mathematics. 2006. *Curriculum Focal Points for Kindergarten Through Grade 8 Mathematics.* Reston, VA: NCTM.

National Governors Association Center for Best Practices & Council of Chief State School Officers. 2010. *Common Core State Standards (Mathematics).* Washington, DC: National Governors Association Center for Best Practices, Council of Chief State School Officers,

National Research Council. 2001. *Adding It Up.* Washington, DC: National Academies Press.

Peterson, P. L., E. Fennema, and T. P. Carpenter. 1991. "Using Children's Mathematical Knowledge." In *Teaching Advanced Skills to Educationally Disadvantaged Students*, edited by B. Means. Menlo Park, CA: SRI International.

Peterson, P. L., E. Fennema, T. P. Carpenter, and M. Loef. 1989. "Teachers' Pedagogical Content Beliefs in Mathematics." *Cognition and Instruction,* 6 (1): 1–40.

Philipp, R. A., V. R. Jacobs, L. C. Lamb, J. P. Bishop, J. M. Siegfried, and B. Schappelle. 2013. *A Study of Teachers Engaged in Sustained Professional Development.* In preparation.

Richardson, V. 1994. "Conducting Research on Practice." *Educational Researcher,* 23 (5): 5–10.

Secada, W. G., and J. L. Brendefur. 2000. "CGI Student Achievement in Region VI Evaluation Findings." *The Newsletter of the Comprenhensive Center — Region VI: Cognitively Guided Instruction and Systemic Reform,* 5(2.12a–12d).

Turner, E., and S. Celedon-Pattichis. 2011. "Problem Solving and Mathematical Discourse among Latino/a Kindergarten Students: An Analysis of Opportunities to Learn." *Journal of Latinos in Education,* 10 (2): 146–68.

Turner, E., S. Celedon-Pattichis, and M. A. Marshall. 2008. "Opportunities to Learn Problem Solving and Mathematics Discourse Among Latino/a Kindergarten Students." In *Promoting High Participation and Success in Mathematics by Hispanic Students: Examining Opportunities and Probing Promising Practices*, edited by R. Kitchen and E. Silver, 1, 19–42.

Turner, E., S. Celedon-Pattichis, M. Marshall, and A. Tennison. 2009. "'Fíjense amorcitos, les voy a contar una historia': The Power of *Story* to Support Solving and Discussing Mathematical Problems among Latino/a Kindergarten Students." In *Mathematics for Every Student: Responding to Diversity, Grades PreK–5*, edited by D. White and J. Spitzer, 23–43. Reston, VA: National Council of Teachers of Mathematics.

Turner, E., H. Dominguez, S. Empson, and L. A. Maldonado. 2013. "Latino/a Bilinguals and Their Teachers Developing a Shared Communicative Space." *Educational Studies in Mathematics,* 84 (3): 349–70.

Turner, E., H. Dominguez, L. Maldonado, and S. Empson. 2013. "English Language Learners' Identity-Enhancing Participation in Mathematical Discussion." *Journal for Research in Mathematics Education,* 44 (1): 199–234.

Verschaffel, L., and E. De Corte. 1993. "A Decade of Research on Word-Problem Solving in Leuven: Theoretical, Methodological, and Practical Outcomes." *Educational Psychology Review,* 5 (3): 1–18.

Villasenor, A., and H. S. Kepner. 1993. "Arithmetic from a Problem-Solving Perspective: An Urban Implementation." *Journal for Research in Mathematics Education,* 24: 62–70.

Webb, N. M., M. Franke, M. Ing, J. Wong, C. Fernandez, N. Shin, and A. C. Turrou. 2013. "Engaging with Each Other's Mathematical Ideas: Interrelationships Among Student Participation, Teachers' Instructional Practices And Learning." *International Journal of Educational Research,* 63; 79–93.

Webb, N. M., M. L. Franke, A. C. Turrou, and M. Ing. In press. "Self-Regulation and Learning in Peer-Directed Small Groups." *British Journal of Educational Psychology.*

Webb, N., M. Franke, T. De, A. Chan, D. Freund, P. Shein, and D. Melkonian. 2009. "Explain to Your Partner: Teachers' Instructional Practices and Students' Dialogue in Small Groups." *Cambridge Journal of Education,* 39: 49–70.

Webb, N., M. Franke, M. Ing, A. Chan, T. De, D. Freund, and D. Battey. 2008. "The Role of Teacher Instructional Practices in Student Collaboration." *Contemporary Educational Psychology,* 33; 360–381.

Wilson, S. M., and J. Berne. 1999. "Teacher Learning and the Acquisition of Professional Knowledge: An Examination of Research on Contemporary Professional Development." In *Review of Research in Education* (Vol. 24), edited by A. Iran-Nejad and P. D. Pearson, 173–210. Washington, DC: AERA.